05/03

Bk # 015438

PERCEPTION AND
COSMOLOGY
IN WHITEHEAD'S
PHILOSOPHY

PERCEPTION AND COSMOLOGY IN WHITEHEAD'S PHILOSOPHY

Paul F. Schmidt

RUTGERS UNIVERSITY PRESS

New Brunswick   *New Jersey*

Manufactured in the United States of America by

QUINN & BODEN COMPANY, INC., RAHWAY, N.J.

To My Mother
Anna Crecely Schmidt
Patient Provider
of
Comfort and Calm

Preface

I FIRST BEGAN to read Alfred North Whitehead with my father in the winter of 1943–44, when I was eighteen. Those winter evenings during the war were long and quiet, affording us time to discuss *Adventures of Ideas*. Our whole family would read in the evenings; this is the strongest memory of my childhood.

During the next winter, 1944–45, I was stationed at Smyrna Air Force Base outside Nashville, Tennessee, and spent long hours sitting in a crash ambulance at the end of the runway. I had discovered the St. John's College list of "One Hundred Great Books" and was reading straight through. For relaxation after the Greeks, I turned again to Whitehead, recalling his statement that all European philosophy "consists of a series of footnotes to Plato." Interrupted every few minutes by a B-24 bomber, taking off or landing, I felt my own way into "process" and "prehension."

In the fall of 1946 I was reading Whitehead once again in an Honor's Seminar at the University of Rochester under the guidance of philosophy professor Robert Trayhern and privately with Professor Alfred H. Jones. I recall vividly that the first ten pages of *Process and Reality* took me several hours to read and how delightful I found the essays in *The Aims of Education*.

During the school year, 1947–48, I had the good fortune, as a first year graduate student, to hear Professor F. S. C. Northrop's lectures at Yale. I often left the lecture hall dazed and inspired. Scattered throughout the lectures were penetrating insights and discussions of all of Whitehead's books, so I dipped in everywhere. On the occasion of Whitehead's death, at a memorial meeting of the Graduate Philosophy Club, Professors Northrop, Weiss, and Blanchard moved us with personal recollections.

The next Yale year, 1948–49, provided me with two golden opportunities: a year of private reading with Professor Northrop of Whitehead's philosophy of science and a seminar of four students with Professor Frederic Fitch on *Process and Reality*. These teachers carried me deep into Whitehead's thought.

Another year of reflection while occupied with other tasks led me to the idea that Whitehead's views on perception were fundamental to his work on the philosophy of science and cosmology. Further exploration reinforced this idea, so I decided to attempt to establish this thesis. With excitement I plunged into a complete rereading of Whitehead and exploration of the writings about Whitehead. Professor Fitch was my sounding board as the thesis took on concrete form. It proved defensible in the spring of 1951. Much of it is incorporated in this book.

Over the next decade my philosophic interests ranged widely, but a periodic seminar on Whitehead kept me thinking along these lines. Influences shifted from great teachers to books on Whitehead by Victor Lowe, William Christian, A. H. Johnson, Nathaniel Lawrence, Robert Palter, Wolfe Mays, Ivor Leclerc, Donald Sherbourne, and Lucian Price. A special stimulus came from correspondence with Victor Lowe. Without his kind prodding, I might not yet have this work ready for the reader. The final text owes much to an unknown reader for Rutgers University Press, who did a marvelous job, and to a last reading aloud with my wife, *née* Gail Ann Baker.

This long odyssey with Whitehead has led me to the conviction that his views about perception are fundamental to his philosophy of science and cosmology. Three views of perception are distinguished here. The first appears in a collection of essays, *The Organization of Thought*. In this view, Whitehead makes good use of logical techniques introduced in the 1905 memoir "On Mathematical Concepts of the Material World" by taking certain sense-objects as a basic class of entities and constructing from them more complex entities for science. His critique of science begun in the 1905 memoir guides the direction of his construction.

The second view of perception appears and develops in the philosophy of science books: *An Enquiry Concerning the Principles of Natural Knowledge, The Concept of Nature,* and *The Principle of Relativity*. It emerges from a critique of scientific concepts and introduces the theory of events and the doctrine of significance. The theory of objects and the constructive method of extensive abstraction are revised and retained. These three books reveal important changes in the continuity of Whitehead's thought. For example, the class theory of objects shifts to the control theory; the doctrine of significance achieves greater internal relatedness. Throughout the books, Whitehead is concerned to show what form would be given to the scientific world picture from his view of perception.

Whitehead's third view of perception makes its appearance in *Science and the Modern World*, gains full form in *Process and Reality*, and acquires a settled maturity in *Adventures of Ideas*. *Science and the Modern World* frames the critique of science based on the fallacy of simple location, which is another form of the "disconnectedness" of *The Principles of Natural Knowledge,* and introduces the novel theory of prehensive unities.

Process and Reality gives us the full doctrines of perception in the modes of causal efficacy, presentational immediacy, and symbolic reference. The earlier theory of objects is developed into the theory of eternal objects. In *Adventures of Ideas* the doctrine of mutual immanence is the mature form of the doctrine of prehensions in *Process and Reality,* which had grown from the doctrine of significance in *The Principle of Relativity.* With these doctrines of perception a full-blown cosmology is elaborated.

Such has been my journey, which I retrace in detail in this work, and invite you to pursue.

PAUL F. SCHMIDT

Capillo Peak Forest Camp, 9000 feet,
Manzano Range, New Mexico,
June 1966.

Contents

List of Abbreviations

When small letters immediately follow page numbers in the references of this book, they refer to paragraphs on the page in question. If a page does not begin with a paragraph, then the remainder of the preceding paragraph at the top of the page is designated by "a."

PERCEPTION AND
COSMOLOGY
IN WHITEHEAD'S
PHILOSOPHY

Chapter I

INITIAL SPECULATIONS AND CRITICISMS
OF SCIENCE

Section I. Introduction

One major theme in the continuity and development of Whitehead's thought consists of his views on perception. In fact, a large part of his total intellectual position after the mathematical-logical years stems from these views. Three fairly distinct periods in his thoughts about perception can be delineated: first, the pre-philosophy of science period reflected in the essays collected in *The Organization of Thought;* second, the philosophy of science period including *An Enquiry Concerning the Principles of Natural Knowledge, The Concept of Nature,* and *The Principle of Relativity;* and, third, the cosmological period embracing *Science and the Modern World, Process and Reality,* and *Adventures of Ideas.*

Whitehead took a very broad view of perception, so that at all times it is crucial to remember that perception is more than mere sense-perception. Exactly how perception and sense-perception are related in his thought forms the subject of detailed discussion in later pages. Furthermore, if we conceive of perception, as I believe I can show Whitehead did, to consist in a grasping together within a single unit of experience, then our account of Whitehead's views of perception must go back at least to the memoir "On Mathematical Concepts of the Material World," delivered to the Royal Society of England in 1905.[1]

Another important feature of Whitehead's views on perception was his persistent interweaving of such views with larger scientific and philosophical problems occupying his attention at those times. His thinking about a problem seems rarely to have occurred in isolation. So we should not be surprised that during his early work in mathematical logic (1900–10) he should take time out, midway, to write a paper weaving that work together with reflections concerning models of the material world, a paper that contains important sources of his later critique of scientific

3

concepts and guidelines for subsequent reflections on perception. Hence, in our study of Whitehead's views of perception, we must keep in focus his broad conception of perception and the interrelations of his views with thoughts about science and cosmology. Nothing less than this can do justice to his insights. These points should make clear why our study begins with a digest of some parts of the 1905 memoir. It launches the criticism of scientific concepts which is essential to an understanding of the earliest theory of perception contained in *The Organization of Thought,* essays published between 1913 and 1917.

The year 1905, already famous in the history of physics and philosophy as the birth date of Einstein's "Special Theory of Relativity," marks the beginning of another train of speculations in philosophy and physics which culminates in that cosmological classic, Whitehead's *Process and Reality,* the Gifford Lectures for 1927–28. His 1905 paper, like Einstein's relativity theory, was revolutionary in scope. It undertook the unification of geometry and physics by means of the powerful new tool—symbolic logic—which was being forged by Whitehead and Russell between 1900 and 1910. The paper constitutes a synthesis unique in the history of ideas at that time. Not until 1916, in the *General Theory of Relativity,* did Einstein express the unification of geometry and physics in his theory of space and theory of matter. But this is not to suggest that Whitehead anticipated Einstein's special or general theory. Whitehead's treatment is quite different. In some respects, for example the theory of time, it is not as novel a departure as Einstein's, but in some other respects, the unification of geometry and physics, it has greater novelty. This paper is so revealing of the man's genius and vision, which were later manifested to the philosophical world, that an effort to summarize his early criticisms of science and cosmological speculations seems important to a proper estimate of Whitehead's place in the history of ideas.[2] Besides the intrinsic importance of this paper as an investigation of axiomatic foundations of geometry and physics by means of the logical apparatus of the *Principia Mathematica,* we can also study the origins of some later doctrines worth noticing in order to dispel the belief that Whitehead changed interests on his way from mathematician-logician to speculative philosopher.

Whitehead tells us that "the object of this memoir is to initiate the mathematical investigation of various possible ways of conceiving the nature of the material world. . . . [In particular] the memoir is concerned with the possible relations to space of the ultimate entities which constitute the 'stuff' in space" (M 465, whᴀ 11a). Whitehead quickly limits the general problem to its purely logical side although he admits that "it has an indirect bearing on philosophy by disentangling the essentials of the idea of a material world from the accidents of one particular concept" (M 465, whᴀ 11–12). This limitation of context allows only a minimum of insight into Whitehead's epistemological ideas and mere hints of his metaphysical ideas in this paper. For example, the epistemological difficulties of ideal concepts like point and instant, which are the backbone of the discussion in his *The Principles of Natural Knowledge* (1919), *The Concept of Nature* (1920) and *The Principle of Relativity* (1922), are not discussed in this 1905 paper. Nevertheless, from the standpoint of logic the later criticism of scientific materialism given in *Science and the Modern World* (1925) is initiated.

In the year 1905, when most physicists and philosophers were thinking in terms of the geometrical and physical concepts of Newton, Whitehead was symbolizing five different theories of the relation between geometry and physics. These formulations were constructed in terms of the possibilities provided by mathematical logic and in particular in terms of its logic of relations, a logical doctrine developed by Whitehead and Russell in the *Principia Mathematica*. Besides the addition of novel physical theories, such a logical formulation itself is most noteworthy. By formulating the Newtonian physics in the logic of relations Whitehead was able to see the disadvantages and inelegance of its synthesis of geometry and physics. The mathematical-logical formulation and analysis of the concepts and basic assumptions of Newtonian physics pointed the way for Whitehead's construction of four additional theories of the physical world.

These five theories are referred to as Concepts I, II, III, IV, and V. Concept I is the traditional Newtonian or classical theory of physics. Concepts II and III are variations of Concept I with interesting alterations. The real originality of Whitehead's 1905 paper becomes evident in Concepts IV and V, for they express the kind of identification of spatial and/or temporal relatedness with the physical field which Einstein achieved, in a technically different form to be sure, in his *General Theory of Relativity* at least ten years later. Concepts IV and V grow out of certain disadvantages of the other three which become especially apparent when formulated in the new manner. These disadvantages are due to the relative disconnectedness of the primitive relations, later in *The Principles of Natural Knowledge* called the principle that extension expresses disconnection, and the large number of extraneous relations which they required, later overcome in the doctrine of significance. Concepts IV and V result from posing the fundamental question, "how can a point be defined in terms of lines?" which initiates the criticism of the concept of point and the hunt for a new foundation in *The Principles of Natural Knowledge* and *The Concept of Nature* (M 466). The geometry in each Concept is three-dimensional and Euclidean, although non-Euclidean systems could be obtained by a correct alteration of the axioms.

The main principle of criticism that Whitehead used to point out the disadvantages of some of these theories is an adaptation of Occam's Razor. Occam's Razor sometimes refers to the least number of entities, but Whitehead has taken the modern approach and postulated relations as primitive, wherein the entities are specified by the fields of the relations, rather than postulating entities as primitive and then looking for relations between them. Hence, for Whitehead, Occam's Razor refers to the smallest number of primitive relations.

Section II. Concepts, Criticisms, and Sources

Each Concept begins with "Fundamental Relations" (M 466, whᴀ 13b) whose fields consist of relata called "Ultimate Existents" (M 467, whᴀ 13e). Concerning each fundamental relation, say aRb, Whitehead speaks of its "sense" as proceeding from one term a, called the referent, to another term b, called the relatum. I suggest that this direction of a relation is a source for what Whitehead, later in *Process and Reality*, called the vector character of a prehension. Each fundamental relation can be conceived as a thought-perception, a grasping together into a single insight. This was very characteristic of Whitehead.

Concept I takes the traditional Newtonian physics and reorganizes it for presentation from its fundamental relations and ultimate existents. The ultimate existents are points of space, instants of time, and particles of matter. Organized in this way, the Newtonian physics requires an indefinite number of relations associating a particle with a point at an instant, and brings into focus the disconnectedness among ultimate existents, which becomes a central point of Whitehead's criticism of Newtonian physics in Chapter I of *The Principles of Natural Knowledge*. He is also critical of the dualism of points and particles (M 475–76, 480, whᴀ 28–29), and of the undue separation of geometry and physics in contrast to other concepts. Both of these concerns continued throughout his intellectual career.

Concept II is obtained from Concept I by abolishing particles from the class of ultimate existents. Whitehead remarks that the only reason for introducing particles seems to have been to give the senses something to perceive. But if we can perceive relations, Concept II will do just as well. In the later books, *The Principles of Natural Knowledge* and *The Concept of Nature*, such a position is adhered to. The fundamental relation of extension is basic. In virtue of extension we can perceive events and from events we can define points and instants. Also in *Process and Reality* concrete relations of prehensions are data in certain perceptions. It is by means of these two methods that Whitehead in these later books is able to avoid a substance philosophy; that is, an adherence to something like the classical physics of Concept I with its particles. Hence Concept II indicates how Whitehead was already contemplating alternatives to a philosophy of substance, which are developed in detail in his later works.

Concept III is a variant of Concept II obtained by abandoning the prejudice against moving points of space (M 480, whA 30b). A more intimate connection of geometry with physics is involved since the moving points at different instants of time can be characterized by different geometrical systems (M 471, whA 18c).

Whitehead proceeds to develop two more Concepts, IV and V, which are opposed to the punctual Concepts I, II, and III; that is, to ultimate existents like points, instants, and particles. Concepts IV and V arise from Leibniz's relational theory of space, which holds that the points of space are not to be taken as fundamental entities. The significant feature about Concepts IV and V is that they show how Whitehead in 1905 was already contemplating alternative schemes of physics and was ready to use a relative or relational theory of space. The core of a relational theory of space or relative theory of space—Whitehead does not distinguish between the two—is that "every true proposition asserting a spatial relation involves a time at which this relation holds between its terms," whereas an absolute theory of space "holds that there are true propositions in which spatial relations are asserted to hold timelessly between certain terms." [3] Whitehead's method of postulating as primitive relations rather than entities allows him to express either type of theory.

In contrast to Einstein, whose criticism was based on physical grounds, Whitehead's criticism of the classical concept or Newtonian physics (Concept I) is based on Occam's Razor and disconnectedness among punctual concepts. The difference between Whitehead and Einstein is reflected in the fact that Whitehead does not in the 1905 memoir contemplate a relative theory of time. An absolute theory of time is accepted by Whitehead without hesitation. In support of this view, he refers to Russell's article "Is Position in Time and Space Absolute or Relative?" [4] But we see that with respect to space Whitehead was in favor of a relational view in 1905, basing his preference on Occam's Razor.

Whitehead's early criticism of the Newtonian physics, as presented in Concept I, combined with far-ranging speculations on types of physical theories, plus the ready use of a relational theory of space, is truly amazing. Here was a man in 1905 working out in mathematical-logical detail a relational theory of space for physics and, further, a physical theory (Concept V) in which the concept of matter (corpuscles) and geometrical concepts are derivative from more primitive relations. Students of Whitehead should not forget this fact in any discussion of his later relativistic views or of the principle of relativity in its philosophical form in *Process and Reality*. We have no indication that Whitehead was influenced by Einstein's 1905 paper, the "Special Theory of Relativity," although it is possible. Clearly, the development of Whitehead's ideas after 1905 were influenced by Einstein's, as he states in later books. The Concepts of Whitehead's 1905 paper seem to have resulted from his own speculations. The independence of his approach seems to me to be indicated by his criticisms of Einstein's theory in *The Principles of Natural Knowledge, The Concept of Nature,* and *The Principle of Relativity,* although they share with it the relationalist approach to physics.[5] Concept V presents a theory of the unification of space and matter in 1905. Einstein did not present such a theory until 1916. How is Whitehead's theory developed?

Points of space are derived from straight lines, which are the ultimate existents in Concepts IV and V. Whitehead calls them "linear objective reals." These primitive entities are postulated and not abstracted from sense experience as Whitehead insisted they ought to be in *The Principles of Natural Knowledge* in 1919. These straight lines are considered throughout their extent as single indivisible entities. "Perhaps, however a closer specification of the linear objective reals of these concepts is to say that they are the lines of force of the modern physicist, here taken to be ultimate unanalysable entities which compose the material universe, and that geometry is the study of a certain limited set of their properties" (M 482, whA 32a). Later in *Process and Reality,* simple physical feelings (prehensions) are said to be the lines of force of physics (PR 177). The simple physical feelings are the cosmological analogue of the linear objective reals. Both serve to bind the universe together.

Certain classes of linear objective reals (straight lines) are sufficient to define a point in a way analogous to that in which the point of projective geometry is a class of straight lines as derived from descriptive geometry. Whitehead generalizes this technique for all points by means of two different methods: the theory of interpoints (intersection points) and the theory of dimensions. These two theories provide different ways of arriving at the basic idea of a point as a concurrence of straight lines. These derivative points are then used to construct the ordinary lines and planes of geometry, which are divisible into points and segments. Recall that our linear objective reals are indivisible.[6] A study of the method of defining points in the theory of interpoints will show that it is somewhat similar to the later method of extensive abstraction employed in *The Principles of Natural Knowledge* and *The Concept of Nature* (M 485, whᴀ 35).

Geometry is much more closely connected to physics in Concept V than in the others, for Concept V deals with the relation of linear objective reals to points, lines, and planes (M 513, whᴀ 60b). This integration of geometry with the dynamics of physics constitutes a life-long goal for Whitehead. In *Process and Reality* the integration of the process of concrescence (the dynamic side of reality) and the co-ordinate division of the satisfaction of an actual entity (which includes geometry) achieves this goal. Another problem Whitehead encountered in Concept IV has to do with the permanence and observability of those ultimate existents which function as matter. His awareness of such perceptual considerations while dealing with logical-mathematical systems is indicative of his wide concerns (M 491, whᴀ 43b). In Concept V the characterization of a corpuscle has striking similarities to Whitehead's later concept of an actual entity in *Process and Reality*, which obtains its being and unity by its peculiar set of prehensions (relations) from its perspective. The prehensions (vector lines) are here the linear objective reals. The same enduring object maintains a basic cohesiveness amid the welter of relations.

Our study of this paper indicates the novel departures in the history of speculative physics that Whitehead contemplated in 1905. First, the creation of a relational theory of space contemporaneous with Einstein's "Special Theory of Relativity." Second, the unification of geometry and physics in a single set of axioms. Third, the application of symbolic logic to the deductive formulation of geometry and physics. Fourth, a reduction in the number of primitive concepts required for a physical theory. Fifth, the creation of alternative conceptions of the material world. Sixth, the initiation of a criticism of the Newtonian classical physics in regard to its dependence on the assumption of a material stuff (particles of matter) and its separation of geometry and physics with the resultant inelegance of the system.

We also notice germs of later ideas in his philosophical development. First, the notion of a point derived from more ultimate entities. Second, the use of relations as perceivable entities to form a perceptual basis in experience for more abstract entities in science. Third, the rejection of substance philosophies which assume a material substratum. Fourth, that the being of an entity is resultant from its relations. These four points indicate the unity of Whitehead's thought from 1905 to *Process and Reality*.[7] These achievements are sufficient to guarantee the importance of the memoir of 1905 in the history of science and philosophy. Despite the brevity of these initial speculations and criticisms of science, we shall see how important they are in the next chapter where they become the pivot for Whitehead's earliest theory of perception.

Chapter II

THE ORGANIZATION OF THOUGHT

Section I. Transition

Between 1905 and the appearance of Whitehead's first philosophical essays in 1915, 1916, and 1917 ("Space, Time and Relativity," "The Organization of Thought," and "The Anatomy of Some Scientific Ideas," respectively [1]) the tendencies and anticipations that we noted in our first chapter have been gathering momentum while other works were appearing before the public. Two geometrical treatises appeared: *The Axioms of Projective Geometry,* 1906, and *The Axioms of Descriptive Geometry,* 1907. In 1910 the first volume of *Principia Mathematica* appeared, written in collaboration with Russell. It is beautifully summarized by Whitehead in the last half of OT and also in the *Encyclopaedia Britannica* article "Mathematics." [2] Two other entries in this famous eleventh edition of the *Encyclopaedia Britannica* were contributed by Whitehead: one on "Non-Euclidean Geometry" with Russell, and another on "Axioms of Geometry." [3] The last-named article is important to his critique of scientific concepts because it presents a summary of Sophus Lie's theory of groups for the definition of congruence without reference to lengths. This is presupposed in the 1905 memoir and is central to the difference between Whitehead's and Einstein's relativity theories. There is also a short incisive criticism of Jules Henri Poincaré's conventionalism with respect to the axioms of geometry. Whitehead remarks that "this point of view (Poincaré's) seems to neglect the consideration that science is to be relevant to the definite perceiving minds of men . . . we have, in fact, presented to our senses a definite set of transformations forming a congruence group, resulting in a set of measure relations which are in no respect arbitrary" (ESP 265). Note again the stress on the perceptual basis for science! The year 1911 also saw the publication of his delightful *Introduction to Mathematics* [4] with its significant chapter on "Periodicity" in nature foreshadowing the chapter on "Rhythms" in PNK. Volumes II and III of the *Principia Mathe-matica* followed in 1912 and 1913. By 1914 the theory of extensive ab-straction had been worked out from the 1905 memoir for the definition of points starting from perceivable events. It is presented in his paper "La Théorie Relationniste de l'Espace," printed two years later.[5] The papers of 1915, 1916, and 1917 can be treated as a unit according to certain topics.

Section II. Introduction

The primary difference between these essays and the philosophy of natural science, as I shall call PNK, CN, and PRel, is that no distinction is made between events and objects. In the light of the emphasis put on this distinction in these books, the omission of it in these essays marks an important forthcoming change in his thought. The analysis of per-ception and science herein marks rather a completion of the 1905 memoir. Ideas typical of empiricism and logical analysis are employed. First, the class concept is used to define objects. "An extended body is nothing else than the class of perceptions of it by all its percipients, actual or ideal" (AE 176b; also 130b, AE 243). Second, the method of logical con-structions for inferred entities is used to derive scientific concepts (AE 191a, OT 214a). Both of these techniques are founded on the British tradition of empiricism (AE 245–46, 159b, 243a). The separation of these ideas from any metaphysical implications is generally affirmed for prac-tical purposes (OT 113–14) but not ultimately maintained (AE 229, 231). The two techniques are provided with a concrete method, the principle of convergence to simplicity with diminution of extent, or what later becomes the method of extensive abstraction (AE 191b). We shall look at these ideas as they occur in this phase of Whitehead's thought and see how they fit into the perceptual groundwork provided for science without the events-objects distinction.

Section III. The Separation of Science and Metaphysics

It is essential to an understanding of Whitehead's philosophy to see why he could insist on the separation of science and metaphysics in the earlier periods and then affirm their close interconnection in the later works. He insists "that the basis of science does not depend on the assumption of any of the conclusions of metaphysics; but that both science and metaphysics start from the same given groundwork of im-mediate experience, and *in the main* proceed in opposite directions on their diverse tasks" (AE 161a, my italics). Most people misunderstand

Whitehead because they overlook the clause following the semicolon. Whitehead was an empiricist at all stages but not in the usual contemporary sense, for many reasons to be revealed as we proceed. Perception, immediate experience, is the starting point. If we concern ourselves only with those aspects of perception besides values felt, emotions, and judgments of value (AE 180a); that is, only with spatial, temporal, material, and causal components, metaphysical thinking (in Whitehead's meaning of metaphysics as the synthesis of nature and value) is not required. Such principles as that of causality, which would traditionally be metaphysical, were for Whitehead part and parcel of the perceptual groundwork. This is still true in PNK and in PR. Prehensions in PR are causal connections and form the basis of experience. But metaphysical "inquiry is a necessary critique of the *worth* of science . . ." (AE 180b, my italics). A total understanding of science would require this critique, as is duly provided in SMW, but "the reasons for its careful separation [in these books] from scientific thought are purely practical; namely, because we can agree about science—after due debate—whereas in respect to metaphysics debate has hitherto accentuated disagreement" (AE 180b). The motive for the pursuit of physical science requires a metaphysical judgment of worth and so does the selection of one field over another (AE 228–29).

Another way in which science needs metaphysics, if science is to be totally understood, concerns what Whitehead has termed "the actuality underlying a possibility"—that is, to understand the factors involved in some possible state of affairs relevant to it. Metaphysics is relevant herein to define the conditions—logical, moral, or aesthetic—which characterize the perceiving consciousness with respect to possible objects appearing to it (AE 229a). Conversely, science aids metaphysics indirectly by "the exposition of the fact that our experience of sensible apparent things is capable of being analysed into a scientific theory . . ." (AE 161b), whereas science collects the classes of actual and ideal perceptions into a system and seeks their interrelations (AE 161b). Science is not concerned with the ontological problem of existence for perceptual data capable of being analysed into a scientific theory . . ." (AE 231b); that is to say, at least part of experience is rational. This is a conclusion any metaphysics would have to incorporate.

Another way of keeping the two disciplines separate is to describe metaphysics as concerned with "how our perceptions of the chair relate us to some true reality" (AE 161b), whereas science collects the classes of actual and ideal perceptions into a system and seeks their interrelations (AE 161b). Science is not concerned with the ontological problem of existence for perceptual data (AE 180b), for it can carry out the function first stated without this. In PNK and CN, Whitehead puts this in another way by saying that all perceptual data are on an equal footing so far as existence goes. He must take them as ultimate existents or fall into the bifurcation difficulty.

These different ways of looking at the distinction of science and metaphysics indicate why Whitehead thought he could construct a sound philosophy of natural science without recourse to metaphysical discussion and still leave room for a later metaphysical discussion of science.

Section IV. General Analysis of Perception

The nature of perception was important in Whitehead's thought because he wanted to construct an empirical system of science and philosophy. "What is really actual are the immediate experiences. The task of deductive science is to consider the concepts which apply to these data of experience . . . This process [of logical construction] builds a common world of conceptions out of fragmentary worlds of experience" (AE 243a). Much emphasis is given to the affirmation of two propositions central to ordinary empiricism: (1) that objects consist of classes of perceptions (AE 176, 243) and (2) that our perceptual experience is fragmentary in relation to the smooth conceptual objects obtained by logical constructions (AE 245–46, 159, OT 214a). These are clearly propositions every British empiricist would assent to. They show where Whitehead started from, but he didn't stay there long, for his analysis of perception soon revealed what his empirical friends never found.

First of all is his doctrine of the "rough world" and the "smooth world," as Lowe has aptly named it (AE 243a). "I insist on the radically untidy, ill-adjusted character of the fields of actual experience from which science starts. . . . This fact is concealed by the influence of language, moulded by science, which foists on us exact concepts as though they represented the immediate deliverances of experience" (AE 157–58). This is the distinction between a world of perceptions and a world of conceptions; between what we actually do experience and what we express in our attempt to communicate that actual experience. Too often contemporary empiricists forget this vague, untidy experience and begin their epistemological analyses with these clear-cut, smooth individual sense data: a particular shade of blue, a note, or some taste. "It is not true that we are directly aware of a smooth running world, which in our speculations we are to conceive as given" (AE 246a). In order to construct a philosophy of natural science, the fundamental problem is "the elucidation of the precise connection between this world [smooth world] and the feelings of actual experience . . ." (AE 158b).

What can we say about the character of this rough world, the real groundwork of perception? We can distinguish a continuous and a fragmentary side. In any given "act of experience we perceive a whole formed of related differentiated parts" (AE 244c). This is the notion of "Fact" and "Factors," which is still retained in PRel. Looked at in this way, perception is of a continuum—fragmentary, yes, but with the components not clearly marked off and actually merging into one another (AE 188–89). Furthermore, all the various durations melt into one another "so, finally, we conceive ourselves each experiencing a complete time-flux (or stream) of sense-presentation. This stream is distinguishable into parts. . . . [but] the parts are not mutually exclusive . . ." (AE 189c). A point like this cannot be argued to a conclusion one way or another. We can just ask the question and then inspect our own experience. To perform some psychological test would be foolish, for that test would employ smooth world concepts obtained from just this realm which the test is trying to ascertain the character of. Metaphysically this whole situation is accounted for in PR in virtue of the fact that no actual occasion can ever have exactly the same set of experiences (prehensions) as another. There is an ultimate privacy.

On its fragmentary side, the rough world must be distinguishable into parts, factors of fact, for otherwise we should have to perceive the whole in order to construct concepts of the smooth world which characterize the rough world, but we do not have a direct perception of the whole. "My point in this respect is that fragmentary individual experiences are all that we know, and that all speculation must start from these *disjecta membra* as its sole datum" (AE 245–46). Although our fragments (sense data) merge into each other, thus forming the continuum, we must assume the fragments as components or else we could have no limited meaningful experience. We have here in the very roots of our immediate experience a polarity of the continuous and discontinuous inextricably welded together.

Section V. Science and Perception

We are now ready to make some general remarks on the connection between science and perception, between the smooth world and the rough world. This connection, Whitehead thinks, must be elaborated into a full-bodied science, the foundation for any empirical philosophy of natural science (AE 158b). This elaboration is just what PNK attempts to achieve.

The task of science "is the discovery of the relations which exist within the flux of perceptions, sensations and emotions which forms our experience of life. The panorama yielded by sight, sound, taste, smell, touch, and *by more inchoate sensible feelings,* is the sole field of activity" (AE 157b, my italics). Are these inchoate feelings the later source of perception in the mode of causal efficacy? It is in the above sense that "science is the thought organization of experience" (AE 157b). The relations and concepts of the scientific world are ab tract; the problem is how they are connected with experience (AE 158b). Logic is the means whereby scientific concepts are derived from perception; a logic of classes building extended bodies from classes of percept ons (AE 175b). The aim of science is to harmonize "our reflective and derivative thoughts with the primary thoughts involved in the immediate apprehension of sense-presentation" (AE 185c). Secondly, it aims to syst ze the derivative thoughts into scientific theory (AE 185c).

The technique which effects this derivation of the smooth world from the rough world employs two principles. First, the principle of convergence to simplicity with diminution of extent is employed to "confine our attention to such parts as possess mutual relations sufficiently simple for our intellect to consider . . ." (AE 191b). This is the later method of extensive abstraction used to define points, instants, lines, etc. The method operates by means of certain theorems in the theory of series with limit values as explained in PNK. Such series are "routes of approximation" to thought-concepts such as points.[6] Think of a series of concentric circles each enclosed in the former. There is convergence and diminution to an element of the series which approximates our intuitive notion of a point. The point is not some member of the series, for there is no end to the series, but the mathematical character of the series itself, or the class of elements defined by this character. It is for this reason we do not have to dream about ideal approximation to some member of the series and its existential status. We know about the existential status of the series of enclosures; they are empirical observables. In this way an empirical basis is provided for abstract concepts.

The second principle employed is the principle of aggregation. It is used to construct serial order relations among homogeneous entities of which some of the relata are not at all times directly observable. Whitehead uses time as an example. The principle is necessitated because "directly comparable relations can only exist between elements of consciousness, both [elements belonging] in that present during which the perception occurs" (AE 190b). How then give an empirical account of the relation of past to present; that is, of the time stream of events? First, Whitehead observes that the present itself is a duration and hence includes directly perceived time relations, say two events *A* and

B such that *A* precedes *B*. When *A* fades (is not directly perceived), *B* and *C* may be directly perceived, *B* antecedent to *C*. Then *A* can be said to precede *C* by logical construction and hence a time series of such aggregates constructed (AE 190–91). In PNK and CN this principle is merged with the principle of convergence into extensive abstraction and time and points are obtained in analogous ways.

We recall that in the 1905 memoir the key principle of criticism was Occam's Razor, but nothing was said in its justification. It might have been purely arbitrary, a part of logical elegance or aesthetic preference, but in an empirically grounded science its justification rests on the fact that every increase in the number of hypothetical entities required "diminishes the claim of scientific reasoning to be the necessary outcome of a harmony between thought and sense-presentation" (AE 218c). Here again, we see how Whitehead was able to base a justification for a principle on an empirical philosophy of science, whereas most appeals to the principle that I know of offer as justification the notion of simplicity; but this is no reason, only an aesthetic preference. In terms of PR this is restated ontologically as "no actual entity, then no reason" (PR 28b).

Section VI. Thought and Perception

Whitehead at this stage denied the distinction which is sometimes made between thoughts and facts. "So far as physical science is concerned, the facts are thoughts, and thoughts are facts" (AE 184b). This certainly sounds like a Berkeleyian phenomenalism, so we shall have to discover what Whitehead meant by these terms. Someone claims to see a certain colored patch, which he says is blue. Perhaps he really didn't see blue at all. But how can we test this? We look and proclaim "red" but our friend replies "no, blue." So far as he is concerned he has had that immediate awareness of a colored, two-dimensional patch which he commonly calls blue. We may think there is something wrong with his physiological mechanism, but it makes no difference in what he claims to report. Whitehead describes this situation by saying that "it is the thought that matters and not that element of perception which is not thought" (AE 181b). Hence, the immediate psychological awareness is what Whitehead called thought. Those elements which are not thought in the total process of perception, be they physiological, physical, or what not, are of no concern. "The field of physical science is composed of these primary thoughts [primary in the sense that we can find none more basic], and of thoughts about these thoughts" (AE 181b). These primary thoughts are the facts of science, the sense data, the immediate awareness. Their ontological status is a metaphysical problem in Whitehead's terms, a problem outside of science. Science is only concerned with the interrelations of these facts. The immediate awareness of redness (the thought of redness) is not perceived in isolation but in relation to the whole perceiving consciousness (AE 182c). We perceive these relations as well as the redness. Recall that Concept II in the 1905 memoir built a physical theory on the basis of perceivable relations. Perception of these primary thoughts is called sense-presentation. Secondary thoughts are derived from, constructed from, primary thoughts.

Next Whitehead distinguishes actual thought-expressions from hypothetical thought-expression. Actual thought-expressions are judgments actually made, such as two plus two equals four, whereas hypothetical thought-expressions are imagined possibilities which are neither affirmed nor denied, such as the one millionth digit of π is seven (AE 183–84). The close relationship of perception and science in Whitehead is revealed when he claims that "science aims at harmonising our reflective and derivative thoughts with the primary thoughts involved in the immediate apprehension of sense-presentation" (AE 185c). These thoughts, primary or secondary, are the so-called material facts which science interprets (AE 184b). The question must surely arise: isn't this a kind of subjective idealism or phenomenalism in science? I think it is not, for the reason that Whitehead has nowhere claimed that reality is constructed out of these thought-objects or that the thought-objects are in some way appearances of the real objects. In fact the question was not faced by him at this time. He wanted an empirical foundation for science, and this was one way to obtain it which seems to do justice to science and perception. But the door was left open on the two metaphysical theses of subjective idealism and phenomenalism. Later in PR he faces the issue of the ontological status of entities similar to thought-objects, namely, eternal objects.

Section VII. Objects

The usual view of common sense and contemporary science is that ordinary objects like pens and sweaters as well as sensed qualities like damp and sour are to be explained by scientific entities and concepts like electrons and chemical structure. Whitehead's desire to locate the foundation of natural science in experience led him to reverse this account by taking crude sensory objects as basic for the construction of perceptual and scientific objects. The task was not an easy one and each fresh difficulty forced a modification of his views until the mature theory of PR.

A distinction must be made between the many direct sense-objects and the derivative object, the pen. Our primary thought-objects are these sense-objects. Sense-objects are correlated to space and time; these latter are obtained by the principles of convergence and aggregation respectively. When a group of sense-objects are simultaneous and spatially coincident we tend to combine them into a single object by a process of "instinctive immediate judgment in general without effort of reasoning" (AE 187d). Objects of common sense are constructed on the basis of a limited number of sense-objects. We can distinguish various kinds of sense-objects such as sight-objects, touch-objects, smell-objects, taste-objects, kinesthetic objects, and emotion-objects.

In a certain way these sense-objects are complex entities (AE 188b). Their self-identity is already a result of perceptual processes. A sight-object, for example, can change as we alter our position in space or time. This point serves to distinguish this theory of objects from that of PNK and CN, in which objects do not change. The sight-object of a burning fire changes from one hour to the next. We can cut down the time interval as much as we desire "but there is no such thing as a sense-object at an instant" (AE 188c), because we have no empirical means of connecting the instants by some observable relation. We perceive durations, not instants. This argument is essential to the understanding of Whitehead's criticism of points and instants in PNK, CN, and SMW. It is what is denied by the fallacy of simple location in SMW. Further, it is this argument which marks one of the changes in Whitehead's development from the 1905 memoir, wherein every concept of the material world assumed instants of time as ultimate existents. What it was between 1905 and 1917 that brought about this change cannot be determined. Was it the impact of Einstein's special relativity theory? Certainly Whitehead studied this carefully, but his own dissent on the definition of simultaneity indicates that he was developing his own approach (OT 203–12). Or was it logical difficulties in science resulting from instants and points (PNK 4–8), or attempts to find an empirical basis for instants and points?

Another consequence of the fact that we perceive durations and not instants is that the distinction between memory and immediacy is blurred. The present fades into the past, for the perceived durations of consciousness overlap. There is not this duration, then the next, and so on. This is a very important point in Whitehead's thought. The fact that memory and immediacy fade into each other is (1) the basis of the doctrine of significance on its temporal side in PNK and CN, (2) essential to the thesis of the uniformity of nature in PRel, and (3) fundamental to the doctrine of mutual immanence in AI. The viewpoint is adapted to the problems in each of these cases, but it is the same root idea.

The complexity attaching to crude sense-objects can be overcome by the principle of convergence, which first restricts the stretch of time to a minimum and second restricts this minimum stretch of time in its spatial aspect. Further restriction is obtained by homogeneity of type of sense (all sight-objects for example), of quality, and of intensity. "Thus the sense-object is the result of an active process of discrimination . . ." (AE 192c). This is surely a different view from Hume's passive impressions of sensation.

Sense-objects can be associated in various ways: (1) we may have a partial stream, forming a time succession, of sense-objects of the same sense that are homogeneous and change only gradually; (2) we may have several homogeneous partial streams of sense-objects of the same sense that are confined temporally to a sufficiently short duration so as to constitute a specious present of perception in which they cohere to form a partial spatial composite; and (3) we can have a combination of associations of partial time-succession streams and partial spatial composites (AE 193a). Such an association of sense presentations as (3) is called a "first crude thought-object of perception." Notice the difference between "thoughts" and "thought-objects." "Thought" in Section VI includes all types of objects. In this section "thought-objects" are one special type of object.

The first crude thought-objects of perception are associations of sense-objects based primarily on the perceived coincidence of their spatial relations (AE 193–94). The coherence of sense-objects in such associations illustrates the fundamental natural law of objective stability (AE 192d). For example, I look at my pen for a brief moment while I am writing. I feel it in my grasp. I chew the end of it; note its spatial relations to the paper. Each of these partial streams of sense-objects, the visual stream, the tactual stream, and so on, is associated and together they form the first crude thought-object of a pen during that brief moment. Sometimes it is the first crude thought-object that we are aware of in perception, and by dissociation we single out the component sense-objects for our awareness (AE 194a). The next step from a number of these very limited spatial and temporal first crude thought-objects of perception to one thought-object of perception extending beyond our specious present requires the two principles of aggregation and hypothetical sense-presentation. The principle of aggregation allows for the temporal extension of our first crude thought-object. For example, a few minutes later, or an hour later, I again see, feel, and taste my pen. The homogeneity and analogy of the first two crude thought-objects coalesce into a third crude thought-object of perception. But, further, I can imagine certain perceptions of my pen without experiencing them. "The world of present fact is more than a stream of sense-presentation. We find ourselves with emotions, volitions, imaginations, conceptions and judgments" (AE 196a). Imagination of hypothetical sense-presentations is necessary to conceive of a permanent collection of first crude thought-objects into a single thought-object (AE 196a). The complete thought-object is a concept (AE 196a). The question as to why certain hypothetical sense-presentations are imagined and not others is not discussed. I suppose that certain scientific presuppositions like permanence, continuity, and simplicity are behind these hypothetical imaginations. But why these and not some others? This is asking for an evaluation of science and would lead to metaphysics, which Whitehead puts firmly aside for the present. These thought-objects are the first data of science.

This analysis of a thought-object is particularly revealing. First, what is here called a thought-object seems to have about the same characteristics as the perceptual object of PNK and CN.[7] If this is true then certain critics of Whitehead's philosophy of science have misunderstood perceptual objects. Northrop claims that Whitehead cannot succeed in deriving scientific concepts from sense-perception alone.[8] His error rests on the strange use Whitehead gives to the term "sense perception." Northrop is thinking of sense-perception along traditional philosophic and empirical lines as that which is immediately given and wholly other than conceptual-imaginative-hypothetical processes. But the passages we have just referred to in Whitehead (OT 143c, 141b, 147c, 151c) clearly indicate that for him sense-perception contains hypothetical imaginative processes which provide aspects of perceptual objects that are not purely given. These are Northrop's concepts by imagination, which are concepts by postulation.[9] If my analysis is correct, at least this is not a point of disagreement between them. Both are saying in different ways that the perceptual object is partly a construct, a theory, or an hypothesis, and partly an immediately given datum. Of course there remain other differences, but this very important issue dissolves and hence allows for a reevaluation of Whitehead's foundation for his relativity theory, which Northrop criticized in the essay previously mentioned.

The hypothetical character of thought-objects of perception cannot be overstressed in this phase of Whitehead's thinking. "The thought-objects of perception which are presupposed in the common thought of civilized beings are almost wholly hypothetical. The material universe is largely a concept of the imagination which rests on a slender basis of direct sense-presentation" (AE 199b). In the light of such a quotation I don't see how anyone can mistake Whitehead's unusual meaning of perception. It includes much of what is ordinarily called conception. We see that direct sense-presentation and hypothetical reasoning are practically inseparable. Isn't this exactly the same position as is maintained in PR in the interconnection of mental and physical poles of any actual entity? It seems to me that a great error has been made in the interpretation of Whitehead's development through neglect of this essay ("The Anatomy of Some Scientific Ideas"). In 1917 perception included direct experiences and hypothetical thinking. What changed is the analysis of how the two aspects are linked together. Whitehead didn't suddenly drag mind into science in SMW as most people think. It was there all the time but hidden by a peculiar use of language, as a careful reading of PNK and CN will reveal. It is not a wavering between realism and idealism as some have maintained.[10] Whether Whitehead is a realist or idealist in various stages was settled in PR, wherein realism and idealism are shown to be falsely considered antithetical. In organic philosophy they are aspects of a whole, and false when taken to be the whole. The key to understanding this view of perception is given in Whitehead's statement in this essay that "fact is thought and thought is fact."

A number of difficulties infect the thought-object of perception. First, we are aware of sense-objects that belong among the coherent parts of some thought-object but that as single properties of it would be inconsistent with the hypothetical thought-object. For example, the different shapes of the penny, the bent stick in water. Second, thought-objects are supposed to be permanent associations of sense-objects, but science demands that they also exhibit change. To provide some account for these difficulties, Whitehead thought that reflective scientific thought was driven to presuppose another kind of object in perception; namely, the thought-object of science. In PNK, this becomes the scientific object.

First, we must "construe our sense-presentation as actual realization of the hypothetical thought-objects of perception" (AE 199b). And then we must construe the thought-objects of perception as requiring thought-objects of science to render their account coherent. These thought-objects of science (molecules, atoms, electrons) are not capable of direct sense-representation in consciousness (AE 200b). They are known only through their associated sense-objects and thought-objects of perception. They are conceived as the cause of these sense-presentations (sense-objects) and sense-representations (hypothetical thought-objects). It is now clear that thought-objects of science are the analogue of scientific objects in PNK. Further we can see how perception includes direct awareness and conceptual entities linked together. Also we see how causality is a relation in perception. The manner of the linkage will change but the general idea is retained throughout Whitehead's writings.

This completes my account of the different kinds of objects at this stage. No such entity as an event is herein explicitly distinguished. It is the addition of this entity along with these objects which provides the basis for the theory of perception in PNK and CN.

Section VIII. Applications: Perceptual Basis of Space and Time

In terms of this theory of perception we can now provide an account of the scientific concepts of space and time. Space and time relations hold between sense-objects. In fact, the relations of space and time are derived from the relations of sense-objects; in particular the relation of whole and part (AE 201b). Sense-objects are parts of the whole stream of sense-presentation. Further, one sense-object can be part of another (AE 202c). The relation of whole to part is a directly presented relation. It is assumed that point-objects of time and space are not direct sense-presentations but hypothetical thought-objects (AE 175b, 205b). Elaborate reasons for the assumption were given two years later in PNK. The aim was to provide a definition of points of space and instants of time based on sense-objects. Then the traditional conceptions of space and time can be used with some corrections necessitated by a relational theory. Sense-space and sense-time must be distinguished from thought-space of perception and thought-time of perception, which involve points and instants (AE 206c). Sense-space and sense-time are relations between sense-objects according to the relation of separation based on whole and part (AE 205–06). They have no points or instants (AE 206a).

The derivation of points of space from sense-objects is accomplished with the principle of convergence. A brief statement of the fundamental idea has already been given. The detailed assumptions of the method are stated in PNK and CN and will be discussed in a later chapter. Its success rests on the nineteenth-century mathematical discovery by Karl Weierstrass and the Berlin School of the definition of a limit without recourse to the notion of infinitesimals.[11] Instants of time are derived in an analogous fashion, but the set of enclosure-objects (sense-objects of a certain kind involving whole-part relations) are different because of the one-dimensional character of time in contrast to the multiple-dimensional character of space.

The definition of a point which results from a set of enclosure-objects yields a hypothetical thought-object of perception. These defined (derivative) points are hypothetical, and are based on the spatial and temporal (whole-part) relations of sense-objects that are extended. These hypothetical points are limited to what might be called "material points" because of their derivation from sense-objects.

What about so-called points of empty space? These can be established by first defining "material lines" as "complete collinear classes of collinear points" (AE 219c) according to the principle of convergence. The intersection of such a set of material lines will be our material point. "Now consider a set of three material lines, such that any two are coplanar, but not the whole three, and further consider the complete set of material lines such that each is coplanar with each of the three material lines first chosen. The axioms which hold for the material lines will enable us to prove that any two lines of this set are coplanar" (AE 219c). Such a complete set of lines gives us an ideal point which may or may not be occupied, a point of empty space, a point of pure geometry. Hence pure geometry can be derived from this relational theory of space ultimately based on extended perceivable sense-objects. Geometry and experience are now united (AE 220b). Or we can say, a perceptual basis has now been discovered for pure geometry. This method is an extension of the theory of interpoints in the 1905 memoir on a perceptual basis not there employed. Hence we have in these essays, as I stated in Section II, a completion of the 1905 memoir on a perceptual basis.

Section IX. Conclusions

A succinct account of Whitehead's first views on perception is now before us. In the discussion of the relations and separation of science and metaphysics I have shown how much of this would not have to be rejected in the light of SMW, PR, and AI, although revisions would certainly be required. Science and metaphysics have a common root in perception, which is the thesis of this work concerning Whitehead's whole thought. Secondly, the root of science in perception was expounded; that is, the derivation of thought-objects of science from thought-objects of perception, and the latter from sense-objects of immediate sense-presentation. An important fact emerging from this discussion concerned the hypothetical nature of thought-objects of perception and science. This revealed the peculiar sense in which Whitehead uses the term "perception" to include conception as well as sense-presentation, and hence the peculiar nature of his empiricism. Further, this interconnection or fusion of hypothetical conception and sense-presentation (thought and fact) served to link this early view of perception to his philosophy of natural science and to PR, wherein we have the fusion of physical and conceptual poles in each actual entity. Finally, in our summary of the manner in which space and time are derived from the perceptual basis of sense-objects, we are presented with a completion of the 1905 memoir on a perceptual basis. We have here an attempt at a philosophy of scientific concepts employing the class theory of objects and logical constructions; namely, the principles of convergence and aggregation, all on an empirical foundation. Phase one of Whitehead's thought is roughly completed. Some aspects linger on in PNK and CN, but new ideas such as events begin to emerge.

Chapter III

CRITIQUE OF SCIENTIFIC CONCEPTS

If one is to understand Whitehead's theories of perception, I think it is safe to say that one must first comprehend his critique of science, especially physics. This is the case because logical difficulties in basic principles or incompatibilities among these principles force him to re-examine the primitive concepts and how these are supposedly related to sense experience; for science claims at least to say something about sense experience, if not about the world. From this it follows that the critique of science has two aspects: (1) the logical difficulties among basic principles, and (2) the erroneous epistemological theories employed to connect the basic concepts to sense experience; namely, the bifurcation problem. For Whitehead this logical criticism extends in two directions. First, it is an extension of the criticism of the classical concept of the material world, which was initiated in the 1905 memoir, and, second, it is a criticism of Einstein's relativity theory concerning the foundations required for a consistent relational theory of space and time.

Section I. Criticism of the Classical Concept

The logical foundations of the classical concept (Newtonian physics), insofar as this could be interpreted as a consistent logico-mathematical system, were presented in the 1905 memoir. The basic concepts (ultimate existents) required are points of space, instants of time, and particles of matter. An absolute theory of space and time is assumed in which space and time extend indefinitely, space being Euclidean and time a one-dimensional serial order. At least, the absolute theory means that any space-distance or time-interval remains unaffected no matter what the conditions of motion or distribution of matter in the universe.

Particles of matter are not assumed to extend continuously and indefinitely, but rather it was generally agreed that not every correlated point-instant was occupied by a particle. But, as will be seen shortly, the further assumption of an ether pervading all space as a fundamental stuff to convey certain wave propagations served to complicate this picture.

"The governing principle underlying this scheme is that extension, namely extension in time or extension in space, expresses disconnection" (PNK 1b). Whitehead does not say why the principle is assumed in the classical view. To provide some justification I must turn to other works.[1] There seems to be an implicit philosophical assumption among physicists that spatial and temporal relations among particles are external. By external I mean that the spatio-temporal relations have no effect on the nature, essence, or character of the particle. The physico-chemical nature of my pen is not altered by my laying it down a moment from now. The justification for holding this assumption rests on the contention that if spatio-temporal relations were internal, then to know the physico-chemical nature of my pen would require a knowledge of all the spatio-temporal relations it has to all objects in the universe; and this they contend is impossible. For, if it were the case, scientific knowledge would be hopelessly handicapped. Hence this *reductio ad absurdum* leads to external spatio-temporal relations.[2]

But further, what about the relation of causality between spatially separated particles? It was generally assumed by classical physics that causal relations did affect the physico-chemical nature of the particles involved. How could this be when the particles are spatially separated, hence disconnected; that is, externally related? It is just this fact which led classical physics to assume in general that action at a distance is impossible and hence that causal action between spatially separated particles is impossible. There must be a continuous line of transmission (PNK 1b).

This disconnection entails another difficulty; namely, that extension in space of an entity is incompatible with unity of being. Such extension involves spatial relations among parts which are externally related, hence disconnected. Classical physics tried to talk about one spatial part causing a change in a contiguous spatial part, in this way trying to form an extended whole entity, but how this fails to do the trick will be made clear shortly. "Thus the extended material (on this view) is essentially a multiplicity of entities which, as extended, are diverse and disconnected" (PNK 1b).

Similarly, in the classical view, multiplicity is not enforced with respect to extension in time. That is, the same particle can endure through a temporal extension. If the particle occupies the same point throughout the time stretch, the time line of successive instants thus formed constitutes the absolute flow of time. If the particle occupies different contiguous points of space at successive instants of time, the particle is said to be in motion in a certain direction, with a constant or changing velocity. But the introduction of the motion of self-identical particles through time and space as an account of physical change leads to a related set of perplexities.

Most of the basic concepts of classical physics are before us: points of space, instants of time, particles of matter, spatio-temporal external relations, no action at a distance, contiguity for causality, self-identity of particles through time, velocity as change of spatial position in time, and acceleration as rate of change of velocity. To this list should be added force as mass of a particle times acceleration and simultaneity as co-existence of one instant of time with a corresponding single set of points of space. Since there is only one absolute time-line for the universe, there is only a single simultaneous spread of points coexistent with any single instant (absolute simultaneity). These basic concepts and relations stated as quantitative formulas provide the rigor of classical physics. What are the logical difficulties that Whitehead finds in these foundations?

First, if we really adhere to our fundamental notions of extensionless points, durationless instants, and point-particles we cannot give a satisfactory account of what is meant by velocity, acceleration, momentum, and kinetic energy. For we must, on these fundamentals, conceive of an ultimate fact of nature as a certain distribution of particles at various extensionless points of space at a single durationless instant of time, and another supposedly related ultimate fact of nature will be another distribution at another instant. Nature, then, on this view, would be a set of such durationless instants each with its fixed distribution of particles in space. But where is change? On the observational level it seems that there is change in nature, but our theoretical foundations provide no change. There is this fixed distribution, then another, followed by another, externally related, disconnected. It remains a mystery how a particle at one point at one instant occupies another point at a later instant. To call this change of position in time motion is to cover with a name what remains unexplained. On the other hand, to incorporate a state of change within the durationless instant itself is equally difficult to understand. But velocity, acceleration, momentum, and kinetic energy all depend on the notion of change. They require reference to the past and future, to stretches of space and time. "Thus change is essentially the importation of the past and of the future into the immediate fact embodied in the durationless present instant" (PNK 2b). But how can a durationless instant include the past and future and remain an instant? This basic inconsistency is in the very foundations of classical physics. It would seem to imply that, if physics is to give an account of change, then durationless instants are not fundamental entities. This argument of Whitehead's seems to depend upon the presupposition that the only real relations are some kind of internal relations.

Second (PNK 2–3), we have to consider whether causal relations can really be asserted among particles located at contiguous points of space. The disconnection (external relatedness) of spatially separated points means that causal connections have to be among contiguous particles, the transmission of some influence across their point of contact. Between two apparently separated particles it is assumed that some chain or medium provides the series of contiguous points. Action at a distance was generally denied, although gravitational effects seemed to provide a counter instance. Consider two points in contact in which two particles are located. According to mathematical ideas, a third point can always be placed between any two previous points supposed to be in contact, just as a real number can be found between any two previously selected real numbers. How is it possible, then, on these assumptions to have two point-particles in contact so that causal reactions can take place? We are once again driven to the wall, this time by having assumed extensionless points of space, which make causal interaction meaningless. Hence we seem to have a *reductio ad absurdum* with the conclusion that extensionless points are not primitive concepts for physical science.

Hume's epistemological analysis of causation fares just as poorly. The configuration of nature at one instant is merely connected to a successive configuration by certain similarities and differences in the identity of material (TSM 45d). If we are to give a satisfactory account of stress or causation we seem to need as a primitive concept an extended quantity of material with a single unity (PNK 3b).

Third (PNK 3c), classical physics does not harmonize very well with the basic biological concept of an organism. An organism is taken to be an extended whole in space and time with some degree of unity of functions. Clearly, such an extended unity in space and time is incompatible with the fundamental disconnection of instants and points in classical physics. This criticism is not affected by assuming any difference in ontological status for these biological wholes. If they are not physicochemical, functioning still takes time, and classical physics is unable to account for their togetherness, just as it is unable to account for its own temporal or causal relations of particles.

Fourth (PNK 18–19), Whitehead assumes that on the traditional definition of mass and force in terms of each other (F equals ma and m equals F/a), these basic equations reduce to such identities as ma equals *ma* and *F/a* equals *F/a*. "It is not easy to understand how an important science can issue from such premises" (PNK 19b).

Even if some of these criticisms seem unsound, they are important for an understanding of why Whitehead constructs his particular theories of perception. He accepts them. I have not intended to raise questions about their validity.

Section II. Criticism of Einstein's Relativity Theory

My statement of these criticisms will be brief. The matter in detail requires a technical knowledge of mathematical physics, but enough can be said to make clear the relevance of these criticisms to the perceptual basis of Whitehead's philosophy of science.

Stated in its most general form the principle of relativity of space and time means that the properties of space and time are ways of expressing relations between entities. For Einstein, properties of space and time were relations between bodily objects.[3] But if points of space are derivative from relations between bodily objects, the foundations of geometry must pay attention to these bodily objects. It became essential that Einstein answer the questions: how is geometry (which assumes points as primitive) related to the experience of bodily objects, and what is the character of these bodily objects? The bodily object for Einstein was a certain class of sense-impressions.[4] Further, conception attributes to the bodily object "a real existence," which enables us to make more order of our sense experience. Hence the bodily object is more than a class of sense-impressions.

It is not necessary to give an account here of how the principle of the additive character of velocities was found inconsistent in the case of light or of the Michelson-Morley experiment's negative result. These difficulties were sufficient to provoke Einstein's special theory of relativity. We can now state Whitehead's criticism, but one must not suppose, because of these criticisms, that Whitehead was opposed to a relational theory of space and time. His whole effort was directed to setting up the foundations of a consistent relational view.[5]

The basic difference between Whitehead and Einstein lay in their use of different fundamental entities. Whitehead maintained that Einstein's bodily object is a derivative and not a fundamental entity. Einstein admitted its hypothetical conceptual character.[6] Such a bodily object is equivalent to one of Whitehead's physical objects, derivative in his special way from sense-objects. But how could Einstein have used the relations between bodily objects to provide space and time when these objects have spatio-temporal characteristics? Furthermore, in claiming to build the concept of a bodily object from recurring similar complexes of sense-impressions, he was already assuming time under the notion of recurrence and space in the juxtaposition of the impressions. Whitehead avoided this circularity by taking as basic the occurrence in sense-awareness of what he called events. Space and time relations are relations among events. Moreover, he claimed that perception shows that events are not instantaneous points but extensive chunks. We just don't perceive points. On the contrary, the events we sense have a "spread-outness" or extension, and it is just this perceptual fact that provides the means of deriving from the relations among events the smooth concepts of space and time. This extension of nature manifest in direct sense-awareness is not scientific space and time and should not be confused with it. Extension is an ultimate character of nature that provides the basis for space and time and many other scientific concepts. In PR this distinction is made very clear in the pairs: process (becoming) and time, extensive continuum and space. This mode of deriving space and time relations allows Whitehead to speak consistently of a physical object in space and time, but such a statement would be inconsistent if space and time relations were derivative from physical objects or bodily objects as Einstein states. The character of this general difference will become clear in the future analysis of events and objects.

A more specific criticism of Einstein concerns the definition of simultaneity (PNK 53–54). In Einstein's special relativity theory the definition of simultaneity for spatially separated events depends upon the uniform velocity of light *in vacuo* (PNK 51–52). Whitehead objects that, if the meaning of simultaneity for spatially separated events depends on the transmission of light, then how am I to account for the sensed simultaneity of an event at my toes and an event at my nose if I should walk into a door? Such events would be recognized as simultaneous by other sight-watchers, but I would not depend upon light signals for my awareness of their simultaneity. Again, would it follow that there could be no recognition of simultaneity in the absence of light signals? In a universe devoid of light it would not be meaningless to speak of simultaneous events. We can comprehend simultaneity in such a universe. However in this criticism Whitehead seems to forget that Einstein distinguished simultaneity for spatially separated events and simultaneity for spatially contiguous events.[7]

Another difficulty with Einstein's definition of simultaneity rests on the specification *in vacuo* when as a matter of fact the universe is not *in vacuo*. We live in air at least, so we could not be aware of simultaneous happenings. But why then should we expect our astronomical predictions of simultaneous happenings ever to be confirmed? And yet they so beautifully are.

Further, a group of entities belonging to the same Galilean frame with its local time (called consentient sets in PNK 31) recognizes the same simultaneous happenings. "The message theory [Einstein's] does not account for the consentience [Galilean frame] in time-reckoning which characterizes a consentient set, nor does it account for the fundamental position of the Newtonian group [Galilean frames in which Newton's third law of action and reaction holds]" (PNK 54c).[8] But isn't this a misunderstanding of Einstein, since he denies that there is any one fundamental frame, and holds that the Newtonian group is merely a limiting case? [9]

It is not a criticism but a mystery as to why light signals should play such an important role in science and why this one velocity should be a key postulate in the special relativity theory.

Whitehead's criticism of the definition of simultaneity can be generalized. The assumption of a uniform velocity for light means that any given stretch of the path for a given length of time is coincident with any such stretch having that time interval; that is, they are congruent. But measurement must be more than such coincidence, for measurement is only of importance in non-coincident circumstances. We have to know that our measuring device is the same at different places and times, or else there would be no sense in making measurements for comparison. Each application of a measuring device requires a direct judgment of constancy (PNK 54–55). Why compare the distance from *A* to *B* with the distance from *C* to *D* if the measuring device is not judged to be constant throughout? The recognition of congruity among distinct circumstances is fundamental for any philosophy of science. No statements about uniformity are meaningful unless the concept of congruence is clear. From Whitehead's point of view, Einstein did not provide a satisfactory theory of the recognition of congruences, although he gave congruence an operational meaning.

Whitehead thought that Einstein's theory was inadequate in its explanation of rotational forces as exemplified in Newton's rotating bucket experiment (PNK 36–37, PRel 87–88, CN 38–39). An explanation of this is crucial since it is one of the main supports of an absolute theory of space. The problem for the relationist is to find a way to define dynamical axes for rotating bodies without reference to other physical bodies, such as the fixed stars in some explanations.[10] Whitehead could achieve this because space-time relations refer to (result from) events, not physical objects. According to Whitehead, Einstein referred such rotational forces to the stars. "But surely this ascription of the centrifugal force on the earth's surface to the influence of Sirius is the last refuge of a theory in distress" (PNK 36b). The doctrine of significance, which leads to the necessary relatedness of events in a uniform matrix of space-time, enabled Whitehead to specify for any single physical object a set of dynamical axes so that rotational forces can be accounted for.

Related to this criticism is a further point. On Einstein's theory we have to assume causal heterogeneity for the spatio-temporal structure since it is dependent on the distribution of matter, whereas for Whitehead the necessary relatedness (significance) of events leads to a uniform spatio-temporal structure of events (PRel 25c, 65a). On Einstein's view, what can we know about nature as a whole beyond the local space-time warping and mass distribution? This point will be discussed when we come to the doctrine of significance.

Finally we can note that there are certain predictions dealing with the shift of spectral lines made by Whitehead's theory and not accounted for by Einstein's that might serve as an empirical test between them (PNK 11).[11]

Section III. Epistemological Difficulties in the Classical Theory

Modern scientific methodology contains a basic confusion. This confusion, Whitehead says, "is the bifurcation of nature into two systems of reality, which, in so far as they are real, are real in different senses" (CN 30b). One system of reality consists of the entities and relations which are thought to constitute the being of a natural object but are never known in perception. The other system of reality consists of the entities and relations known in perception and supposedly caused by the former group. Stated in another way, the bifurcation of nature is the division of nature "into the nature apprehended in awareness and the nature which is the cause of awareness" (CN 31a). The former includes the immediately felt sense-impressions; the latter includes the hypothetical entities like electrons which are the cause of these impressions. "The meeting point of these two natures is the mind, the causal nature being influent and the apparent nature being effluent" (CN 31a).

Galileo made the classic statement of this doctrine at the dawn of modern science, concluding: "Hence I think that these tastes, odours, colours, etc., on the side of the object in which they seem to exist, are nothing else than mere names, but hold their residence solely in the sensitive body; so that if the animal were removed, every such quality would be abolished and annihilated. Nevertheless, as soon as we have imposed names on them, particular and different from those of the other primary and real accidents, we induce ourselves to believe that they also exist just as truly and really as the latter." [12] Newton reinforced this viewpoint in the beginning of his *Principia* (*Mathematical Principles of Natural Philosophy*), in the first scholium, with his distinction between sensed space and time and mathematical space and time, although this is not quite the same division as Galileo made, since Newton did not speak of mathematical space and time as the cause of sensed space and time.[13] Locke put this bifurcation view into systematic form in his *Essay Concerning Human Understanding*, with the distinction between primary and secondary qualities. The bifurcation view has several variant forms, which we shall distinguish shortly, but I do not think contemporary science has escaped from it. Let us see what it means in terms of the notion of causality.

Two kinds of causation have to be distinguished in the light of the bifurcation theory (cn 31c). First, there is the causal connection between some natural object and the effect of the object on the mind to produce immediately perceived sense data (cn 31c). This type of causal connection became clear with the advent of the transmission theories of light and sound (cn 26–27). The sense datum, some particular sound or color, is caused in the mind (or brain or whatever we want to call the location of the perceptual experience) by its relation to certain nerve impulses set off by the impinging of some wave pattern on the ear or eye (cn 32a). Second, there is the causal connection between one natural object and another. This is an interaction within nature.

Consider an example with both types of causation: someone strikes a bell with a hammer. The bell reacts in a certain way so as to set off a series of waves in the surrounding medium. The waves travel outwardly from the source and perhaps impinge upon the ear. A series of reactions takes place which set off certain impulses to the brain. These impulses are finally converted and perceived as certain sounds. What are some of the consequences of such a view of perception? First, what we directly know about nature is restricted to perceived sense data (causation in the first sense). The causal reactions between the hammer and bell, the bell and medium, and the medium and ear, are not perceived (causation in the second sense). They are hypothetical relations specified by certain postulates in different scientific theories. We have only elaborate indirect means of checking on such relations in terms of causal relations of the other type. If nature is restricted to perceptual experience we have no direct experience of these causal interactions in nature. Some theoretical superstructure is required to explain them. But of course there are good reasons for the bifurcation theory. We seem to need publicity, objectivity, and postulated entities to explain the tones of the bell and the motion of the molecules. The problem is how to get the two together inside nature.

In a relational view of space and time, we would have to have one set of space relations resulting from the relation of perceived events and another set of space relations resulting from the relation of hypothetical causal events (cn 21b,c). But these space systems would then belong to two different orders of reality. "Hence there is no pointwise connection between the two and it is meaningless to say that the molecules of the grass are in any place which has a determinate spatial relation to the place occupied by the grass [greenness] which we see" (cn 42a). And matters are worse if we also admit a relative theory of time.

There are various forms of the bifurcation theory. In its traditional form of Lockean dualism we are to suppose that some of our sense impressions are copies or true representations of the natural objects, such as shape and solidity, while other sense impressions are the result of causal actions on the mind, such as colors and sounds. On this theory we still have some contact with the natural object, but there are psychic additions to nature provided by the perceiver (cn 27c, 29–30, 43b,c). Or we may have a purely causal theory in which there are no copies or true representations but all our sense impressions are assumed to be caused by the postulated natural objects. On the purely causal theory we have no direct knowledge about the causal objects. Whitehead calls this the "Berkeleyan Dilemma": "Perceptions are in the mind and universal nature is out of the mind, and thus the conception of universal nature can have no relevance to our perceptual life" (pnk 8–9). Another extreme form of the bifurcation theory maintains that natural objects like electrons are purely conceptual (cn 45a). The bifurcation, in this case, is between sense perceptions and conceptual entities, and even if we call them fictions we still have bifurcation. It is not difficult in contemporary science to find these variants of the bifurcation fallacy. Certain quantum physicists advocate considering electrons as mere names for conceptual formulas necessary to connect sense impressions. Einstein advocated a purely causal theory but maintained the realist assumption of an external world of physical objects. Many chemists are Lockean dualists. They think that the shapes of molecular models have some approximation to the shape of these chemical compounds. And finally, many biologists still are naive realists, who believe that the muscle tissue they are dissecting is a direct picture of that anatomical structure.

The mention of naive realism connects our foregoing discussion of variants of the bifurcation theory with epistemological analysis in general. We have been discussing several steps in what is known as the dialectic of idealism, which begins with naive realism and ends in absolute idealism, having passed through dualism to Berkeley's phenomenalism and Hume's skepticism. If the bifurcation fallacy is a part of this larger whole, then it is relevant to ask what is the source of naive realism, and by what principle does the dialectic move to the bifurcation variants and finally to its recognizable untenability in Hume's skepticism? The explicit discovery of the principle will then show why "the attempted bifurcation of apparent nature into two parts of which one part is both causal for its own appearance and for the appearance of the other part, which is purely apparent, fails owing to the failure to establish any fundamental distinction between our ways of knowing about the two parts of nature as thus partitioned" (CN 44b).

Naive realism, and hence bifurcation, has its probable historical root in the doctrines generally attributed to common sense and presented in systematic form by Aristotle (CN 18). According to this simple theory of perception we are directly aware of qualities, or the properties of objects which they characterize. This is the assumption of an underlying stuff or matter which is a location for and support of the common-sense world of solid objects (CN 16b). Certain qualities (properties, characteristics, attributes) are predicated of some substance. Aristotle gave this view a metaphysics and a logic. In fact, Indo-European languages seem to be built around this view. We have statements with subjects qualified by certain predicates which tell us something about certain substances possessing certain attributes (CN 20–21). "The unquestioned acceptance of the Aristotelian logic has led to an ingrained tendency to postulate a substratum for whatever is disclosed in sense-awareness . . ." (CN 18b). In modern times the notion of matter (material) has been substituted for substance. Matter has properties which we can investigate through measured experiments. Galileo repudiated Aristotle's vocabulary and physical doctrines and implicitly rejected naive realism, which he replaced with a dualism. However, Aristotle's logic continued to dominate logical, physical, and epistemological analysis. One version of subject-predicate physics was substituted for another by changing laws appropriately. This Aristotelian logic severely restricted the development of logic until mathematical speculations opened the way for the *Principia Mathematica*'s generalized logic of relations. The source of naive realism in common sense with its systemization by Aristotelian logic set the stage for the dialectic of idealism.

Naive realism is refuted on the ground that it leads to logical contradictions. The same stick can look bent and at the same time feel straight. But how can a single self-identical object have these different qualities at the same time? The solution was to assume that the shape was a subjective sense datum causally linked to its self-identical object.

The relativity of the shapes of a coin to different observers indicates that the shapes are subjective in the minds of the observers because of their particular relations to the coin. How else explain this on the two-termed logical system of Aristotle, in which perception is a two-termed relation of perceiver to perceived (CN 150)? If the contradictions in naive realism are to be avoided, then what is perceived must be separated from the self-same object. This is the case because, if it is assumed that ultimate metaphysical relations are two-termed relations of subject and predicate, then relativity of the perceived to the perceiver implies the subjectivity of the perceived. Since there are only two relata, the relative shapes must belong to one or the other. Not to the object, because it is assumed to be a single self-same object. Hence to the perceiver. Relativity implies subjectivity. This assumption is required by the two-termed Aristotelian logic and is the key to the dialectic of idealism (PRel 27b). If the assumption is given up, the dialectic fails. But with the multiple relation logic of the *Principia Mathematica* the assumption need no longer be true, and the way is opened for a new theory of perception, namely, objective relativism. This theory retains a kind of bifurcation (objects and events) which is not vicious; it does not lead to contradictions, as the older bifurcation theories did.

The problems which a new theory of perception must face in the foundations of physics and epistemology have been presented, together with hints toward their solution. We are now ready to understand why Whitehead formulated his theory of perception as he did in PNK and CN and its connection with science.

Chapter IV

THEORY OF PERCEPTION

There is a sense in which the construction of a theory of perception obeys the proverb: "you can get out of it only what you put into it." Much depends on how you define perception. On the other hand, it is not just a game but an analysis of a certain aspect of our experience, and the analysis can be done correctly or incorrectly. Whitehead's analysis certainly departs from traditional views and is essential to an understanding of his empirical philosophy of science, because "Nature is that which we observe in perception through the senses" (CN 3b).

Section I. The General Structure of Perception

The analysis of perception in PNK, CN, and PRel is fairly stable, but there is a gradual expansion of the concept with increasingly detailed analysis. A clear presentation is given only in PRel; it is condensed into a few pages and often overlooked. The key to this is to be found in the comparison of statements in CN with those in PRel. In CN, Whitehead talks about sense-perception and sense-awareness (CN 3) while in PRel he talks about perception and awareness (PRel 19c). The question arises at once: are these the same or not? It has often been assumed that they are, with the result that people cannot understand the change from CN to PR. But Whitehead states that sense-awareness is only a part of awareness (PRel 20b). Hence what is said in PNK and CN about perception, perceiving, and nature is only part of his whole view of perception. The result is that we must dig out his theory of perception from a very condensed discussion in PRel and then use this theory to interpret the discussion in CN.

The need to turn to PRel is revealed in another way. Points on which Whitehead hesitates in CN are given a definite answer in PRel. In CN sense-perception contains an immediately given element, namely, sense-awareness. But it remains a question at this time whether sense-perception involves thought (cn 3e); if it doesn't, then sense-awareness and sense-perception are identical (cn 4d). In the expanded doctrine of prel this question is answered. Perception contains more than awareness; it contains thought, *i.e.*, cogitation (prel 19c). But cn allows for this possibility (cn 3e), and its theory is not affected by the answer to this question. Hence for the mature statement we turn to prel. The terminology shifts, as in all Whitehead's works, serving to confuse the hasty reader but also to add valuable connotations for the patient reader.

To see this gradual expansion of ideas one should compare pnk 59–61, cn 3–5, and prel 14–19, and further insert before pnk the earlier position of ot 135–42. In pnk Whitehead simply breaks up our perception of nature as a whole into related entities according to distinct procedures. Such a diversification of nature yields radically distinct entities like events, percipient objects, sense-objects, perceptual objects, and scientific objects. In cn sense-perception is realized to be more complex. Though it may contain thought, the emphasis is on sense-perception with its sense-awareness, while in prel he talks about perception, not sense-perception, awareness, not sense-awareness. Whitehead realized, I think, that things he said in cn required that sense-perception include thought. Finally, the full range of the transition is seen when we consider the view of ot, before pnk, wherein it was held that "facts are thoughts and thoughts are facts." Thus the analysis of perception widens and deepens. First we shall expound the full view of prel and then relate the others to it.

Prel declares that " 'perception' will be the name given to the consciousness of a factor when to full awareness cogitation of it as an entity is also superadded" (prel 19b, whа 309c). We have now to explain the parts of this definition. Factors are elements of fact involved in relationships within fact (prel 14b, whа 306b, pnk 59a). Fact is an ultimate primitive including all diversification (pnk 59a). It is *the* totality. It "is not an entity of cogitation, since it has no individuality by its reference to anything other than itself" (prel 15b, whа 306e). It contains all contrasts and cannot be contrasted with anything else. There is just one fact; we might call it "factuality." Factuality is what there is, considered as one single whole, and this totality is inexhaustible, infinite (prel 15b, whа 306e). It contains all concepts as well as percepts, in the traditional way of speaking (prel 15b, whа 306e). Factuality "cannot be exhausted by any definite class of factors" (prel 15b, whа 307a).

The term "awareness" is used for consciousness of factors within fact (prel 14c, whа 306c). Consciousness is taken as a primitive term. We shall see shortly how the sense-awareness of cn is part of awareness.

According to our explication of fact, "awareness is itself a factor within fact" (PRel 14c, whA 306c). Awareness, then, is one aspect of perception in which factors are discriminated, and always seen in relation to other factors of fact. Sometimes awareness focuses more on the factor than the relatedness and vice versa. "Full awareness" occurs when factors are clearly apprehended and their mutual relations are jointly apparent (PRel 19c, whA 309c). The clear awareness of the apparent factor is called "cognisance by adjective," while the awareness of its connection with other factors of fact is called "cognisance by relatedness" (PRel 64a, whA 338–39). In CN these are respectively "the discerned" and "the discernible" (CN 49c).

The process of considering a given factor of fact in and of itself abstracted from its relatedness in fact is termed "cogitation" (PRel 14d, whA 306d). In CN cogitation is called thought; hence the question posed in CN as to whether thought was a part of sense-perception is now answered. The factor cogitated upon as an individual is called an "entity" (PRel 14d, whA 306d). Perception then is concerned with fact, factors, and entities as they function in awareness and cogitation (CN 13c). For cogitation of an entity, there need not be full awareness of that factor. For example, the awareness of red as clearly presented but vaguely related still allows for cogitation of red as an entity (PRel 19d, whA 309d).

The above definitions make it clear that before cogitation can take place there must be awareness of factors of fact. Further, cogitation is limited by the process of awareness, for what we are not aware of we cannot cogitate about (PRel 15a, whA 306d). Cogitation is the refinement and further limitation of awareness. "Thus awareness is crude consciousness and cogitation is refined consciousness" (PRel 15a, whA 306d). This was Whitehead's view in 1922. Already cogitation (thought) and awareness were part of the same process of perception. It is strange that philosophers were so surprised at the doctrine of perception in SMW and PR. With some further refinements and an ontological doctrine the transition is easily made to SMW and PR. The concept of ultimate finite velocities in relativity physics leads directly to the splitting up of awareness into causal efficacy (because transmissions take time) and presentational immediacy; the rest is not so different.

"For awareness all relations between factors are internal and for cogitation all relations between entities are external" (PRel 15a, whA 306d). The major effort of cogitation is to get hold of the factor in its individuality, to catch its "itness," to see it standing alone by itself. This is the "individual essence" of SMW. On the other hand, awareness singles out the factor by seeing it in contrast to other factors of fact or as a focal point within fact. This is the "relational essence" of SMW (CN 13a).

The most general notion of limitation is of a focal point (factor) in fact (PREl 16c, whA 307c). The limitation of fact in various ways leads to different kinds of factors and entities. "Finite consciousness is a limitation of fact, in the sense that it is a factor canalising fact in ways peculiar to itself" (PREl 16d, whA 307d). Cogitation is a limitation of consciousness divesting it of the crudeness of awareness (PREl 17b, whA 307e). The important point here is that limitation expresses the negative side of the relatedness of factors in fact. To be aware of a factor is to have a focal point in fact in relation to other factors; that is, "any factor, by virtue of its status as a limitation within totality, necessarily refers to factors of totality other than itself" (PREl 18d, whA 308b). The whole doctrine of significance, so important to the success of this theory of perception, flows out of this concept of limitation.

We are now ready to make the transition to CN. If we eliminate from awareness the consciousness of logical, aesthetic, and moral awarenesses of factors within fact we are left with sense-awareness. Then we define nature as the "system of factors apprehended in sense-awareness" (PREl 20b, whA 309e). Thus sense-perception is that part of perception which focuses attention (cogitates) upon those factors of fact discriminated in sense-awareness (CN 12e). Nature, then, consists of those entities which we observe in sense-perception (CN 3e). Sense-awareness is not identical with sense-perception, since sense-perception requires cogitation (thought) to separate out entities according to our original definition (CN 3e). Natural science is concerned neither with thought (cogitation) nor with sense-awareness by itself but with the factors which are the termini of sense-awareness (CN 4a,b). For this reason Whitehead can speak of nature as closed to mind, that is, self-contained in contrast to sense-awareness (CN 4d). But the fact that nature can be studied as a system closed from mind does not imply that the two are completely independent or ultimately divorced. "It means that in sense-perception nature is disclosed as a complex of entities whose mutual relations are expressible in thought without reference to mind, that is, without reference either to sense-awareness or to thought" (CN 4-5). It is admitted that the factors of nature can be significant of factors not included in nature (PREl 21a, whA 310a). Nature can thus be considered as a closed system, or as a part of a larger system (the integration of mind and nature) in which those aspects of perception which were dropped to form sense-awareness are included in the analysis. The moral and aesthetic values may be the means of integrating mind and nature (CN 5b). Hence the stage is set for the work of smw.

According to our definition, sense-awareness is other than thought and precedes thought (cogitation) in perception. Now, if rational explanation is a process of thought, then the factors discriminated in sense-awareness cannot be explained, since thought follows awareness (CN 13b). They seem to be given and ineffable; given because thought arises from them and ineffable because they cannot be explained. The essential relatedness of a discriminated factor to other factors of fact provides its individuality or, we might say, the awareness of a factor constitutes a perspective on the whole of fact of which our awareness is an essential part. This private particularity of our awareness is just what is dropped out in the transition from awareness to cogitation, from factor to entity. In cogitation the entity is a public communicable thought, an abstract (CN 13b).

Just as fact itself is inexhaustible, so that part of fact discriminated by sense-awareness is also inexhaustible. There are relations between factors which are also factors and relations of relations which are factors and so on (CN 14a).

The analysis of perception in PNK is less subtle than in CN or PRel. Nature as closed to mind is expressed by saying that perception takes place within nature, "here within nature" and "now within nature" (PNK 13a). The analysis of fact into factors and then entities is called the diversification of nature, but at this stage fact, factor, and entity are hardly distinguished. Different modes of diversification yield different types of entities (PNK 60a). The complexity of fact is recognized but not described (PNK 69b). The vividness of perception depends on continual stimulation from the side of awareness and from the side of thought (PNK 98c).

In conclusion, this analysis of the general structure of perception indicates how Whitehead's thinking progressed from PNK through CN to PRel. Each work is a more detailed analysis of perception, and PRel is not the end. Further analysis leads directly into SMW. Problems solved at one stage are reopened and solved again at a later stage. The whole development shows a nice continuity.

Section II. The Structure of Events

The development of Whitehead's analysis of events is like that of his analysis of perception. This is made clear in the notes to the second edition of PNK (PNK 2d ed. 202). In PNK, Whitehead at first takes the notion of extension as fundamental, but the working out of his ideas leads him to see that it is process (passage of nature) that is fundamental and that extension is derivative from process. Sometimes PRel seems to take events as four-dimensional space-time units (PRel 21e, 29b, UC 6c), but Whitehead is quick to reaffirm the derivative character of space and time from events (PREL 29b, UC 15c). Arthur Murphy has contended that Whitehead made a fatal slip in advancing spatial and temporal aspects as basic to events rather than considering them as being just two of the many characteristics of events, and that this error is carried over into PR.[1] We shall consider this criticism later.

The general analysis of perception revealed the process of sense-awareness. Sense-awareness conveys the information that something is going on, namely, nature. What is going on can be discriminated in two ways. Some factors of fact are discriminated in their status as individual peculiarities directly perceived, while other factors are discriminated only in virtue of their relation to the factor directly perceived, such as the side of the door opposite the side we see (CN 14c). Hence, the occurrence which is the terminus for sense-awareness in a given sense-perception is a whole with two aspects. We are aware of certain directly perceived individualities, in CN called the "discerned," in PREL called "knowledge by adjective." On the other hand, we are aware of certain factors as relata of the directly discerned factors, in CN called the "discernible," and in PREL called "knowledge by relatedness" (CN 49c). For example, we are aware of this page we are reading with certain characteristic marks upon it; that is, we directly discern certain adjectives of this occurrence. But also we are aware of the reverse side of this page as related to the discerned side. We do not know any specific adjectives about the reverse side but we do have knowledge of it as a bare relatum. Sense-awareness is in contact with such occurrences. Also, the discerned components can be characterized in virtue of certain recognizable aspects which are called objects. It is the fact of recognition which enables us to separate the characters from their occurrence. The occurrence is called an event.

PNK defines events as "the relata of the fundamental homogeneous relation of extension" (PNK 61b). Extension is a primitive notion. Whitehead tries in this work to get everything out of extension (PNK 2nd ed. 202c), but the actual working out of his ideas in PNK requires the introduction of "cogredience" as another primitive. In CN "This structure of events is the complex of events as related by the two relations of extension and cogredience" (CN 52a). In PREL the analysis of sense-awareness has cut deeper. "Nature presents itself to us as essentially a becoming, and any limited portion of nature which preserves most completely such concreteness as attaches to nature itself is also a becoming and is what I call an event" (PREL 21b, WHA 310b). In PREL process is the fundamental notion. Extension and cogredience are derivative from process (PNK 2nd ed. 202b). This change from extension as fundamental to process is very important. It indicates Whitehead's break with the class theory as a means of constructing objects, the consequences of which we shall discuss later. Yet the views expressed in PNK, CN, and PRel with respect to events are little changed by this transition, since after extension is derived from process the analysis of events is the same, although a greater symmetry is achieved with respect to the definition of moments and points (CN 198c). The description of events which follows should be considered from two standpoints: (1) we should inspect our own perceptual experience to see whether the description is true and (2) we should remember the critique of science for which this theory is trying to provide a new foundation.

One of the first characteristics of events revealed in our analysis of the termini of sense-awareness is their spread-out-ness. We are aware of occurrences which have extension in two ways (PNK 61c). First the event occurs spread out over an area in our specious present, which means that we do not perceive points. This is extension in its spatial aspect, but it should be emphasized that it is not the homogeneous space of physics and mathematics. Spatiality must be distinguished from space. Secondly, an occurrence stretches through a duration containing the parts of our specious present. This means that we do not perceive instants of time (CN 57a). This aspect of extension is its temporality. The above comment about space applies equally to this distinction of temporality from time. Space and time are abstractions from the spatial and temporal aspects of extension. It may be asked: "But how do we know we are aware of extension and not points or instants?" The answer is simply to look and see. To this it is objected: "If I touch the end of a needle am I not aware of a point?" Not a mathematical point; and even if only a single nerve ending is touched, this too has size.

Events extend over and are extended over by other events. This sheet of paper extends over a part of the desk on which I am writing and the whole surface of the desk extends over this sheet of paper (PNK 61b). Similarly, the duration of time it takes to write this sentence extends over the duration of writing any word of the sentence and, conversely, the duration of forming any letter is extended over by the duration of writing the word in which it occurs. This aspect of extension is called the passage of nature. Two events can now be defined as separate from each other "if there is no event which is part of both" (PNK 61b). Two such separate events are said to be mutually external. Hence the externality of nature results from the fundamental relation of extension. But each of us as a perceiver is also an event, a percipient event, immersed in this externality. Events are both the medium in which our experience takes place and the development of that experience (PNK 63c).

Insofar as events have a spatial aspect they are said to be actual, and insofar as their temporal aspect is concerned they are said to participate in the becomingness of nature or the passage of nature. Thus events embody actuality and becoming (PNK 61c). In this sense events are the unity of being and becoming. Events are said to be concrete because each event embodies actuality and becoming and stands in a definite, unique relation to other events. Each event is ultimately related indirectly to all events, as will be made clear in our discussion of significance, and this guarantees the uniqueness of any event. An event is what it is in just that relation to everything else (PNK 61c). Events are quite similar to what are usually called particulars, but particulars are thought of as definite chunks of reality whereas events are not definite. Their boundaries are vague, shifting; they blend into one another. Further, a particular has traditionally a fixed characteristic, which would make it akin to Whitehead's objects, but an event is a locus for the ingression of many characteristics. Awareness of red "here-now" would be an example of a traditional particular, but for Whitehead this is a complex in which the red is repeatable while the "here-now" marks an unrepeatable event. For these reasons it is an error to identify Whitehead's event with the usual notion of a particular.

Events are neither wholly nor partly hypothetical (PNK 62a). It might seem that events grasped by knowledge by relatedness are in part hypothetical. This error arises because we are tempted to think of such an event in the light of certain characteristics it might have, but we are not aware of any definite adjectives in knowledge by relatedness. We are aware of it as a bare x, as a term in relation. Hypothetical thinking belongs to cogitation about entities and awareness precedes cogitation. It is true that we can imagine certain events (a process of cogitation) "but there is nothing actual about such events, except so far as imagination is actual" (PNK 62a). Objects, however, can have a hypothetical character, as will be shown later. Let us try to imagine the occurrence of a centaur. This act of imagination is complex. A centaur is a perceptual object which is hypothetical, recognizable, and repeatable, but the occurrence of the imagination must belong to the systematic interrelations of events; that is, be an event. Not to separate events and objects is what leads one to suppose there might be hypothetical events.

Events do not change (PNK 62b). We are aware of a certain event, say e^1, which is the occurrence of this sheet of paper through the interval of writing the last word of this sentence. The event does not change into another event e^2 which is the occurrence of this sheet of paper from the writing of that word to this word. Instead we say that event e^1 is part of this more inclusive event e^2. There is development in nature in the sense that one event becomes part of another event. The original event e^1 may be said to change only in the sense that it changes its relations to other events which had not yet become but now are. Whitehead calls this type of change the passage of nature. There is a passage of events but not change in the ordinary sense. One event becomes part of another but does not itself grow into some other event. The idea of becoming must not mislead us into wondering how some event comes into actuality from somewhere. Events just are, and it is a fundamental fact of awareness that some events are parts of others and that one way in which events are parts of others reflects the temporal side of extension in nature. Events are not to be conceived as in some sense potential until they become actual. The concept of potentiality did not enter Whitehead's thinking at this stage. Our sense-awareness reports the static quality of events. To say that events do not change is not to affirm that they are permanent, for they come to be and pass away in the ultimate becomingness which is the creative advance of nature (PNK 63b), but the becomingness is not in an event per se.

We have so far looked at an event from the standpoint of extension. An event is also defined in PNK as a factor which possesses certain characteristics called the "constants of externality" (PNK 72a). There are six major constants which we now want to consider. "Externality and extension are the marks of events," says Whitehead (PNK 62c). "The constants of externality are the conditions for nature, and determine the ultimate concepts which are presupposed in science" (PNK 72c). Whitehead considers only those constants from which the concepts of space, time, and material arise.

The first constant of externality asserts "that what has been apprehended as a continuum, is a potentially definite complex of entities for knowledge" (PNK 74b). Potential here is used in the special sense of the transition from awareness of factors to cogitation of entities. Whitehead insists that if we examine our sense-awareness carefully we shall find that what we are aware of is indefinite in its boundaries and highly complex in its relationships (PNK 73b). Consider, again, our awareness of this page. Can we fix definite boundaries to the awareness? For me, the awareness spreads over parts of the desk, perhaps even to the walls and a view out of the window. What thought (cogitation) does is to focus on the page in its individuality, mark it off with definite boundaries, and seize upon certain prominent relations. But the awareness itself is blurred. Before identities and other judgments can be asserted thought requires that some definiteness be achieved. One of the problems this theory of perception faces is how to get from the indefiniteness of awareness to the definiteness of thought. But on the other hand this indefiniteness of awareness leaves the door open for revisions in the fundamental concepts of science. The demarcation of an event reveals the transition from awareness to thought, from perception to science. The assignment of demarcation is arbitrary. Thought requires definite entities, events with definite boundaries, while awareness does not apprehend such. Hence this definiteness, the contribution of thought in perception, is a necessary assumption, requisite for the successful application of the principle of extensive abstraction. Those who criticize Whitehead's method of extensive abstraction on the empirical ground that perception does not provide such definiteness for events are really agreeing with Whitehead but forgetting that he includes an element of thought in perception which can provide the definiteness required. This criticism will be considered in the next chapter.

The second constant of externality concerns the fundamental relation of extension such that "an event x may 'extend over' an event y . . ." (PNK 74c). The explication of an event according to our first definition was based on the relation of extension. This fundamental characteristic of events provides the basis for the derivative concepts of space and time. It seems reasonable that concepts of such wide applicability in nature should be derivative from a characteristic common to all events. The formalization of the various properties of the relation of extension is the basis for the principle of extensive abstraction, which is used to define derivative concepts like space, time, event-particle, routes, and moments. These then provide the basis for the usual beginnings of deductive physical science.

The next three constants of externality have to do with the awareness of a duration and percipient events. The third constant of externality states that an apprehended event is related to a complete whole of nature, called a duration, which extends over it (PNK 77b). In perception we are aware of events which are related by extension. If we consider some given event we can choose among its extensive relations certain groups that lead to important properties. For example, we can consider the event, say this sheet of paper during the interval of writing this sentence. Further, we can single out for consideration those related events such that they have the same interval (PNK 68c): the top of the desk during that interval, my study, the city of Albuquerque, earth, the planetary system, and our galaxy. We may know nothing about the character of these related events; that is not important. But we can perceive them as bare relata in relation to this sheet of paper here-now, whose characteristics we do discern. Such a related complete whole of nature is a duration. According to Whitehead simultaneity is a characteristic of such a complete whole (PNK 68b, CN 53b). There is no question here of some separate event being simultaneous with the perceived event and hence the need of a transmission definition for simultaneity like Einstein's. Rather each one of these events is perceived, and extends over this sheet of paper in a special way. Whitehead is talking about the sensed simultaneity of events "now-present" (PNK 68b). "A duration is a concrete slab of nature limited by simultaneity which is an essential factor disclosed in sense-awareness" (CN 53b). A duration is a definite natural entity of perception, not an abstract stretch of time. A duration is a special type of event which is unbounded in its spatial aspect but limited in its temporal aspect by the condition of the sensed simultaneity "now-present" (PNK 69a, 111b).

The key factor which provides the basis for the apprehension of such a complete present whole of nature, a duration, is that the demarcation of events is not definite. They shade off into one another so that for any discriminated event brought into focus by cogitation, there always remains an awareness of a beyond whose presence we are aware of but whose qualities we do not discriminate (PNK 69b). This "beyondness" is the basis of externality.

A duration includes other events which are limited in both their spatial and temporal aspects. Those events which share the same temporal limitation are said to be simultaneous with the duration and in a derivative sense with each other (CN 53b). Further, a duration can include (extend over) other durations and be extended over. This leads to the notion of families of durations. The duration marked off by the temporal stretch of this sentence extends over the durations marked off by any word in the sentence and is extended over by the duration marked off by this paragraph.

"The fourth constant of externality is the reference . . . of the apprehended event [which defines a duration] to the percipient event . . ." (PNK 77c). The temporal limitation "now-present" which is required for the definition of a duration yields on analysis the fact that a duration is related to something else, for the "now" means a sensed simultaneity; that is, some thing to do the sensing, and the "present" means presented to something (PNK 69c). That with which the duration is simultaneous and to which it is presented is the event "here-present" which is called the percipient event. The percipient event must not be confused with what in traditional philosophic thought has been called the perceiver or mind (CN 107b). Nor does the notion of a percipient event argue in favor of realism or idealism. An event is neither mental nor physical, but the physical and mental are somehow abstractions from the concrete event (IET 131, 133b). The percipient event is an event in nature along with other events. It is one of the finite events limited in both its spatial and temporal aspects included in the duration defined by the apprehended event (PNK 70a).

The fifth constant of externality states that the percipient event has a definite station within the duration, or is at rest in the duration, or cogredient with the duration (PNK 78a). It has a definite station within the duration because otherwise we should be able to be aware of adjectives elsewhere in the duration as well as bare relata. Later, in PR, the percipient event becomes the "seat" of a "focal region" (PR 476a). That is to say, if the percipient event could be anywhere in the duration, we ought to be aware of adjectives as well as bare relata anywhere in the duration. But we are not. This indicates that the percipient event is here at some place in the duration.

Furthermore, the percipient event has the same temporal limitation as that event defining the duration. The duration is "now-present" and the percipient event is "here-present"; the same specious present is referred to (PNK 70b). The percipient event is the area of focus for that act of awareness (CN 107b). For example, the occurrence of this sheet of paper for the temporal stretch of this sentence defines an event which in turn defines a certain duration having the same temporal stretch. My act of awareness of this occurrence is another event with the same temporal limits, since it is marked out by the sheet-of-paper event. Hence, it is a finite event belonging to the same duration. Further, the percipient event is said to be at rest in the duration since it has the same temporal limitation as the duration; otherwise the meaning of "here" in "here-present" for the percipient event would be vague (PNK 70b). In more technical terms the percipient event is said to be cogredient with the duration because they both have the same temporal limitation (PNK 70b, CN 108d). The notion of "cogredience" is very important for working out the space-time system of physics.

"Cogredience" is another fundamental relation of perception in addition to extension. We do not define cogredience by saying that it is the relation between an event and a duration when they have the same temporal stretch, because in this context the word "same" means cogredience. This was, perhaps, the point at which Whitehead first saw that he could not build a philosophy of science (give an account of natural entities) in terms of extension alone. Further, their close connection may have provided the impetus to find a more basic notion from which they are derivative; namely, process, or the passage of nature (PNK 2d ed. 202c).

"An event can be cogredient with only one duration" (PNK 70c). Since it serves to define that duration, the event is temporally but not spatially present throughout the duration. The event and the duration have the same temporal limitation. "But a duration can have many events co-gredient with it" (PNK 70c). Each one of these is a finite event included in the duration having the same temporal limitation. It is "there-present" in the duration. A duration also extends over other events which are not cogredient with it (PNK 71b). Perceptual examples of these various statements about cogredience are readily thought of. The relation of cogredience specifies an absolute position for an event in a duration, and hence of absolute rest (PNK 71b). "The notion of motion is derivative from that of inclusion within a duration without cogredience with it" (CN 188b).

The sixth constant of externality states that there is a "community of nature"; an association of events which gives rise to the notions of continuity and publicity in nature (PNK 78c). The continuity of nature follows from the extension of events (CN 59a) and the lack of definite demarcation of events. When we are aware of a given event, this event has vague boundaries which are only made precise by the role of thought. It extends over other events and is extended over, and the lack of boundaries means one cannot say where one event leaves off. The knowledge of other events by relatedness gives both a temporal and spatial continuity (CN 197–98). Events provide a continuous background of nature. The spatial continuity of nature is especially revealed in durations, while the passage of nature, which forms families of overlapping durations, reveals the temporal continuity (CN 59a,b). Insofar as the percipient event is cogredient with its duration it is enmeshed in the continuity of nature. But, so far, this continuity of nature relates only to a given percipient event. How does this continuity achieve a public status? The publicity of nature for different observers results from the notion of durations (CN 55–56). It is true that the discerned characteristics (knowledge of adjectives) of any given act of awareness are different from any other such act because each such act of awareness involves a complex of related events in relation to that percipient event as a focus (CN 55a). But the percipient event defines a duration which does involve other events, some of which may be percipient events for other acts of awareness. Some of these other possible percipient events could define the same duration. It is this possible identity of durations which provides publicity among percipient events; provides a community of nature for all awareness.

These six constants of externality express the general nature of events. Later on after we have discussed the objects of perception we shall consider the nature of some important events relating to various objects. We have also postponed any discussion of the doctrine of significance, in which events play a key role, since we need in addition some information about objects for its complete exposition. With respect to the development of Whitehead's thought the point to be emphasized in this section is the introduction of the notion of events into the analysis of perception—in contrast to OT, which confined its analysis to objects. But the doctrine of objects also underwent changes which we shall now consider.

Section III. Objects in Perception

In harmony with previous sections, we can begin by stating in a general way the development or change in Whitehead's notion of an object in PNK, CN, and PRel. The change has been pointed out before and carefully discussed by L. Susan Stebbing in her articles.[2] It is explicitly remarked by Whitehead in the notes to the second edition of PNK in 1925 (PNK 2d ed. 204b). But the change is not clear-cut. The analysis of objects in PNK, the first work of the group, "is confused by a wavering between the 'class-theory' of perceptual objects and the 'control theory' of physical objects, and by the confusion between perceptual and physical objects" (PNK 2d ed. 204b). As Whitehead develops, he turns more and more to the control theory in PRel and UC. By 1925, the year he published SMW, he says: "I do not hold the class theory now in any form, and was endeavouring in this book to get away from it" (PNK 2d ed. 204b). The class theory of objects was adhered to in OT, and in PNK (1919) but in CN (1920) with hesitations. The class theory holds that a perceptual object is a class of sense-objects. But the sense-objects are said to be private and the perceptual objects public. So the problem arises as to how a class of private things in an irreducible multiple relation constitutes a public thing. The control theory of PRel (1922) and UC (1922) states that a perceptual object is a "pervasive adjective" of its situation for the control of the ingression of sense-objects. With the general situation before us, we can now proceed to a detailed analysis of the perceptual recognition of objects according to both theories and the reasons for Whitehead's shift from the one to the other. Although there are inconsistencies the two theories have much in common. We look at the common elements first.

Objects are the recognizable permanent characters of events (PNK 62–63, CN 143–44, PRel 26a). "Objects enter into experience by recognition and without recognition experience would divulge no objects. Objects convey the permanences recognised in events, and are recognised as self-identical amid different circumstances . . ." (PNK 62–63). "An object is an ingredient in the character of some event. In fact the character of an event is nothing but the objects which are ingredient in it and the ways in which those objects make their ingression into the event" (cn 143–44). The general notions to be clarified about objects are recognition, permanence, and ingression (ingredient). The last sentence quoted above makes it clear why the description of an event is so difficult; namely, because the description is made in terms of characteristics or objects, and these entities are not the event. An event devoid of its characteristics (objects) is an indefinable particular of which nothing can be said. It is a mere "it," an occurrence. Any characteristic of it is an object. Thus, in a sense, even extension, and consequently space and time, are objects (cn 189c).

Whitehead nowhere says so, but it seems a reasonable interpretation of his ideas to conceive of awareness as having two aspects: (1) the apprehension of events and (2) the recognition of objects (pnk 67a,b). Hence sense-awareness of nature would include sense-apprehension and sense-recognition (cn 143a). I interpret this to mean that, if the object focused upon in sense-recognition as a part of sense-awareness is divested of its connection with that particular event and considered by itself, then thought (cogitation) performs this isolation. The object discriminated in that sense-recognition can function in the intellectual procedure of comparison, which is a component of cogitation (cn 125c). This interpretation solves a possible difficulty. For if recognition (sense-recognition) required that we perceive the object before recognizing it then "there never could have been a first knowledge" (pnk 64a, tsm 51b).

"Recognition is an awareness of sameness" (cn 143a). But this sameness is not an intellectual act of comparison (cn 124d). Rather we must emphasize that we perceive an event of which some object is a characteristic, and this event defines a duration. The duration contains many smaller durations. The recognition of the permanence of the object throughout these included durations is what is meant by the awareness of sameness (pnk 64a, tsm 51b, cn 124d).

Recognition is not the comparison of the object in this perceived duration with some previously perceived duration, for this would lead to the infinite regress mentioned above about first knowledge. Recognition, which is carried beyond the present perceived duration, involves recollection, memory, and comparison (pnk 64a, 82c). Notice how closely recognition in sense-awareness is connected with comparison in cogitation as a hint of the close connection of the mental and physical poles of an actual occasion in pr.

Recollection can be defined as "the indefinite recognition . . . which is the awareness of other perceptions of the object as related to other events separate from the specious present, but without any precise designation of the events . . ." (pnk 82c). Recollection is thus an intellectual procedure of cogitation involving recognition and awareness of several events. Memory can now be defined as "the definite recognition . . . which is an awareness of perception of the object as related to certain other definite events separate from the specious present" (PNK 82c). These definitions are important because they reveal how Whitehead can define two intellectual procedures on an empirical basis of sense-recognition and sense-awareness of events.

The theory of recognition extends beyond the recognition of objects (PNK 57a). The theory of congruence for Whitehead is a part of the theory of recognition (CN 124d). "Our recognitions are the ultimate facts of nature for science, and the whole scientific theory is nothing else than an attempt to systematize our knowledge of the circumstances in which such recognition will occur" (PNK 56–57). Congruence depends upon judgments of constancy for measuring devices, and a judgment of constancy is a recognition of objects as permanent.

Recognition provides the ground from which abstraction enters into perception. In our experience, we apprehend events as the concrete factors and recognize objects in such events. To recognize any single object of an event is to abstract from it and to abstract requires the recognition of diverse objects in the whole event (CN 189b).

The second notion in our definition of an object that needs clarification is permanence. The permanence of an object results from the recognition of sameness throughout some duration (specious present of perception). In another sense, objects are permanent because they are outside space and time. Space and time are particular relations belonging to the extension of events; "space and time are abstractions from events" (PNK 63b). Objects change in the sense that a single object can have diverse relationships to diverse events (PNK 63b). Events are neither permanent nor changing, for change and permanence are themselves characteristics or objects abstracted from events. Events just are. Hence physical change has to be defined in terms of objects. The knowledge of the permanence of any object, regardless of whether in fact it is ever recognized again, results from the fact that we perceive durations which contain smaller durations. Hence recurrence in separate perceptions is not necessary for knowledge of permanence.

If we ask how objects are related to events, the answer is, by the relation of ingression. "The ingression of an object into an event is the way the character of the event shapes itself in virtue of the being of the object" (CN 144c). Ingression is the general relation between any object and any event (PRel 37b, whA 321b). Since there are many kinds of objects, perhaps an indefinite number (CN 149a), and each kind has a different sort of relation to events, there are various modes of ingression

(CN 145b). Every event has objects ingredient in it and every object is ingredient in some event.[3] But sometimes we are aware of events in knowledge by relatedness, wherein the objects evade our recognition (CN 145a). Such objects are known to science by indirect inferential procedures, but they are nevertheless objects in perception, although strictly speaking not in awareness. Whitehead's position that such inferred objects are given in perception has served to confuse many of his critics who do not take time to distinguish awareness and cogitation in perception. It is even true that the same kind of an object can ingress into events in different ways (CN 145c). Common sense has not bothered to distinguish these different ways in any detail. This is the task of science. The fact that events extend over and are extended over by other events leads to the view that the ingression of an object in some event exercises an influence on the related events. This gives raise to the notion of a field of influence of an object (CN 145c, 190a). Moreover the general extension of events drives us to the conclusion that the object's field extends to all nature, although its quantitative effect may be irrelevant (CN 145c).

Among the various modes of ingression of objects in events there is one which common sense and science have singled out as very important: the relation of situation. The table is said to be in a certain place; the molecule is at some place (CN 146–47). But the relation of situation is not the same for different kinds of objects, and science has suffered from not recognizing this fact. We shall treat the relation of situation along with each type of object we discuss.

A few more points about the general interconnection of events and objects can be noted. An event need not have a clearly demarcated object in it (CN 78b). The recurrence of an object in different events follows from its permanence. This recurrence need not happen, but the fact that it can leads to the notion of possibility, which belongs to all objects (PNK 64c). Since objects are not in space and time because space and time are themselves abstractions of events, it follows that an object can be in many places at the same time and at many times in the same place (PNK 65c, CN 125c). The object green can be in many plant-events for several separate durations. Objects do not have parts. The leg is not a part of the chair-object but another object; namely, leg-object (PNK 65c). Lastly, at this stage of Whitehead's thought, the atomicity of nature derives from objects, and, as already explained, the continuity of nature resides in events. The reason for this atomicity will be shown in the section on significance. In PR atomicity and continuity derive from the nature of actual entities.

"A sense-object is a factor of nature posited by sense-awareness which

(1), in that it is an object, does not share in the passage of nature and (2) is not a relation between other factors of nature" (CN 149b). In the sense that a sense-object is not a perceived relation, it is the simplest type of permanence (PNK 83c, PRel 28). Such sense-objects are colors, tastes, sounds, or other particular feelings. External events cannot be apprehended without the recognition of sense-objects and conversely (PNK 83d). Sense-objects are a basic type of object insofar as they do not express any permanence of relatedness between objects of another type (PNK 84a).

The primary thing to notice about sense-objects is that they do not have a simple two-termed relation to nature (PNK 84b). The persistent dogma resultant from Aristotelian logic that relations in concrete reality are two-termed has caused much error in philosophy. The assumption that relativity implies subjectivity is closely connected with it. The analysis of sense-objects is an explicit challenge to this dogma (CN 150–51). The events involved in the multiple relation of a sense-object to nature can be classified into three groups not mutually exclusive: percipient events, events which are situations of sense-objects, and conditioning events (PNK 84c). In CN four groups are mentioned by dividing conditioning events into active and passive conditioning events (CN 152b).

The reason why sense-objects exist in multiple relations to nature is that Whitehead wishes to avoid the subjectivity of sense-data. Consider, for example, just the shapes involved in the perception of a coin, which are visual sense-objects. The manifest fact is that from different positions different shapes are perceived, and the old problem is how the same coin can have different shapes. The usual answer has been that the visual shape is a subjective factor due to some relation between the perceiver and the coin. Shape is not to be considered as indicating something about the coin but about the perceiver's relation to the coin. If it is admitted that such relativity implies subjectivity, Hume's skepticism follows, except perhaps for the objective idealists. Whitehead's effort is to re-do Hume's analysis in order to avoid Hume's conclusion (UC 14).

Whitehead's answer to Hume is put in two ways. In UC and PRel he tries to show that the perception of a given event is significant of other events; that there is knowledge contained in one individual instance about other instances. This is the doctrine of significance which we will discuss shortly. In CN and PNK, Whitehead proceeds to point out the erroneous character of the two-termed Aristotelian logic relating a sense-object to nature. These amount to the same thing in the end, for significance entails the erroneousness of the two-termed doctrine.

Consider our perception of the shape of the coin. First, we are aware of a given event via the recognition of a certain shape as ingredient in that event. Second, we are aware of the percipient event which includes our awareness of that recognition. What is essential for perception is that the duration defined by the percipient event include the event which is apprehended by the recognition of that shape (PNK 84–85). There is no simple case of a particular shape qualifying a given thing. Instead our concrete occurrence in nature involves at a minimum a percipient event, an object, the situation-event for the recognition of the object, and intervening events (CN 152a). To abstract certain relata from this multiple inherence of events and objects is to falsify the concrete occurrence in nature. The concrete occurrence is objective, which means that it is a part of the system of nature and not all inside our head. Further, it is relative, since the multiplicity of relations makes reference to the percipient event a necessity.[4] On this theory, objects by themselves are not concrete, self-sufficient things but characteristics of events. Hence we cannot talk about the contradictory objective shapes of the coin. Each perception of the coin is a complex occurrence involving multiple relations, some of which are the same but many of which are different. Each such complex occurrence is an objective facet of nature relative to the percipient event because of the necessary specification of that event in the complex multiple relation of the concrete occurrence.

If this seems a most difficult and paradoxical answer, Whitehead would remind us how deeply ingrained such basic presuppositions as "relativity implies subjectivity" are. Philosophy has usually taken objects as concrete and made events derivative as being a certain complex of objects. Whitehead reverses this. He makes events concrete, internally significant of each other, forming the whole interrelated system of nature, and makes objects the recognizable characteristics of events. However, either one without the other is a falsification of nature.

Thus in the polyadic relation of a sense-object to nature one important set of events involved is the set of percipient events; namely, those events which have the awareness of recognition of that sense-object as characterizing that situation-event.

Another important set of events in these polyadic relations is the set of situation-events; that is, *where* we see or feel or perceive the sense-object (PNK 85, CN 152b). Consider the perception of the color of a star. The color sense-object is situated in a certain event belonging to the duration defined by the percipient event, but that same color sense-object is also situated in a certain event in the past of the percipient event, for the light from the star took time to reach us. These two situation-events of that color sense-object are closely connected in science, but the perception of the two situations needs to be carefully distinguished (PNK 85d). Their connection in nature is affected by other kinds of objects and conditioning events. The situations of sense-objects vary greatly for different types. Sound sense-objects have a very vague situation affected by many conditioning events (PNK 86a).

Suppose we restrict our considerations to a single percipient event and a single situation, then our polyadic relation is completed by the conditioning events, active and passive. The active conditioning events are those events particularly relevant for that situation-event as the locus for that percipient (CN 152b) or the cause of that situation (PNK 86b). The passive conditioning events include the rest of nature, which is systematically internally related to the situation-event but has negligible effect on it (CN 152b, PNK 86b). Scientific laws of nature have thus far been concerned only with the active conditioning events and percipient events. This accounts for the seeming externality of relations in nature. But in Whitehead's view it would follow that a finished science would require knowledge of the minute effects of passive conditioning events. Further, science "depends on the fact that in general certain simple types of characters of active conditioning events repeat themselves" (PNK 87a). The difference between active and passive conditioning events is a matter of their degree of relevance in the determination of the situation-event. Active conditioning events are generally antecedent to the situation-event (PNK 87c).

It follows from what we have said about sense-objects, their situations, durations, and percipient events, "that in general the situation of a sense-object is not only the situation of that sense-object for one definite percipient event, but is the situation of a variety of sense-objects for a variety of percipient events" (PNK 154b). For example, in the case of a single percipient event the same situation event may be involved for a sense-object of sight, touch, sound, etc., and further that situation-event may be involved in other polyadic relations to other percipients. At this stage of his development (PNK, CN) Whitehead held that there is a correlation of sense-objects ingredient in the same situation (CN 154b), which is a habit of experience (CN 155b), such that one sense-object can convey another sense-object (CN 145b, PNK 88–89). Such an association of sense-objects in the same situation is called a "perceptual object" (CN 155b, PNK 88c).

The definition for the complete recognition of a perceptual object in PNK and CN involves (1) the primary recognition of an association of sense-objects in the same situation; (2) the conveyance of other sense-objects by these primary recognitions; and (3) the perceptual judgment as to the general character of the perceptual object (PNK 89b). The perceptual judgment has two aspects: (1) that the association of sense-objects in that situation with certain limited modifications be recognizable by other percipient events; and (2) that this common situation be an active conditioning event for these recognitions (PNK 89c).

Some elaboration of this definition is in order. What is recognized in the association of sense-objects in the same situation is the permanence of the group. We perceive this desk as a perceptual object in which are associated a certain color sense-object, a shape sense-object, a characteristic sound and hardness when rapped with the finger, and when I return tomorrow the same group of sense-objects are associated in a similar situation. But the association conveys other sense-objects perceived in other circumstances, like other shape sense-objects from different perspectives, and color sense-objects under changing illumination. On the other hand, sense-objects do not have to be perceived as belonging to an association forming a perceptual object, and when perceived in such an association the sense-object can be recognized as itself or as conveying the perceptual object (PNK 78c). The perceptual judgment, by dropping out fine distinctions which would serve to restrict the perceptual objects to a private basis, adds to the sense-awareness of the perceptual object both clarity and precision. It is just such a point as this that forces Whitehead in SMW and PR to the view of eternal objects as abstract.

In PNK and CN, Whitehead provides no real explanation of how a group of sense-objects, each with its unique polyadic relation of ingression into nature, can through association form a perceptual object which he maintains is a public, recognizable object. Apparently he felt this difficulty, for in PRel and UC another definition of a perceptual object is given; and the incompatibility of the two definitions is first explicitly recognized in the notes to the second edition of PNK in 1925, although there is a hint of the inadequacy of the first definition in PNK when Whitehead says: "the [perceptual] object is *more* than the logical group; it is the recognisable permanent character of its various situations" (PNK 91a, my italics). A study of UC indicates that this difficulty with the first definition was recognized by him in his analysis of Hume's doctrine of the association of sense-impressions (UC 14c,d,e). If no single sense-awareness of a sense-object is significant of other sense-objects, what reason can there be for any recognizable permanence of association or publicity of perceptual objects? There must be significance in a single instance of sense-awareness (UC 14–15).[5]

In PRel and UC a perceptual object is defined as "a true Aristotelian adjective of some event which is its situation" (UC 15b), or as a true pervasive adjective such that it is an adjective of every stretch of the route (PRel 32a, whA 317b), or "an adjective of any temporal slice of that event" (UC 15b). An adjective is a factor of fact or object recognized in sense-awareness as qualifying the situation-event. It is an Aristotelian adjective in the sense of being an adjective related to the event by the two-termed Aristotelian relation of adjective qualifying substantive (uc 17c). A route is "an event with only one dimension of finite extension . . ." (prel 29e, wha 316c). A stretch is a finite section of a route. Thus the pervasive adjective must be present in any stretch of the route regardless of the situation of the percipient event. The difference between an adjective which is a sense-object and one which is a perceptual object is that the former is involved in a polyadic relation of which the percipient event is an essential relatum while the latter does not involve the percipient event as a relatum. Hence the relation of any percipient event to a perceptual object is external. The definition of pervasive adjectives given in prel is more restricted that that in uc since it involves the restriction of such pervasion to historical routes, whereas tables, chairs, and trees, for example, are not strictly speaking historical routes, since routes have only one dimension of finite extension (prel 32a). But Whitehead states that this restriction can be overcome (prel 33–34) and refers to the definitions for a uniform object in pnk.

This new definition of a perceptual object accounts for its publicity, since the percipient event is not a necessary relatum in its ingression. Hence the difficulty of accounting for how the association of private sense-objects can form a public perceptual object is avoided. But we have now to find a new relation between sense-objects and perceptual objects, since it is the sense-objects which convey the perceptual objects. "Thus the ultimate character of perceptual objects is that they are Aristotelian pervasive adjectives which are the controls of ingression" for sense-objects (uc 17b).

The control theory of perceptual objects is a part of the general doctrine of significance. "The ingression of a sense-object into nature is significant of perceptual objects, so that thereby perceptual objects are known by relatedness" (uc 15c). We are aware of sense-objects in nature because they are the result of perceptual objects ingredient in events (uc 16e), or we can say that the perceptual object is a permanent factor of nature which conditions the appearance of sense-objects (prel 73c, wha 318c). Hence, according to uc and prel, perceptual objects are known as signified by sense-objects, but nevertheless the sense-objects are supposed to be the result of or conditioned by the ingression of perceptual objects which are their controls. For example, we recognize certain sense-objects like white color, rectangular shape, and smooth feel whose ingression into nature is controlled by the ingression into nature of a perceptual object; namely, the sheet of paper. The perceptual object is the condition for the appearance of those sense-objects. Thus in a sense we can speak of the perceptual object as the cause of the appearance of the sense-objects. Whitehead extends this type of analysis to the perceptual object, whose appearance is conditioned or caused by the scientific object which is its control or cause. These perceptual objects (pervasive adjectives) mark a breakdown in the reign of relativity in nature, for no reference to the percipient, his motion or position, is required (UC 17c). When Whitehead states that perceptual objects are common-sense tables, chairs, flowers, and birds we must be careful, for the common-sense theory does not possess the subtlety of Whitehead's although both theories are trying to account for the same perceptual phenomena. Whitehead's rejection of any simple substance-attribute philosophy replaced by his complex events and objects should make clear the different characters of common objects.

The change in the definition of a perceptual object marks the end of Whitehead's use of the class theory in any form (PNK 2d ed. 204c), and we are forced to resort to the doctrine of significance for the perceptual basis of the second definition. Here again is evidence of the gradual development of Whitehead's ideas. It seems impossible to tie his ideas down at any point. In the end it seems more reasonable to view PNK, CN, and PRel and their theories as experimental stages on the way to PR and AI. We return now to PNK and the definition of a physical object.

In our awareness of perceptual objects we are struck by one fundamental distinction: with respect to some perceptual objects our perceptual judgment is in error while in others our judgment is true. In the case of an awareness of a perceptual object in a mirror, (1) the association of sense-objects is not the same for different percipient events (CN 155c), and (2) the situation event of the perceptual object behind the mirror is not an active condition for the ingression of this association of sense-objects (CN 155c). Recognition of these two fundamental groups leads to another group of objects called physical objects, which are the group of non-delusive perceptual objects (PNK 90b).

In PNK and CN a perceptual object is defined as a physical object "when (1) its situation is an active conditioning event for the ingression of any of its component sense-objects, and (2) the same event can be the situation of the perceptual object for an indefinite number of possible percipient events" (CN 156b). Comparison will show that these are the two conditions making up a perceptual judgment (PNK 89c). Before we explore the consequences of this definition it should be noted that the shift in the definition of a perceptual object from the class theory to the control theory entails a change in the conception of a physical object (PNK 2d ed. 204c). This change will be discussed shortly.

A physical object is often called a cause because the event of its situation is an active condition necessary for its perception via the associated sense-objects. But the active conditioning event should not be confused with the object, as has happened in modern science (PNK 90c). The active conditioning events, which are the situations of physical objects, are either generating conditions or transmitting conditions. For example, a glass of water is a perceptual object in a certain situation. This situation is the generating condition-event for the associated group of sense-objects of shape, color, and wetness. At the same time, the glass of water is a transmitting condition-event for the light waves passing through it, which are refracted. But the situation of the glass of water is a passive conditioning event for me (a perceptual object) who happen to be mirrored in it. I, as situated in the glass of water, am a delusive perceptual object.

Physical objects like perceptual objects are perceived via the associated sense-objects and are Aristotelian adjectives in the sense that their ingression into nature does not require reference to the percipient event (PNK 90–91). But sense-objects are not merely attributes of physical objects as Aristotle and the Scholastics thought (CN 156b). Every physical object has associated sense-objects but not conversely. The difference rests on their different types of situations.

The situation of a physical object has the properties of uniqueness and continuity (CN 157a). By uniqueness Whitehead means that, in progressively smaller and smaller durations approximating to a moment of time, the situation of the physical object is within that duration alone. By continuity he means that in two separated durations, each of which is the situation of the physical object, a set of events can be found linking the two durations such that each is the situation of the physical object (CN 157b). The situations of sense-objects do not have these properties. Sense-objects can be situated at different places in the same duration and in different durations without any continuity or connection.

Physical objects are infected with vagueness. On the one hand, vagueness arises from the unique situation of such objects in a duration (PNK 91b). This has led to the confusion of the object with the event which is its situation. When we concentrate attention on the situation-event, we erroneously divide the objects into parts by considering the events included in the situation-event cut down finally to a durationless instant with all the attendant errors this brings. This vagueness is overcome by remembering the distinction between object and situation. On the other hand, vagueness arises from "the impossibility of submitting the group of associations, forming the object, to any process of determination with a progressive approximation to precision" (PNK 92b). Consider a chair: at what moment in its deterioration is it no longer a chair?

With the advent of the control theory of perceptual objects in PREL and UC a new definition of the physical object is also required. Physical objects are controls for the ingression of perceptual objects in nature. They are no longer a subclass of perceptual objects as in PNK and CN (PNK 2d ed. 204c). If we perceive a perceptual object in a mirror, that object's ingression into nature is controlled by a physical object of which it is the appearance. Hence we can also speak of the physical object as the cause of the perceptual object. To be precise, the one is the cause of the other only in an indirect fashion insofar as the situation-event of the physical object is an active conditioning event for the situation of the perceptual object (PNK 92a). Likewise the perceptual object is an indirect cause of sense-objects insofar as the situation-event of the perceptual object is an active conditioning event controlling the situation-events of the sense-objects.

Scientific objects are recognized in perception in an effort to overcome the vagueness of physical objects. They result from the effort to recognize the characters of the active conditioning events of physical objects. "Scientific objects are not directly perceived, they are inferred by reason of their capacity to express these characters, namely, they express how it is that events are conditions. In other words they express the causal characters of events" (PNK 95c). Their hypothetical status results from the fact that the perceptual judgment introduces the notion of hypothetical percipient events perceiving this character of some active conditioning event as a permanent causal character of events (PNK 93–94). This causal influence of a scientific object is effected in two ways: (1) by its permanence and (2) by its field (PREL 35a, whA 319d). Since it influences events in the future it is to be contrasted with sense-objects which qualify events only in the present directly perceived duration (PREL 34–35, whA 319d).

The permanence of the scientific object which is the character of some active conditioning event for a physical object and hence for the directly perceived sense-objects results from the fact that some historical route has that scientific object ingredient in it (PREL 35a, whA 319e). An historical route is a route which lies in the past and future of each and every event in the route (PREL 30c, whA 316f). That is to say, an historical route is the abstract one-dimensional extension of time, a time-line. But this permanence only tells us that some pervaded route will stretch into the future and past. The determination of the character of this scientific object depends upon knowledge about other objects and events.

The field of a scientific object consists of those events whose characters are affected by the ingression of that scientific object into that event

(PNK 95d), or by the pervasion of that adjectival particle into that historical route (PRel 35c, whA 319f). Ultimately the field of a scientific object includes the whole of nature because of the systematic inter-connectedness of all events. But for the present purposes of science this all-inclusiveness is negligible. This field-effect depends upon that aspect of the doctrine of significance which finds events significant of objects in mutual relations (PRel 26a, whA 313–14). "The particular objects and their particular relations belong to the sphere of contingence; but the event is essentially a 'field', in the sense that without related objects there can be no event. On the other hand related objects signify events, and without such events there are no such objects" (PRel 26a, whA 314a).

To specify in more detail the nature of certain scientific objects like electrons, as Whitehead does, goes beyond the general theory of perception as a foundation of natural science to the investigation of the results of a certain stage in the history of science. This particular exemplification of the general theory is reserved for the next chapter. It is not a part of the general theory.

Whitehead sees no reason why upon further analysis of perception we may not find other types of objects not yet discriminated just as, beginning with sense-objects, we found perceptual, physical, and scientific objects (CN 163a). There are some further definitions concerning the location of objects, uniform objects, components of objects, material objects, and adjectival particles which depend upon the derivation of space and time from events and pertain more to the application of the general theory of perception to current scientific doctrines. Insofar as they are important to our discussion we shall treat them in the next chapter dealing with applications.

There is one additional type of object mentioned by Whitehead in PNK called the percipient object, to be distinguished from the percipient event. It is not strange that a theory of perception should have some reference to a percipient or perceiver or mind. Whitehead distinguished five different ways of diversifying nature: (1) events, (2) percipient objects, (3) sense-objects, (4) perceptual objects, and (5) scientific objects (PNK 60a). We have discussed all but percipient objects. What he has to say about the percipient object is brief. "The percipient event is discerned as the locus of a recognisable permanence which is the 'percipient object'" (PNK 83b). There is nothing strange about this definition. The percipient object is a particular kind of recognizable permanence of an event just as a sense-object is a particular kind of permanence of an event. The percipient object "is the unity of the awareness whose recognition leads to the classification of a train of percipient events as the natural life associated with one consciousness" (PNK 83b). Since the specious present is a temporal duration, "the self-knowledge of the percipient object is a knowledge of the unity of the consciousness within other parts of the immediate present" (PNK 83b). Whitehead does not continue the discussion of percipient objects, for they take us beyond the limits of this inquiry (PNK 83b), since a percipient object is in some sense beyond nature (PNK 195a).

The similarity of the percipient object to mind is manifest, but Whitehead claims that nature is closed to mind. This looks like an inconsistency. An answer may be found by recalling the sense in which nature is said to be closed to mind; namely, that nature can be considered as systematically interrelated and rationally comprehensible without reference to mind. If the percipient object is identified with what is usually called mind, this would involve in Whitehead's terms a metaphysical discussion which he by-passes in these books. But he realizes the incompleteness of the study (*cf.* the preface of the second edition of PNK, where he hints at the forthcoming complete study of SMW). Finally, the close connection of the percipient object with nature points toward the doctrine of prehensions in PR, wherein he makes explicit how nature and mind can be related. The whole question of mind and the closure of nature to mind is discussed by Stebbing,[6] but she seems reluctant to turn to PR for Whitehead's answer and wants a completely consistent view in PNK, CN, and PRel. This is to ask of Whitehead what he never intended to do. It is only the theory of prehensions which really makes understandable what Whitehead means by the closure of nature to mind. "Closure" is a bad word for it.

Section IV. The Doctrine of Significance

At crucial points in our discussion of this theory of perception we have had recourse to the doctrine of significance in order to explain our point. It is safe to say that without this doctrine Whitehead's theory would have no foundation. It is the means whereby he can remain an empiricist yet avoid Hume's skepticism, and later construct a cosmological system. To understand the development of this doctrine is in large part to understand the development of Whitehead's philosophy. In PR it becomes the theory of prehensions and in AI the doctrine of mutual immanence. But certain important points about its empirical basis are presented in PRel and also certain answers to objections which are not repeated later. Further, the doctrine undergoes an expansion from PNK through CN to PRel, which Whitehead recognized (CN, notes to 1930 reprint, pp. 197–98).

Whitehead tells us that there are two ways in which he arrives at the doctrine of significance (uc 8–9). In uc he proceeds to show that Hume's analysis of experience contains presuppositions which Hume's conclusions denied, and that a re-examination of Hume's analysis in an effort to make explicit the hidden presuppositions leads to the internal relatedness of events and the mutual significance of objects. In prel Whitehead proceeds from general philosophical considerations concerning our perception of nature; that is, our perception of particular items of awareness called factors of fact (uc 9a).

Whitehead's analysis of Hume in uc leads to significance in two ways: (1) to the uniformity of space and time relations, and (2) to the significance of one instance (object) of another. Hume says: "It appears, then, that this idea of necessary connection amongst events arises from a number of similar instances, which occur, of the constant conjunction of these events, nor can that idea ever be suggested by any one of these instances surveyed in all possible lights and positions." [7] Thus Hume assumes a spatio-temporal character of nature in the idea of constant conjunction; otherwise the contiguity account of causality is meaningless (uc 3c). For if time and space relations cease to be, then the texture of experience which gives rise to all these ideas is destroyed (uc 3d); whereas the destruction of other impressions does not have this effect.

Besides the basic status of space and time relations, we can also show that any segment of space and time relations establishes a whole uniform scheme of space and time. For consider dreams, which present an alternative space and time scheme. Whitehead maintains that it is a manifest fact that the dream-scheme cannot be correlated with the awake-scheme (uc 5b). But, if we assume that space and time relations are contingent (not uniformly significant), then we have no ground on which to discriminate the dreams from awake-experience. Under Hume's doctrine of the contingency of sense-impressions just this inability to discriminate would follow (uc 5b). Hence Whitehead concludes that we are aware of a dominant scheme of space and time relations (uc 6c) because we are able to fit together isolated portions of space and time experience in a uniform scheme; this morning with this afternoon. That is, the relations among relata revealed this morning can be extended to include this afternoon (uc 7b). Thus, "the discrimination of reality from dream requires an apprehended dominant space-time continuum, determined in its totality, and this determination requires that it be uniform. We have here the primary ground of uniformity in nature" (uc 8c).

If induction is to be possible, there must be a further significance besides the uniformity of the space-time continuum (uc 12c). Hume's justification of induction is the instinct of habit, which he admits is fallacious (uc 13a). Under his own doctrine he cannot offer a rational justification because "there is nothing in a number of instances, different from every single instance, which is supposed to be exactly similar; except only, that after a repetition of similar instances, the mind is carried by habit, upon the appearance of one event, to expect its usual attendance, and to believe, that it will exist." [8] Hence, if there is any ground for an inductive conclusion it must be in the single instance; the accumulation gains nothing since the impressions are all contingent and similar (uc 14c). The single instance of knowledge by adjective must thus be significant of knowledge by relatedness of something besides itself, if induction is to be possible (uc 14d). Such significance is found in Whitehead's control theory of the perceptual object, whereby the sense-objects are significant of the perceptual object as previously explained (uc 15c). This significance provides a basis for induction and also puts causality back into nature (uc 17c). This conclusion leads us to see that knowledge does not begin with bare entities and then discover relations, but that we begin with the relatedness of nature and find the contingent adjectives (PNK 12c, 61a).

Second, consider the general approach of PRel. "'Significance' is the relatedness of things" (PNK 12c), or more explicitly it is the thesis that it is impossible to find "any entity for cogitation, which does not in its apprehension by consciousness disclose relationships to other entities, and thereby disclose some systematic structure of factors within fact" (PRel 17–18, whA 308b). The technical meanings of the terms involved in this thesis have been explained in Section I of this chapter. Significance is the reverse side of the notion of limitation insofar as "a factor is a limitation of fact in the sense that a factor refers to fact canalised into a system of relata to itself, *i.e.* to the factor in question" (PRel 16c, whA 307c). The notion of significance seems to involve that which is signified and that which does the signifying, but this is not to say it is a two-termed relation, for what is signified may involve many terms. Nevertheless, significance leads to a fundamental distinction between awareness of a factor as signifying and awareness of a factor as signified. The former is "cognisance by relatedness" (PRel 18, whA 308–09). The same distinction of signified and signifying is stated in CN in terms of the "discernible" and the "discerned" (CN 49c).

Previously, we divided awareness into the apprehension of events and the recognition of objects. These distinctions must not be taken to be the same as the above, as has sometimes been done. The factors discriminated in the awareness of adjectives are objects, while the occurrences of which these adjectives (objects) are characteristics are events, so that in this sense adjectives are significant of events. On the other hand, factors known by relatedness are events in the sense that we are not aware of any specific characteristics of these related factors; lacking recognition of such characteristics (objects), we are left in knowledge by relatedness with the bare "it"—the occurrence, a part of the becomingness of nature, an event. But insofar as these events known by relatedness may be active conditioning events controlling the ingression of certain objects we have an indirect significance of other objects on the basis of those objects discriminated in knowledge by adjective (uc 14e). Events are systematically related because of the fundamental relation of extension. Since every event extends over and is extended over by other events, events are thus all systematically related, hence significant of each other, in virtue of the relation of extension. To sum up: objects are significant of events; events are significant of other events; events are significant of objects; and objects are indirectly significant of other objects. Each of these cases of significance occurs in a particular way.

The complete analysis of full awareness involves knowledge by adjective and knowledge by relatedness. Each type of knowledge presupposes the other (PREL 19b). Let us illustrate these four aspects of significance. In the awareness marked out by this specious present I recognize certain adjectives (objects), say the color, shape, texture, and so on of this sheet of paper, which are sense-objects in a polyadic relation with the percipient event "here-now" while I write this sentence. These objects, as characteristics of a certain chunk of the becoming of nature, mark out an event which is their situation—objects significant of events (PREL 24–25).

Second, the event marked out by these objects extends over the events marked out while writing words in that sentence. The event is also part of (included in) the event marked out by this paragraph and recognized by roughly the same group of sense-objects. Hence these events are significant of each other, that is, related; and further their relatedness is uniform in order that they may mesh together—events significant of events (PREL 25c). Thus, events are mutually significant of each other.

Third, events are significant of objects in a special way insofar as the event is a field for related objects, and without the related objects there could be no events (PREL 26a). Our recognition of some sense-objects of the sheet of paper signifies an event, and this event is a field which is significant of other objects not yet recognized. This aspect of significance is rather vague.

Fourth, objects are significant of other objects in an indirect fashion. The recognized sense-objects of color, shape, and so on signify a certain event. This event is an active conditioning event for those objects and has a character which we recognize as the perceptual object (this sheet of paper). The perceptual object is a control for the ingression of the sense-objects we recognized. In this indirect way via active conditioning events the sense-objects are significant of the perceptual object. Similarly perceptual objects are significant of physical objects, which are their controls, and physical objects are significant of scientific objects, which are their controls (uc 14e).

The third and fourth aspects of significance involve a limitation; namely, we recognize that events are significant of objects, and objects significant of objects, but we don't know precisely what the signified objects are (prel 64c, whA 339e). We are required to indulge in further analysis to determine their specific character. Whitehead calls objects in this status "contingent" (prel 26a, 64c), and for a good reason, to be seen shortly. On the other hand, the mutual significance of all events requires knowledge of only a limited set of events because their relations are uniform (prel 64d, whA 339f); otherwise they would never mesh together into a single dominant scheme. Further, "the factors of nature are also significant of factors which are not included in nature" (prel 21a, whA 310a). Thus, the door is left open for the metaphysical significance of PR.

Once again Whitehead considers and answers the old and serious objection which any theory of knowledge dependent on relatedness must answer. If for knowledge of some factor (event or object) we require knowledge of its relations to other factors and hence to all factors, then how can we as finite beings achieve this knowledge of relations to all factors? Again, if any proposition is either true or false or meaningless, then, if relatedness to all factors is necessary to knowledge, how can we attain truth in any finite form (prel 23b, 73b, whA 311, 345d)? This form of objection has often been made to a coherence-theory of truth, particularly against idealism with its doctrine of internal relatedness. If everything is internally related, then to know one thing we have to know everything, since the nature of each is determined by all the others.

Whitehead holds such a view of relatedness indirectly involving all factors of nature in his doctrine of significance. How does he meet the objection? The key to his solution is a distinction "between the essential and the contingent relationships of a factor" (prel 23a whA 311e). The essential relationships are those the lack or alternation of which would change the character of the factor. They are essential to its peculiar individuality. Contingent relationships are those which, if they were other than they are, would not change the peculiar individuality of the factors related. Significance concerns only essential relationships (prel 23a), although in another context (uc 14e) Whitehead talks about the significance of objects to those objects which fall in the category of contingent relationships. This point is clarified by recalling the indirect character of this significance and further by remembering that although some object is signified its character is not revealed. The similarity of this distinction to that between internal and external relations should be mentioned but not pressed, since there are differences. Also note for later discussion that in smw the relations between objects are internal.

This distinction, coupled with the doctrine of significance, entails that an awareness of any factor necessarily involves awareness of its essential relationships but not of its contingent relationships. On this level the objection stated above could still be pressed, for we need some way to determine when we are aware of all the essential relationships (prel 23d, wha 312d). The solution proposed is that the essential relatedness is uniform and depends upon the distinction between knowledge by adjective and knowledge by relatedness. We perceive some factor, say X, through knowledge by adjective; that is, we recognize some object (characteristic). This factor has significance; that is, involves essential relatedness; however, we do not need to know the related factors through knowledge by adjective but only through knowledge by relatedness (prel 23d); and, further, we do not need to distinguish individual factors in this knowledge by relatedness (prel 24a). It is sufficient for our awareness if we know the structure of the uniform scheme of relations of which our perceived factor is a part. This will give us the information required to understand the factor before us in terms of its significance. The adjectives of the related factors are not required. They are contingent. The uniform structure of the scheme signified in knowledge by relatedness is guaranteed by the necessity of a dominant scheme to distinguish dreams and reality in such a way that its sections mesh together. Thus Whitehead's answer to this objection is twofold. First, he distinguishes two kinds of relationships; second, he shows that essential relatedness does not involve reference to particular factors since it is a uniform structure. The reason for the uniformity has been previously stated. This uniform structure, which solves the problem raised by the objection, is similar to a later view expressed in pr, whereby the internal relations between eternal objects are generic, and hence the specific character of the relata need not necessarily be known.

Whitehead's answer to this objection seems to have placed rather severe restrictions on essential relatedness or significance (prel 23a), which are not in harmony with other expressions of the doctrine of significance (uc 14e). There seems to be a confusion. One possible solution would be to distinguish essential relatedness from significance in general, making it a special form of significance. Then we could speak of other forms of significance in which the relatedness was such that *what* was signified required further analysis to discover; but *that* something was signified was an element in the awareness. The physical field of an object may signify *that* other objects are related and even in some cases how they are related without specifying what the objects are. Laws of nature express the conditions of limitation as to how other objects may be related (PRel 71c,d). Significance could then be understood as a generalization of the notion of relatedness in which the character of the relata is not determined but *that* there are relata and perhaps how they are related are determined. Such an interpretation would be in harmony with Whitehead's method of generalizing notions formerly applied in a limited context. Awareness of a factor would thus involve (1) the essential relatedness of the situation of that factor in a systematic uniformity of events and (2) the awareness that the factor was related to other factors and perhaps how it was related, but not what the character of the other relata was. These two points would constitute the generalized notion of significance. The following statements in CN seem to support this interpretation. "This disclosure of an entity as a relatum without further specific discrimination of quality is the basis of our concept of significance" and "thus significance is relatedness, but it is relatedness with the emphasis on one end only of the relation" (CN 51b). Some such view as this seems to me to be present in SMW, where this whole objection is raised again and answered in the framework of the ideas of that book. The second quotation expresses a view similar to one in PR, where the relation of an eternal object to an actual entity is said to be internal only on the end of the actual entity.

The three major aspects of Whitehead's views on perception at this stage of his development have now been discussed, namely, events, objects, and significance. Throughout I have tried to show how his thoughts develop, to systematize his remarks into as consistent a view as possible, and to extend and fill in his doctrines in order to gain a better understanding. We must next see if the theory provides an answer to his critique of science.

Chapter V

APPLICATIONS TO SCIENCE

The purpose of this chapter is twofold: (1) to present Whitehead's answer to his criticism of science given in Chapter Three in terms of the theory of perception presented in Chapter Four; and (2) to canvass briefly some implications of this theory of perception for contemporary scientific theories. Beginning with the latter point, we discuss the derivation of space and time by the method of extensive abstraction.

Section I. Foundations of Extensive Abstraction

A preliminary statement of the methods of extensive abstraction was given in Chapter Two dealing with the 1916 paper "The Anatomy of Some Scientific Ideas," but the details of the method are found in PNK. The fundamental relation which the method utilizes is the relation of extension (PNK 101a). Some basic properties of the relation of extension are: (1) every event extends over other events and is extended over by other events; (2) extension is transitive and asymmetrical; (3) the field of extension is dense or compact—that is, between any two events A and B, one of which extends over the other, there is always a third event which is extended over by A and extends over B; (4) events include other events and are included by other events; (5) any two events are included in a third event such that it has no parts not included in the other two events; and (6) events have exact demarcation instead of vague boundaries.[1] The last property listed is not given by Whitehead along with the others on page 101 of PNK but earlier (PNK 73–74), and has been the source of much controversy and confusion about the method. Critics like Lenzen argued that this last assumption made the whole procedure of extensive abstraction circular in the sense that to talk about a definite demarcation of an event requires implicitly the notion of a point, which concept the method proposes to define.[2] Grünbaum has made the same criticism in greater mathematical detail, arguing that we cannot sense the distinction between the sets of abstractive classes which serve to define two points indefinitely close to one another, and hence that points cannot be defined in this empirical manner without already presupposing the notion.[3] Hammerschmidt has raised the same objection.[4]

Whitehead seems aware of this whole problem, and it acts as a driving force in the evolution of his thought. It is first discussed at the end of the 1914 paper "La Théorie Relationniste de l'Espace."[5] Again in the 1916 paper "The Anatomy of Some Scientific Ideas" (AE 213–14) the exact demarcation of events is considered not as a thought-object of perception but as a thought-object of science; that is, in some sense hypothetical. In PNK the following comment on the problem is offered: "This demarcation of events is the first difficulty which arises in applying rational thought to experience. In perception no event exhibits definite spatio-temporal limits. A continuity of transition is essential. The definition of an event by assignment of demarcations is an arbitrary act of thought corresponding to no perceptual experience. Thus it is a basal assumption, essential for ratiocination relating to perceptual experience, that there are definite entities which are events; though in practice our experience does not enable us to identify any such subject or thought, as discriminated from analogous subjects slightly more or slightly less" (PNK 74a). On the surface it looks as if Whitehead is agreeing with his critics. Two remarks can be made to support Whitehead at this period of his development: (1) we must remember that in CN and PREL thought (cogitation) is a part of perception, and hence the assumption of exact demarcation is not an importation into perception from some other source of knowledge, namely thought; and (2) even though we lack an apprehension of this exact demarcation it may still be a part of sense-awareness, for cogitation may assume it on the basis of the analysis of sense-awareness while sense-awareness cannot practically apprehend such exact demarcation.[6] Extensive abstraction is an exact idealization of a procedure we may never precisely carry out in practice. Murphy has given an answer to Lenzen similar to the two points above, emphasizing the distinction between what is given in sense-awareness and what is found by logical analysis of this given.[7]

By the time of PR, Whitehead has modified the notion of extension to meet this demarcation problem. The fundamental relation is now "extensive connection" among regions rather than extension among events. Victor Lowe aptly states it: "Whitehead introduces the idea of regions in exact contact only as the case to be excluded in his definition of a point, which is then made in terms of non-tangential enclosure, and this does not require the assertion that any region actually has exact boundaries."[8]

What happens in PR is that the notion of extension, which is primitive in the method of extensive abstraction, becomes a notion, derived from the primitive notion of extensive connection. "Two regions *A* and *B* are extensively connected if there is no region completely separating them." [9] From this primitive notion the notion of inclusion, which is the counterpart of extension in the earlier books, is derived. (See definitions 9 and 10 in PR 434 for non-tangential relation and inclusion of abstractive sets, respectively.)

The method of extensive abstraction has also been criticized because of the third defining property, namely, that the field of extension is dense. Lenzen argues that we do not perceive in sense experience infinite sets of elements as required by the assumption of a dense field.[10] Grünbaum, again, offers the same criticism in more detail.[11] The criticism hinges on the assumption that there is a threshold of perception, a limit to the number of perceivable events making up an abstractive class. Hence the assumption of denseness is not warranted by sense-experience. The line of Murphy's reply to this objection has already been stated. Ushenko holds that "the infinite number [of regions] is allowed not because it is observable but because it is a legitimate concept of formal mathematics" and "the requirement is that *any* constituent region should be, in principle, observable." [12] The core of this debate seems to me to center on whether we restrict ourselves to what is given in sense experience or allow as a legitimate part of perception the intellectual analysis of the given with the drawing out of implications. Since Whitehead clearly affirms the latter alternative in PRel, there is, I think, a basis for his assumption about extension. The opposing sides of this debate have been stated because it is crucial to the method of extensive abstraction, the rest of which seems to be sound except for minor points.[13]

Section II. The Derivation of Time, Space, and Particles

In the previous chapter I explained the nature of events and durations and how these were related. It is in terms of durations that the notion of time can be derived. A "family" of durations is such that "one contains the other, or they overlap each other in a subordinate duration without either containing the other; or they are completely separate. The excluded case is that of durations overlapping in finite events but not containing a third duration as a common part" (CN 59b). Asymmetry and transitivity hold for families of durations.

We can now define an "abstractive set" of durations in which the following properties hold: "(1) of any two members of the set one contains the other as a part and (2) there is no duration which is a common part of every member of the set" (cn 60d). In pr an abstractive set is defined on the basis of the new primitive of extensive connection relating regions. "A set of regions is called an 'abstractive set' when (1) any two members are such that one of them includes the other non-tangentially, [and] (2) there is no region included in every member of the set" (pr 454d). The new element introduced, the non-tangential criterion, eliminates the reference to boundaries, which was one point of criticism in the earlier definition.

Returning now to the definition of cn, such an abstractive set differs from a set of Chinese boxes in that there is no smallest box (duration) and from the mathematical notion of convergence to a limit, for it does not "converge towards a duration as its limit" (cn 61a). This would violate the second condition previously stated for such sets. Admittedly the procedure tends to converge to the ideal limit of nature at an instant but in fact no such limit can be stated. Instead, the consideration of the set leads one to consider the progressive simplicity of natural relations as the temporal extension of the durations decreases. Call this series of durations, $d_1, d_2, d_3 \ldots , d_n$. Correlated with this series, that is to each duration are the quantitative expressions of the natural entities, say $q(d_1), q(d_2), q(d_3) \ldots , q(d_n)$ which "do converge to limits though the abstractive set does not converge to any limiting duration" (cn 61b). This quantitative limit represents the instant of time necessary to express the laws of physics, although in nature there is no such instant but only the abstractive set. An analogous procedure utilizing events can be developed to define the notion of a point.[14] The technique involved in the principle of convergence with diminution of extent should now be clear.

The method can also be employed to define a notion similar to a particle in physics, called by Whitehead, an event-particle. "The event-particle associated with π [where π is some given punct] is the group of abstractive classes each of which has the two properties (1) that it covers every abstractive set in π, and (2) that all the abstractive sets which also satisfy the former condition as to π and which it covers, also cover it" (cn 93b). The event-particle has position in virtue of its association with a punct. It is indivisible by virtue of its location in a moment.

The method of extensive abstraction allows Whitehead to provide an answer to his criticisms of Newtonian physics presented in Chapter Three, Section One. The method shows how we can start with the extended events of sense-awareness and with the aid of cogitation derive the durationless instants, extensionless points, and point-particles which are the fundamental notions in the usual axiomatic developments of mathematical-physics. Such a mode of derivation enables Whitehead to answer the criticism involving points, instants, and particles. R. M. Palter has written an excellent, detailed, technical account of these matters.[15]

Section III. Functions of the Doctrine of Significance

The doctrine of significance developed in the last chapter, which was found to be essential to this theory of perception, plays just as important a role in Whitehead's new foundation for natural science, especially with respect to the notions of causality and uniformity. Whitehead maintained that it was one of the assumptions of Newtonian physics that extension in time and extension in space expressed disconnection (PNK 1b). This assumption, coupled with the durationless instants and extensionless points, makes the notion of causality most difficult to comprehend (see p. 29), and, further, the notion of unity of being seems to lack any interpretation.

The doctrine of significance provides a new theory of causality based on a new view of internal relatedness. As already shown, objects are significant of other objects; they are controls for their ingression (PNK 186, 187, 94b). Further, objects insofar as they are situated in events are affected by related active conditioning events which exert a causal influence (PNK 183b, CN 158a). Appearance and causation are inextricably mixed, for what is appearance in one respect may be cause in another (PNK 185a). A perceptual object is the cause (control) of sense-objects and the appearance of some physical object. Significance is causation in the sense that (1) knowing some objects signifies knowledge about other objects, and (2) existence of some objects controls the existence of other objects. Thus significance is epistemological and ontological. Significance is the denial of the Newtonian assumption of disconnectedness based on the re-analysis of perception, which yielded extended events internally related. If events were extensionless, the relations between them would suffer the same difficulty as the classical points.

The doctrine of significance also makes understandable the unity of being, which is a fundamental notion of biological science (see p. 29). For a given natural entity now possesses in a definite expressible sense internal parts necessarily related in a definite manner, or else that natural entity would not be what it is. The events which are the situations of these parts belong to a pattern of relatedness. Such extended interrelated wholes revealed in the analysis of perception provide the foundation for the key biological concept of an organism.

Besides causation, significance provides the foundation of spatio-temporal uniformity. The lack of a uniform space-time continuum is one of Whitehead's criticisms of Einstein's theory of relativity. Einstein's general relativity theory holds that the space-time curvature depends upon the distribution of matter in the universe.[16] Our knowledge of the space-time structure of the cosmos is dependent upon knowledge of the distribution of matter. But such knowledge is difficult to come by. Further, would it not be difficult to assign the location of this distribution if the spatio-temporal structure was not already known? Approaching in another way, Whitehead admits that in science there are both contingent and necessary facts, but he insists that the only correct approach is to begin with the necessary facts and then determine the contingent ones.[17] Hence we must begin, on Whitehead's view, with the necessarily uniform space-time structure determined by the significance of events and proceed to the determination of the distribution of matter, not conversely. The result is that the geometry of Whitehead's theory of relativity is uniform throughout, whether Euclidean, hyperbolic, or elliptic, as opposed to the geometrical heterogeneity of Einstein's theory (PREl v).

Section IV. Functions of Events and Objects

The fundamental awareness of events and the derivation of space and time from events enables Whitehead to solve a basic difficulty which he finds in Einstein's definition of relative space and time. Einstein had defined space and time as the relations between bodily objects, but such objects can have space-time characteristics. Hence, how can they be used to define space and time? Whitehead avoids this problem by deriving space and time from events, which are the situations of objects (see pp. 30–31).

Another criticism of Einstein dealt with his definition of simultaneity (see p. 31). Whitehead holds that simultaneity is a definite natural entity recognized in sense-awareness (CN 53b). The natural entity is a duration. "A duration is discriminated as a complex of partial events, and the natural entities which are components of this complex are thereby said to be 'simultaneous with this duration.' Also in a derivative sense they are simultaneous with each other in respect to this duration" (CN 53b).

Further, the discussion of simultaneity reveals the need of the notion of congruence. If we assume a uniform velocity of light in our definition, we require that two separate stretches have the same length or be coincident, but this requirement presupposes a direct judgment of constancy. Whitehead's theory of recognition in perception provides a basis for these direct judgments of congruence. The essence of the theory of recognition is the judgment of sameness for objects. Simultaneity is the recognition that many events are alike in the respect that they are members of the same duration, a concrete temporal slab of nature. With the notion of duration we can define moments and rects, and thus a complete theory of geometrical and physical congruence follows (CN, Chap. VI).

The theory of events and objects also solves a major difficulty in the traditional methodology of science; namely, the bifurcation of nature. The bifurcation is a dualism of apparent objects and causal objects in which our sense-knowledge is limited to the apparent objects. The consequences of this dualism were presented in Chapter Three, Section Three. Events and objects form another dualistic theory of perception but one in which there is sense-awareness of both types of entities, each of which can function as cause or appearance. Further, by relinquishing the assumption that relativity implies subjectivity, the objective status of the apparent objects is restored, with the effect that what we are aware of does constitute nature.

Whitehead's own summary of the applications of his analysis of perception is as follows: "(1) It explains the differentiation of the one quality of extension into time and space. (2) It gives a meaning to the observed facts of geometrical and temporal position, of geometrical and temporal order, and of geometrical straightness and planeness. (3) It selects one definite system of congruence embracing both space and time, and thus explains the concordance as to measurement which is in practice attained. (4) It explains (consistently with the theory of relativity) the observed phenomena of rotation, *e.g.*, Foucault's pendulum, the equatorial bulge of the earth, the fixed senses of rotation of cyclones and anticyclones, and the gyrocompass. It does this by its admission of definite stratifications of nature which are disclosed by the very character of our knowledge of it. (5) Its explanations of motion are more fundamental than those expressed in (4); for it explains what is meant by motion itself. The observed motion of an extended object is the relation of its various situations to the stratification of nature expressed by the time-system fundamental to the observation" (CN 194-95).

Section V. The Passage of Nature

In the notes to the second edition of PNK, Whitehead makes it clear that his views regarding the ultimacy of the relation of extension have changed: "the true doctrine, that 'process' is the fundamental idea, was not in my mind with sufficient emphasis" (PNK 2d ed. 202c). Since the notion of process plays such an important role in all his later thinking, it will be well to consider the germs of the notion in these earlier books so as to bring his philosophical development into better focus.

The passage of nature, or its creative advance, is closely connected with perception. There are two sides to nature, seemingly antagonistic, yet both essential: becoming and permanence (PNK 98b). Apprehension of events deals with the passage of nature, which contains spatial extension as well as temporal extension (CN 54b). In this sense, extension is derivative from process (PNK 2d ed. 202c). On the other hand, the theory of recognition in perception deals with the permanent side of nature, with what occurs again. Thus nature exhibits both being and becoming. Perception depends upon both the process-side of nature and its permanence, or the apprehension of events and the recognition of objects. "Perception fades unless it is equally stimulated from both sides of nature" (PNK 98c). At this stage of development, process or the passage of nature means the becoming of events. Is all this so different from the concrescence of actual occasions in process and the permanence of eternal objects?

We can approach the connection of process and perception in another way. "Natural knowledge is merely the other side of action." And "the sense of action is the direct knowledge of the percipient event as having its very being in the formation of its natural relations" (PNK 14b). The relations of the percipient event to the rest of nature are perceived because the percipient event is involved in the passage of nature and, further, the relations are those particular relations because of the interplay of the percipient event in the process. This fact about the percipient events means that perception takes place at the front edge of process or creation (PNK 14b, CN 54b). Perception is a particular relation, resulting from the passage of nature and the mutual significance of events and objects, of the percipient event to nature (CN 55a). In PR perception belongs to the doctrine of prehension (significance), which is intimately bound up with the process of actual occasions.

PNK also contains the important distinction between the general passage of nature and any particular time-system derivative from some particular set of durations involving a particular percipient event (PNK 80–81). Thus a particular time-system expresses certain characteristics of the passage of nature but not all (CN 54b). The complete set of time-systems derivative from nature contains those characteristics of process which can be considered by thought (PNK 81a). Hence no particular time-system is fully concrete. This distinction is retained in PR in the general process of reality and the particular time-systems determined by particular actual occasions.

The process of nature is a primitive notion in the system (CN 53c).

It cannot be explained by other notions. We can only portray its character by showing its relation to other factors of nature and indicating how some features are derivative from it. The occurrence of events and durations is the best evidence of this fundamental process. This fundamental passage of nature accounts for the uniqueness of events (CN 54-55). Further, the passage of nature offers a connection "of nature with the ultimate metaphysical reality" (CN 55a). For Whitehead holds that passage (process) extends beyond nature to mind. For example, the procedure of sense-awareness involves process. In another place the passage of nature is identified with "the creative force of existence . . ." (CN 73c). These last few sentences all contain metaphysical hints which are developed in PR. Whitehead, even at this stage, considers the metaphysical questions but takes one problem at a time. In our next chapter we shall begin to see these hints elaborated.

Chapter VI

SIMPLE LOCATION, PERCEPTION, PREHENSION, AND INTERNAL RELATEDNESS

The locus of discussion for this chapter consists mainly of *Science and the Modern World*. Smw contains no detailed theory of perception but merely scattered remarks which indicate changes from earlier views and provide hints of the mature theory of *Process and Reality*. More important, smw contains significant discussions of two topics central to the later theory of perception: the theory of prehensive unities or occasions, and a new theory of internal relatedness. These are our main concern in this chapter. Smw is also important in that it sums up Whitehead's critique of science, which we have followed since the 1905 memoir, under the heading of the assumption of simple location as an instance of the fallacy of misplaced concreteness. It is necessary to follow this critique in our work on perception because Whitehead's answer to scientific materialism, namely, the philosophy of organism, provides a framework for his mature theory of perception.

Section I. The Assumption of Simple Location

"Scientific materialism" or "materialistic mechanism" is the cosmological outlook so beautifully expressed in the physics of Newton but dating back in its origins to the Ionian philosophers (smw 71c). It "presupposes the ultimate fact of an irreducible brute matter, or material, spread throughout space in a flux of configurations. In itself such a material is senseless, valueless, purposeless. It just does what it does do, following a fixed routine imposed by external relations which do not spring from the nature of its being" (smw 25b). Criticism of the Newtonian physics in the 1905 memoir utilized Occam's Razor and related to the indefinite number of extraneous relations required to specify the position of particles. In PNK, CN, and PREL, Newtonian physics is further criticized from a perceptual and logical angle. We do not perceive instants, points, or particles. The assumption that extension implies disconnectedness leads to logical difficulties in the notions of causality, velocity, and acceleration. These specific criticisms or difficulties in Newtonian physics are now (SMW) taken to be symptomatic of some basic cosmological outlook which does not harmonize with our concrete experience (SMW 71b). Analysis of the specific criticisms indicates that they have to do with space, time, and matter; of the relation of matter to space and time. It makes no difference whether we talk about matter, material, mass, particles, or substance so long as we are concerned in each case with the fundamental stuff of the cosmos. The basic question is, what is the nature of this stuff? The answer, assumed by various philosophical or scientific systems falling in this epoch, is that stuff has the fundamental property of simple location in space and time (SMW 71–72). This property of simple location "common both to space and time is that material [stuff] can be said to be *here* in space and *here* in time, or *here* in space-time, in a perfectly definite sense which does not require for its explanation any reference to other regions of space-time [or space and time]" (SMW 72b; *cf.* also 84b).

It makes no difference whether our theory of space and time is relative or absolute; the assumption is compatible with either.[1] We might think that this is not so in a relational theory of space in which space is defined as a relation between particles, but, so long as the positions of these particles requires no reference to other particles for their explanation, the assumption of simple location is still present (SMW 72b, 84b). Hence, no matter what our system of space-time, or space and time is, once we have defined the notion of place or position so that we can speak about stuff located at that position without specifying any other relations as necessary to its being in that place, the assumption of simple location has been made (SMW 72b).

The assumption of simple location has some minor but important characteristics. With respect to time, if some stuff has existed for a given stretch of time, then it is assumed to have existed during any fraction of that stretch, or, to put it in another way, the division of time does not divide the stuff (SMW 73a). On the other hand, if some stuff has occupied a certain volume of space, then there will be only a part of that stuff in any fraction of the volume; in other words, division of space divides the stuff (SMW 73a). All this may seem to make beautiful common sense, thereby showing how neatly we are caught in the assumption. Some interesting consequences of this assumption follow. For mathematical description, division of time functions with respect to stuff in a different way from division of space. Again, since division of time does not affect the stuff, it follows that the passage of time is a contingent fact having no effect on the nature of the stuff (smw 73b). As will be seen clearly in pr, the process of becoming is essential in determining the character of actual entities. One might well single this out as a primary difference between a materialistic and an organismic philosophy.

Another consequence of simple location relates to the question of induction. For, if the passage of time has no effect whatsoever on the nature of the basic stuff and if the location of configurations of the stuff at a place requires no reference to any other time, then it follows that the configuration of the stuff by itself at one time contains no information about any other time. But this is just the kind of connection that a sound theory of induction requires. Hence induction for Newtonian physics, which assumes simple location, is a mere hunch, as Hume made clear. But science worked, and the philosophical analyses that Hume's conclusions demanded were by-passed by science.

It is readily seen that these minor characteristics combined with the core of the assumption of simple location lead directly to the specific criticisms of Newtonian physics in the opening chapters of pnk. As has been shown in previous chapters, the theory of perception therein presented is designed to meet these scientific criticisms. It is difficult to understand how some critics can maintain that Whitehead changed his views on these points from pnk to smw.[2]

Stebbing has correctly pointed out that the assumption of simple location is an instance of the fallacy of misplaced concreteness.[3] The fallacy involves "mistaking the abstract for the concrete" (smw 74b) or taking as fundamental and primitive what is derived and abstract. Other instances of this fallacy are the notions of substance and quality, and the conception of sense-data as given or primitive. In the light of this, one could say that the philosophy of organism is a correction of these instances of the fallacy. It is to be noted that Whitehead's correction of these instances of the fallacy roughly marks out the three periods of his development: *Principia Mathematica* corrects the mistaken notion of subject and predicate logic; pnk, cn, and prel utilize the theory of events and objects with the method of extensive abstraction to correct the notion of simple location (smw 76–77); and pr corrects the mistake of supposing sense-data to be primitive given elements of experience, a view still adhered to in the second period. These three cases of the fallacy seem to me to give an interesting insight into Whitehead's development.

Someone might well remark at this point, "But if the assumption of simple location is a fallacy, how do you propose to account for the rather extensive confirmation of Newtonian physics and for the scientific cosmology associated with this view?" The question clearly requires an answer. Although Whitehead holds "that among the primary elements of nature as apprehended in our immediate experience, there is no element whatever which possesses this character of simple location" (SMW 84–85), this does not lead to the conclusion that Newtonian physics is wrong. Rather he maintains that the abstractions of Newtonian physics are derivative entities having simple location and that they are derived by a method of constructive abstraction from concrete elements of our experience which are not simply located (SMW 85a). The main requirement is that our abstract entities incorporate the important aspects of our concrete experience so that, when they are manipulated in logical fashion, the deductions which follow exhibit some approximations to the truth found in our concrete experience.

Whitehead's critique of the assumption of simple location should surprise no one acquainted with his earlier books, for it is an integral part of the theory of events and objects.[4] On the other hand, it must not be assumed, as it often has been, that, because the later views developed out of the earlier, we can attack the later position by showing mistakes in the earlier works. These deficiencies provide the motivation that drives Whitehead forward to new positions and, if our previous generalization about the stages of his thought is right, the correction of the last instance of the fallacy of misplaced concreteness will make a difference throughout his mature system. A glance at the interpretation and criticism of Whitehead will reveal two types of errors: (1) an assertion of the autonomy of PR and AI, and (2) an assertion of the identity of PNK and PR as far as basic ideas go. Both views are wrong. They miss the beauty of Whitehead's development, the continuity amid change.

The theory of events and objects rests upon three propositions: "(1) a thoroughgoing acceptance of the relativity of space-time; (2) a rejection of all forms of the bifurcation of nature; and (3) the inclusion within the one system of nature of everything that is observed."[5] As a result of these propositions the traditional notion of substance must be rejected. It is replaced by the notions of events and objects. In order that the sense-data we perceive should have an objective status in nature it is necessary to reject the principle that relativity implies subjectivity. But to account consistently for the objective status of sense-objects it is also necessary to reject the simple subject-predicate view of their location in nature and to affirm a theory of multiple relatedness for sense-objects. That is to say, sense-objects cannot be supposed to be simply located in nature "here-now"; their natures necessarily depend upon the specification of additional relations to the perceiver and eventually to all the rest of nature. These propositions require that the definition of an event include a denial of its simple location. The details of the attack on bifurcation and the multiple relatedness of objects in events have been explained in the previous chapter. It is clear that the theory of perception in PNK, CN, and PRel is an attempt to avoid the consequences of the assumption of simple location for objects and events. But our present task is to show how the views of SMW on perception avoid the assumption of simple location and its consequences in science.

Section II. The Analysis of Perception in SMW

Whitehead begins his discussion of the character of perception by reference to some quotations from Bacon's *Sylva Sylvarum* (*Natural History*). These quotations, he thinks, are significant because although they came from a person usually associated with the foundations of modern scientific method they show Bacon as contemplating viewpoints not adopted by the subsequent historical tradition of scientific materialism (SMW 61b). In PR, Whitehead is concerned to show that most of his doctrines are the development of discarded aspects of the philosophical tradition from Descartes to Kant. This reference to Bacon initiates this use of discarded ideas.

On the distinction between perception and sense Bacon says: "It is certain that all bodies whatsoever, though they have no sense, yet they have perception . . . and sometimes this perception, in some kind of bodies, is far more subtle than sense; so that sense is but a dull thing in comparison of it . . . It is therefore a subject of very noble enquiry, to enquire of the more subtle perceptions; for it is another key to open nature, as well as the sense; and sometimes better" (SMW 60–61).[6]

Herein perception seems to be more basic and widespread than sense. It is attributed to all actual entities. If we could generalize the term "reaction" so as to include what is common to physical reaction, mental reaction, emotional response, and sense-awareness we would approach what Bacon seems to mean by perception. Whitehead renders it as "taking account of" (SMW 61b). Sense for Bacon seems to mean a particular kind of perception limited to certain classes of things, involving a cognitive aspect. It approximates Whitehead's concept of perception in PRel as involving awareness and cogitation.

Whitehead in his agreement with Bacon's remarks reveals in SMW for the first time a significant change in his views on perception (SMW 61b). Perception is not to be restricted to any particular class of entities. PRel did not deny this but neither did it assert it, for PRel was not concerned with this aspect of the discussion of perception. The move from perception in relation to scientific foundations to perception in relation to cosmology brings this question to the surface for discussion. Moreover, perception now seems to mean a process more basic and fundamental than sense-awareness. These are the new elements in the discussion of perception in smw with which we must concern ourselves.

The first point, that perception in its new, wider meaning is not restricted to any particular class of actual entities, has an important connection with the problem of induction. Perception now concerns the way one actual entity "takes account of" or "reacts" to another entity or entities. This new idea of Whitehead's expands and evolves through his works beyond smw. In S it is the doctrine of the conformation of the present to the past; in pr it is the doctrine of causal efficacy; in ai it is the doctrine of the conformation of feeling, which is closely linked with the doctrine of mutual immanence. It is this new view of perception which provides an answer to that instance of the fallacy of misplaced concreteness which maintains that sense-data are primitive, concrete, given elements in immediate experience. How does this connect with the problem of induction? "Either there is something about the immediate occasion which affords knowledge of the past and the future, or we are reduced to utter skepticism as to memory and induction" (smw 64a). The new view of perception provides that any immediate occasion does "take account of" or "react to" past occasions so that there is a knowledge of the past on which to rest a rational basis for induction.[7] One caution needs to be stated. Whitehead does not think that induction arrives at general laws but only that it discovers characteristics of a particular future from the characteristics of a particular past (smw 65b).

Considering Whitehead's interpretation of Bacon's meaning of perception as "taking account of" we can ask, "Taking account of what?" The answer is, "Taking account of the essential character of the thing perceived . . ." (smw 101a), since Bacon tells us that "for else all bodies would be alike one to another . . ." (smw 101a). That is to say, something is perceived that entails the real diversity of the entities, some difference between them that is essential to their natures. In a further effort to explain Bacon's meaning of perception as not dependent on any cognitive element of experience Whitehead derives the word "prehension" as the root idea in the term "apprehension" (smw 101b), and I would also add its derivation from the term "comprehension." Prehension, apprehension, and comprehension might be looked upon as designating three levels of feeling in which cognition is not necessarily present at one end (prehension) but forms a large part of the other end (comprehension).

The exact role which cognition plays in these three levels of feeling, particularly in prehension, if it plays any at all, determines whether or not a given philosophical construction is reared on an objectivist or subjectivist basis (smw 128–30). The subjectivist maintains that "the nature of our immediate experience is the outcome of the perceptive peculiarities of the subject enjoying the experience" or that "what is perceived is not a partial vision of a complex of things generally independent of that act of cognition; but that it merely is the expression of the individual peculiarities of the cognitive act" (smw 128b). The objectivist maintains "that the actual elements perceived by our senses are *in themselves* the elements of a common world; and that this world is a complex of things, including indeed our acts of cognition, but transcending them" (smw 128–29). Whitehead in smw attempts to state a modified objectivist position which also does justice to the subjectivist contention. He is able to do this because he denies the assumption that relativity implies subjectivity, which is the essence of the subjectivist's attack on objectivism. He succeeds in this denial, as I have said before, because he holds that the subject-predicate (substance-attribute) logic is not adequate to the analysis of concrete experience; that is, it is an instance of the fallacy of misplaced concreteness. Hence he can admit relativism and yet maintain objectivism (see Chap. III, Sec. III). Only in pr is the exact nature of this synthesis made clear.

Whitehead rejects the subjectivist position in smw on three general points. The first reason is based on the direct deliverance of our experience in which we have an awareness of ourself as a perceiver and also an awareness of ourself as just another factor of nature (smw 129–30). The second reason depends upon the lack of content in our experience; for example, our knowledge of past geological ages, of distant galactic systems; that is, our experience of occurrences without knowledge of the content of such occurrences (smw 130b). Thirdly, Whitehead cites the instinct for action as an instance of self-transcendence involving a world beyond (smw 130–31). Readers of pr, wherein Whitehead adopts a reformed subjectivist principle (pr 252b), may wonder if this doesn't indicate a change of view, or, if pr and smw are taken together, an internal inconsistency in his system. I hope to show later that neither supposition is correct but that the same basic doctrine is expressed in both places (pr, Pt. II, Chap. VII).

In concluding his derivation of the new notion of prehension Whitehead asserts the following definition, which we must interpret: "Perception is simply the cognition of prehensive unification; or more shortly, perception is cognition of prehension" (smw 104a). This definition forces us to draw a careful distinction between prehension and perception. In interpreting Bacon's use of the term "perception" Whitehead is concerned to show that he means "taking account of," regardless of any cognitive element that might be involved. For this use of the term "perception" by Bacon, Whitehead substitutes the term "prehension" (SMW 101b). He is now free to assign to the term "perception" a meaning other than Bacon's, which he does in the above definition. This definition seems to me to incorporate the view of PREL, wherein perception consists of cogitation and awareness, which are now referred to as cognition and prehension, but it also expands that earlier view insofar as the term "prehension" designates a wider meaning than "awareness." What this wider meaning is we have tried to state in interpreting Bacon's remarks; prehension is possessed by all occasions, while awareness is restricted to percipient events. This discussion of terminology allows us to see precisely how the views of SMW are continuous with PNK, CN, and PREL, and how the widening of horizons constitutes a change in viewpoint. Part of the core of his philosophical development is revealed in this way.

Section III. The Nature of Prehensive Unities

"The actual world is a manifold of prehensions; and a 'prehension' is a 'prehensive occasion'; and a prehensive occasion is the most concrete finite entity, conceived as what it is in itself and for itself, and not as from its aspect in the essence of another such occasion" (SMW 104–05). To one familiar with the doctrine of PR this definition must appear confusing, for PR makes a distinction between a prehension which is a "concrete fact of relatedness" (PR 32d) and an actual occasion (PR 27–28). The distinction in PR seems implied in SMW in other passages (SMW 103a, 227c, 233c). This seems to me to indicate that SMW represents a phase of transition in Whitehead's development. The vocabulary and ideas are in flux.[8]

In SMW Whitehead is concerned to follow out the insight that what is fundamental in nature is process (SMW 106b). Out of this fundamental fact we are to derive a new cosmology. We can start by asking two questions: what constitutes the process, and what gives it structure? In each case the answer is: prehensions. From any given standpoint in nature there is a "reflection" of the rest of nature as unified at that standpoint (SMW 106a). This is what is meant by prehensive unification in the process of nature and such a unification of "modes" or "aspects" is a prehensive unity or prehensive occasion (SMW 102a). There is nothing permanent about such prehensive unities; they are and are not. We have a transition from prehension to prehension (SMW 106a).

By consideration of certain "modes" or "aspects" of the prehensive unity constituting our standpoint in nature we can derive the structure of space-time (SMW 95a). We can consider, for example, three prehensive unities, *A*, *B*, and *C*, from the angle of what might be called their extensional prehensions. From the standpoint of *A* we have an aspect of *B*, and also of *C*. The relation of *B* to *C* also has an aspect from the standpoint of *A*. These aspects of other prehensive unities from *A* are of the essence of *A*; that is to say, they have no independent existence but form a connected structure (smw 95a). "The aspect of *B* from *A* is the *mode* in which *B* enters into the composition of *A*" (smw 95a). One such key mode is that of extension and with this key the reader can return to pnk for the construction of the uniform system of space-time.

Besides the interconnected structure of prehensive unities, insofar as each is an aspect in every other (smw 133b), we can consider those definite characteristics which we are aware of in any act of perception. Such a character is a sense-object. "The cognitive perception of a sense-object is the awareness of the prehensive unification (into a standpoint *A*) of various modes of various sense-objects, including the sense-object in question. . . . A mode of a sense-object at *A* (as abstracted from the sense-object whose relationship to *A* the mode is conditioning) is the aspect from *A* of some other region *B*. Thus the sense-object is present in *A* with the mode of location in *B*" (smw 103b; *cf.* also 233c, 247c). This theory of aspects or modes is another attempt on Whitehead's part to explain how sense-objects have ingression in nature. It is another way of stating the multiple relatedness of a sense-object to events described in pnk. The effort on Whitehead's part to state in more detail the ingression of objects in nature and their relations to each other leads to a discussion of internal and external relations, which we will treat shortly.

In smw an event is defined as a prehensive unity (smw 106c): "the grasping into unity of a pattern of aspects" (smw 174b). Contemporary events as well as past events are aspects of or modes "mirrored" in a given present event (smw 106–07). The way in which contemporary events are aspects of each other is not stated (smw 177b). The view of pr is that we do not have direct perception of contemporary actual occasions, and if the theory of relativity is accepted it is hard to see what Whitehead means by this relationship between contemporaries. An event could contain aspects of a contemporary event in the indirect fashion of pr, but this is not stated. Contrast this definition of an event as a prehensive unity with the definition in pnk by means of the constants of externality; namely, definite demarcation, extension, duration, percipient event, cogredience, and the community of nature.

Besides the new explanation of an event as a prehensive unity arising out of the process of nature in contrast to the definition of an event in pnk given by the constants of externality, we also want to compare the notion of an enduring thing and of eternal objects in smw with the position taken in PNK. "Enduring things are thus the outcome of a temporal process; whereas eternal things are the elements required for the very being of the process" (SMW 158b). Consider some prehensive unity (event): it has a certain structure pervading it in accordance with its particular standpoint as a focus of prehensions. But this prehensive unity can be divided into temporal parts, and when each such part is pervaded by the same eternal objects in a structural pattern we have an enduring thing (SMW 175b). The extent of the original event can vary, allowing cases of prolonged or brief endurance (SMW 158b).

One very important restriction is indicated by the substitution of reiteration for endurance (SMW 175b). The pattern cannot "endure in undifferentiated sameness through time" (SMW 193a). If it did so, we would have an instance of simple location for enduring things with respect to instants of time. The structure may be one of contrasts, which requires a lapse of time for its unfolding (SMW 182b). "Thus the endurance of the pattern now means the reiteration of its succession of contrasts" (SMW 193a). It is not hard to see how this philosophical notion of endurance as reiteration fits in with the findings of the quantum theory under the technical notion of vibration (SMW 193a).

Perception carried on by enduring things, that is, cognition of prehension, may vary greatly in its depth and width, depending on the particular standpoint of the prehensive unity (SMW 155a). It may range from the faintest insignificant contrast to conscious thought making judgments about abstract possibilities of value. Most intermediate perceptions envisage without self-consciousness that possibility of attainment which most closely resembles their present pattern. They seek the least change, which in physics becomes the principle of least action (SMW 155a).

A prehensive unity or event serves to define the notion of a duration. "Thus a duration is spatialised; and by 'spatialised' is meant that the duration is the field for the realized pattern constituting the character of the event" (SMW 183a). By "field" Whitehead means the indefinite spatial extent marked out by the temporal boundaries of the event. The notion of an enduring thing as a repetition of pattern in successive events, each of which defines a duration, leads to the notion of a succession of durations exhibiting the field of the pattern.

Time is distinct from temporality and divisibility, which are characteristics of extension. "Time is sheer succession of epochal durations" (SMW 183a). An epoch corresponds to a duration which is "the field of the pattern realized in the actualization of one of its contained events . . ." (SMW 183a). Such an epoch is not indefinitely divisible. The realization of events which define durations is the becoming of time in the field of extension made up of durations (smw 185a). The duration as sheer extension is divisible, but time is not, for it depends on the endurance of realized patterns which mark out definite durations. Time is atomic in the sense that it is realized by an epoch marked out by an enduring object, but the temporal extension of the epochal duration is divisible (smw 185a). In pnk, cn, and prel, time was also defined in terms of durations according to extensive abstraction. But nothing was said there about the atomic character of time. In a certain sense a duration was a realized pattern of the systematic interrelationships of all the events in it, but the atomicity resulting from the reiteration of pattern was not stressed. Smw seems to make explicit what was really involved in the notion of the systematic interrelationships of events in a duration. By passing over this fact pnk and cn seem closer to the views of modern physics, but the chapter on "Rhythms" in pnk is a large hint toward the development of smw.

Our explanation of a prehensive unity as the unification of aspects at a standpoint in nature requires a further explanation of these aspects. "An eternal object will be an ingredient of one event [prehensive unity] under the guise, or aspect, of qualifying another event" (smw 151a). The eternal objects required to effect the aspects of one prehensive unity in another are required for nature and not emergent from it. These aspects are the characters of other prehensive unities which are grasped together in the nature of this prehensive unity. The common-sense notions of change, endurance, and eternality reflected in all our concrete experience are expressed and explained in smw by the technical notions of event, enduring thing, and eternal object respectively (smw 126a).

Eternal objects are said to be abstract. This means that they are completely understandable without reference to any prehensive unities (smw 228a). In this sense they transcend experience, but they are also connected with prehensive unities by the relation of ingression (smw 229a). Moreover, any given eternal object is related to other eternal objects (smw 229a, 230b). Every eternal object has an individual essence and a relational essence. Its individual essence is the peculiar character which constitutes its uniqueness in abstraction from all relationships—its is-what-it-is-ness (smw 229b). Being abstract it is a possibility for actuality. The relational essence of an eternal object concerns its relation to other eternal objects and its general relation to prehensive unities, but not its specific relation to any one prehensive unity (smw 230a). The details of the relational essence will be explained in our next section on internal relatedness.

Contrast this view of an eternal object in smw with that of an object in pnk, cn, and prel. The primary difference is that eternal objects are

potentialities (abstractions) for the determination of the nature of prehensive unities, while objects are permanent elements in nature that do
not pass.[9] In PREl objects are said to be significant of other objects,
but this significance seems to differ somewhat from their internal relatedness in SMW.[10] The examples given of objects and eternal objects
are frequently the same, but their status in their separate systems seems
to be different. SMW again indicates that a transition is in progress.

To say that a prehensive unity "mirrors" other such unities or is a
grasping together of aspects of other unities clearly involves some theory
of essential relatedness among prehensive unities. Further, such a theory
of aspects requires the notion of eternal objects, which form the definite
character of the aspects in the relations between prehensive unities.
Hence there is another kind of relatedness joining eternal objects to
prehensive unities. Lastly, the fact that each eternal object has a precisely definite character or essence means that there are definite relationships between it and other eternal objects. An important part of the
role of SMW from the standpoint of our discussion is the exposition of
these interconnected relationships, for (1) it completes the discussion of
prehensive unities, (2) it develops the doctrine of significance in PNK,
CN, and PREl one step further in the direction of the doctrine of prehensions in PR, which reveals again the transitional character of SMW,
and (3) it provides a new view of the nature of perception.

Section IV. Internal Relatedness

L. Susan Stebbing has maintained that Whitehead greatly confused
students of SMW by the introduction of the terms "internal" and "external"
relations in order to explain the relations among events and objects—a
vice he was careful to avoid in PREl, since "a different philosophic outlook
radically affects all meanings" (PREl 23, whA 312c).[11] These terms were
certainly a part of the different philosophical outlook of idealism, which
was based in part on the assumption that relativity implies subjectivity—
an assumption Whitehead was concerned to deny. In the explanation
of the doctrine of prehensions in PR there is no recourse to these terms,
yet it is clearly the same viewpoint as that of SMW, much expanded.
Further, as the view itself is explained in SMW it is clearly not the same
as the theory of internal relations as, say, it is expounded by Brand
Blanshard in *The Nature of Thought*.[12] But in AI these terms appear
again in the discussion of law as immanent, a position which Whitehead
follows in general (AI 144a). The use of these terms seems to me an
effort to turn the reader's thinking into certain general channels before
a carefully revised theory is offered. After all, contact with the history

of philosophy must be maintained. In order to understand in a full sense how prehensive unities are internally related we must first discuss the relatedness of eternal objects.

An eternal object is a determinate entity. This determinateness has two sides: its individual essence and its relational essence. What an eternal object is in itself determines what it is in relation to other eternal objects. If we have before us a group of entities each with a determinate character, then the relationships between these entities are determined. On the other hand, these determinate relationships are constitutive of the essence of the eternal object (SMW 230b). If this were not the case, then Whitehead would be holding that colors, sounds, and spatial relations could be unique, independent qualities simply located in a substance-attribute universe. But we know that this is not his view.

It seems to me that this is the point at which Stebbing's discussion becomes confused.[13] The point is worth careful attention because it marks the spot where early admirers of Whitehead like Stebbing and Murphy part company with him. Stebbing wants to maintain that eternal objects have definite relations to each other but that they are not internal in the sense that the object is what it is because of its relation to other objects. "Nor is A [an eternal object] what it is because of its relations to B [another eternal object]; but seeing that A is what it is, and its characteristics are fixed, it has to B, which is also of fixed character, an unalterable relation of some kind or other. This relation is not the relation of 'entailing'; it is merely the relation of contrast, or of similarity, or of such and such a grade, that must hold between simple terms." [14] This false interpretation of SMW depends upon two points: (1) on a false separation of the relational essence from the individual essence (SMW 230b, 180b) and (2) on taking the individual essence of an eternal object to be a simple, that is, a unique, independent character. But Whitehead says that "the individual essence is merely the essence considered in respect to its uniqueness" (SMW 229b). On the other hand, this essence of an eternal object must be considered in respect to its relatedness, which is its relational essence. With regard to this second point, Stebbing unconsciously commits the error of simple location with respect to the essence of eternal objects. To consider the eternal objects as unique simples with an independent "itness" is to assume that the essence of an eternal object can be completely understood without knowing its relations, and this is to assume simple location. They are unique, but their uniqueness results from their internal relatedness.

Whitehead says: "If A be an eternal object, then what A is in itself involves A's status in the universe, and A cannot be divorced from this status. In *the* essence of A there stands a determinateness as to the relationships of A to other eternal objects . . . Since the relationships of A to other eternal objects stand determinately in *the* essence of A, it follows that they are internal relations. I mean by this that these relationships are *constitutive* of A; for an entity which stands in internal relations has no being as an entity not in these relations" (SMW 230b, my emphasis).

It is hard to understand how Stebbing could interpret this passage the way she did. We must accept her statement that "what I am about to say may misrepresent his views." [15] But I would further contend that her interpretation is not consistent with the earlier view of PNK, CN, and PREl, on the ground that the way in which a perceptual object controls the ingression of (is significant of) sense-objects will never be understood unless some view of internal relations is adopted. Before this, it remains an unanalyzed phrase like Hume's "habit of association." Whitehead seems to confirm this point, for he says that "the internal relationships of A conjointly form its significance" (SMW 230b).

It is clear that the various types of objects in PNK, CN, and PREl correspond to the eternal objects of SMW. To say that one object is significant of another means that the two objects are internally related, such that the being of one necessarily involves the being of the other. In this sense they are significant of each other. Hence, part of what is involved in the control theory of ingression, so far as the relation of objects is concerned, is explained by the internal relatedness of eternal objects, such that the ingression of one eternal object in some event necessarily involves the ingression of other eternal objects. Further, the internal relatedness of eternal objects means that all eternal objects are internally related to each other so as to constitute a single systematic mutual relatedness. From the standpoint of prehensive unities or actuality this is the realm of possibilities (SMW 231c), as will be explained shortly.

This reference to ingression leads to the relation of eternal objects to prehensive unities or actual occasions, or of objects to events, but we must remember always the slight differences in the meanings of these terms. Ingression allows for the novelty in Whitehead's doctrine of internal relatedness. Briefly, the relation between an eternal object and a prehensive unity is internal on the side of the prehensive unity and external on the side of the eternal object (SMW 231b, 180a). Or, to put it another way, the relation is a constitutive part necessary to the being of the prehensive unity, but the relation is not a constitutive part of the being of the eternal object.

By external relations Whitehead means that a given entity is indeterminate with respect to its relations to certain other entities. It may be in this possible relationship or some other possible relationship. The concept of possibility takes its meaning from the notion of external related-ness, from relations which are not settled or determinate. To say some-thing is possible is to say that, from among alternative relationships, no one relationship is necessarily the case. The situation is patient for any one of the alternatives (smw 230c). Actuality, on the other hand, takes its meaning from internal relations. The actual situation is settled, definite, unique. The relationships embodied are necessarily just what they are or else the entities would not be precisely what they are.

"Thus the general principle which expresses *A's* [an eternal object's] ingression in the particular actual occasion *a* is the indeterminateness which stands in the essence of *A* as to its ingression in *a,* and is the determinateness which stands in the essence of *a* as to the ingression of *A* in *a.* Thus the synthetic prehension, which is *a,* is the solution of the indeterminateness of *A* into the determinateness of *a.* Accordingly the relationship between *A* and *a* is external as regards *A,* and is internal as regards *a"* (smw 231b; *cf.* also 233c).

We must now state the sense in which prehensive unities are internally related to each other (smw 235a, 180a). What has already been said about the theory of aspects indicates that they are so related. One pre-hensive unity is internally related to another in the following way. Every prehensive unity prehends (perceives) other prehensive unities in that it is aware of aspects of the other unities, and these aspects or characteristics are eternal objects ingredient in the prehended unities (smw 174b, 217c). Since these aspects (eternal objects) are internally related to the prehended unities of which they are aspects, as explained in the previous paragraphs on the relation of eternal objects to prehen-sive unities, and also are internally related to the prehending unity as a part of its synthesis of these aspects, then it follows that the two prehensive unities are indirectly internally related, because any change in the aspects (eternal objects) common to them in different ways would enforce a difference in their beings (smw 151a). Or to put it in another way: a given prehensive unity is a grasping together of eternal objects in such a way that these eternal objects are necessary to its being what it is (smw 217a). But this prehensive unity is perceived (pre-hended) by other prehensive unities in virtue of the aspects it presents. These aspects or characteristics or modes are eternal objects ingredient in it (smw 217c), and are a part of the grasping together of eternal objects constitutive of the being of the perceiving prehensive unity, and hence are internal to it (smw 174a). One prehensive unity *a* is internally related to another prehensive unity *b* in virtue of its necessary aspects, which are an integral part of the being of the other prehensive unity *b* (smw 180a). "Each event [prehensive unity] corresponds to two such patterns; namely, the pattern of aspects of other events which it grasps into its own unity, and the pattern of its aspects which other events severally grasp into their unities" (smw 151a).

It seems to me that Stebbing is also wrong in her interpretations of the relation of prehensive unities, at least wrong according to the view of smw which I have tried to express. The question of whether she is wrong with respect to pnk, cn, and prel is difficult to answer. Probably not with respect to the class theory, but, if my interpretation of what is really involved in the control-theory of ingression is correct, then she is at least wrong about prel and uc. She states that "whatever is actual is an event and thus what is actual *could* not be otherwise," and "this characteristic of events might be described as a certain 'fixedness of relations'; it is misdescribed as an 'internal relation.'" [16] I do not see how she can say this when Whitehead in smw specifically states that the relations between events are internal (smw 179c). And, further, we have explained how this internality is effected by means of eternal objects functioning as aspects.

Those who argue for the externality of relations often cite as typical examples the relations of space and time. Whitehead holds the opposite view (smw 180a). The ground for his position is that space-time relations are derivative from the extensive characteristics of prehensive unities and that such characteristics are aspects involved internally in the constitution of the prehensive unities. Their seeming externality depends on their being abstractions from the concrete interconnectedness of prehensive unities (smw 180–81). The details of the internality of space-time relations are not presented until pr.

In our discussion of significance (Chap. IV, Sec. IV) we had to face the problem of how finite truths are possible if every event is internally related to every other. We there proposed Whitehead's answer as contained in prel and uc. Now that the doctrine of internal relatedness has been extended to the relations of eternal objects, and eternal objects to prehensive unities, we must tackle once again the question "how any particular truth is possible . . . [if] we cannot know about anything till we equally know everything else" (smw 235b)?

First, consider the internal relations among eternal objects. "The reason for the existence of finite relationships in the realm of eternal objects is that relationships of these objects among themselves are entirely unselective, and are systematically complete" (smw 236c). By "unselective" I interpret Whitehead to mean that within the realm of eternal objects (possibilities) there is no process, no grasping together of aspects into a whole, no growing or change. Each eternal object is precisely determined. By "systematically complete" I interpret Whitehead to mean that no creation or dissolution takes place in this realm. It is complete in its totality and systematic in structure because of the internal relations throughout.

Consider some eternal object, say the color green. The eternal object has an individual essence which can be described by saying that it is what it is. It is the eternal object considered from the standpoint of its uniqueness (smw 229b). This unique eternal object green as a determinate entity has a set of definite relations to all other eternal objects since they too are determinate in character. The whole web of eternal objects and relations is determinate. Green with respect to other colors is "lighter than" or "darker than" or "warmer than"; with respect to other eternal objects it is "above," "below," "left of," "between," "on the surface of from this percipient event," and so on. Each of these relations is constitutive of the eternal object green in the sense that each relation belongs to the relational essence. If any one of these relations were altered then the relational essence would be different.

Each of these relations is generic in the sense that the other relata need not be known in their individual essences but merely as bare relata so long as the determinate relation is sustained; that is, "the relational essence of an eternal object is not unique to that object" (smw 237a). For example, green is darker than x, and x, a bare relatum, could be a number of different colors which satisfy this generic relation. Thus a uniform scheme of relations is determined but their individual essences are not. The generic character is what Whitehead means by "unselective," and the uniformity results from the "systematic completeness" and determinateness of eternal objects. Although the relata are bare "its," whose individual essences are not determined, nevertheless the generic relations are internal for (constitutive of) the eternal object under consideration. Further, this web of generic relations, systematically complete, uniform, and unselective, is constitutive of and internally relates all eternal objects, as is apparent from the above description (smw 237a).

This view of the relations between eternal objects as generic—a fact that is not strange, considering that eternal objects are abstract—allows us to know something about a given eternal object without requiring knowledge of the individual essences of all other eternal objects that are related to it. We need to know only the uniform structure of the web of relations involved in its relational essence. This much of Whitehead's answer is stated in the metaphysical principle "that the relationships of any eternal object A, considered as constitutive of A, merely involve other eternal objects as bare relata without reference to their individual essences . . ." (smw 238b).

Whitehead contends that a second metaphysical principle follows from the above: "that the divisibility of the general relationship of A into a multiplicity of finite relationships of A stands therefore in the essence of that eternal object" (SMW 238b). These finite relationships, he contends, are possible because of the generic character of the relations, their non-uniqueness. Consider arithmetic: a given natural number, say six, which is an eternal object, stands in certain definite relations to other numbers. It is half of some other number, twice another, the square root of another, and so on. Each of these relations is constitutive of the relational essence of six. This relational essence is determined by the individual essence of six and is not unique to six, for it can be the relational essence of some other numbers; the web of relations (half of, twice, square root, etc.) can belong to other numbers as well. Finally, the web of relations has an analytical character in the sense that its uniform structure can be stated in a multiplicity of finite propositions, one basic example of which is the postulates for natural numbers (SMW 239a). Alternative sets of postulates constitute a different analysis of this web of relations in another finite group of propositions belonging to the total multiplicity of relations constitutive of the relational essence of six. Whitehead seems to hold that it is possible to find such finite groups of propositions to express any web of relational essences (SMW 236b) because of the uniform structure and generic character of the relations between eternal objects. His example of the most general set of limited propositions concerning relational essences applicable to actuality is the four-dimensional spatio-temporal scheme (SMW 239a).

Whitehead's answer to the question of how we can have finite knowledge about eternal objects and yet hold a theory of their internal relatedness is a difficult one to comprehend. In SMW it is very brief. I have tried to give an interpretation which would be consistent with PR and the general direction of his development as I understand it. The best one can say is to echo Stebbing: "what I say may not be Professor Whitehead's view." The truth of this second metaphysical principle, which I have just endeavored to explain, is by no means apparent. It seems to hold in a number of cases like arithmetic, but its generality is far from established. If the second principle could be established it would provide an answer to the problem.

The same problem does not exist with regard to the relatedness of eternal objects to prehensive unities, since the relation is external for the eternal object, as already explained.

In the case of the internal relatedness of prehensive unities the above solution is not possible, since those eternal objects (aspects) which are grasped together in the prehensive unity are unique for that unity. The relation is not generic but concrete; the individual essence of the eternal object is constitutive of the unique being of the prehensive unity. Hence, as regards prehensive unities we can never know the concrete being of another prehensive unity. We grasp only certain of its aspects into our own concrete being. There is then an ultimate privacy of prehensive unities. This will be made clear in detail in our discussion of the doctrine of prehensions in PR.

This chapter was concerned with tracing the transition in Whitehead's development from the early phase of PNK, CN, and PRel to the mature phase of PR and AI with respect to four interrelated major topics. First, the entire critique of traditional scientific thought is summed up in the discussion of the assumption of simple location, an instance of the Fallacy of Misplaced Concreteness. Second, the enlargement of the notion of perception with the introduction and derivation of the notion of prehension. Third, the notion of prehension and the enlargement of perception leads to the new entities called prehensive unities, which link the events of PNK with the actual occasions of PR. Fourth, the theory of aspects with respect to prehensive unities necessitates a discussion of internal relatedness, which is the link between the doctrine of significance and the doctrine of prehensions in PR. We now have completed our bridge to the mature discussion of perception in PR and AI.

Chapter VII

FUNDAMENTAL CATEGORIES
AND THEORIES

Process and Reality is, without qualification, a magnificent and almost superhuman achievement in the field of speculative philosophy. It is the culmination of a stream of speculative thinking which we saw begin in the 1905 memoir. It will be the core of our discussion from here on. Two more works are important for this discussion. S is a brief statement of Whitehead's mature theory of perception, lacking the details and systematic completeness of PR. Besides, it is not wholly consistent with PR, as will be shown. *Adventures of Ideas* is a marvelous exposition of PR in nontechnical terms, with applications to history, culture, and science. It is a literary masterpiece. In MT little is added on the subject of perception, although the work has many other interesting things to say. Our discussion would be hopeless without some explanation of the basic categories of this system. These basic categories are in part the result of Whitehead's effort to correct a number of basic philosophical errors of modern philosophy.

Section I. Basic Categories

As previously stated, it seems to me that Whitehead's philosophical thinking falls into three parts, determined by his attempted answers to three instances of the fallacy of misplaced concreteness; namely, (1) the assumption that the subject-predicate form of logic and the substance-attribute forms of metaphysics are the most adequate means to analyze and represent reality; (2) the assumption of simple location for the fundamental entities of reality; and (3) the assumption that "the primary activity in the act of experience is the bare subjective entertainment of the datum, devoid of any subjective form of reception. This is the doctrine of *mere* sensation" (PR 239c). Frequently this bare subjective entertainment of discrete data passes under the title of the "given" element in perception. This is the assumption that sense-data are primitive elements in our experience, on the basis of which logical constructions of other entities are to be accomplished. But Whitehead's contention is that they are derivative from causal efficacy; hence their "misplaced concreteness."

In PR, the subject-predicate, substance-attribute assumption is shown to be a consequence of the subjectivist principle, which states "that the datum in the act of experience can be adequately analyzed purely in terms of universals" (PR 239b). Thus, substance has been thought of as having an independent existence, to which the qualities (universals) are somehow related. Subject-predicate statements have led to two misconceptions: "*one* is the concept of vacuous actuality, void of subjective experience; and the *other* is the concept of quality inherent in a substance" (PR 253b). In PNK, CN, and PRel this subject-predicate assumption was met by the polyadic relation of the ingression of sense-objects in nature. The assumption was first attacked in the purely logical work of *Principia Mathematica*.

In PR the assumption of simple location is closely linked with the substance-attribute view. The substance-attribute assumption is "the employment of the notion of an actual entity which is characterized by essential qualities, and remains numerically one amidst the changes of accidental relations and of accidental qualities. The contrary doctrine [Whitehead's] is that an actual entity never changes, and that it is the outcome of whatever can be ascribed to it in the way of quality of relationships" (PR 122d). The claim that a single substance with its qualities can be by itself both meaningful and actual is one form of simple location and is denied by Whitehead. His view is that relatedness among a plurality of entities is essential to concreteness.

The consequences of the substance-attribute view and simple location with respect to science and perception have already been discussed. The cosmological scheme of PR incorporates with modifications the alternative views. Our main task is to consider the third instance of misplaced concreteness: the assumption that sense-data are the immediately given primitive elements in experience. The correction of these three instances of misplaced concreteness provides the framework of ideas for the cosmological system.

But why should the solution of an epistemological problem require a recourse to metaphysics? This depends on our notion of "togetherness." If our meaning of togetherness is such as to allow no other meaning besides "experiential togetherness" then we cannot hope to separate our account of truth and falsity from our intuitive perceptions of truth and falsity. They must be together in experience. If on the other hand we hold that there is a form of togetherness not derivative from experience, then we are left with a disjunction of the component elements of the external world (ontology) on one side and the component elements of perceptual experience (epistemology) on the other (PR 288). The difficulties of epistemology flow from this disjunction, because there is no bridge uniting the two kinds of togetherness (PR 289a). Hence Whitehead asserts that "all difficulties as to first principles are only camouflaged metaphysical difficulties" and "the epistemological difficulty is only solvable by an appeal to ontology" (PR 288a). Hence, for Whitehead, the separation of epistemology and ontology is repudiated. To understand his solution to the problem of perception we must immerse ourselves in his basic metaphysical notions.

In the notes to the second edition of PNK, Whitehead made it clear that he then thought that process is the fundamental notion by means of which we can understand concrete actuality. Actual entities are the concrete stuff which issue from process or are involved in process (PR 33, category of explanation I). "'Actual entities'—also termed 'actual occasions'—are the final real things of which the world is made up. There is no going behind actual entities to find anything more real" (PR 27–28). They are complex, different, organic, synthetic, and creative; each one is a process of becoming. The process of becoming, termed "creativity," is that by means of which the disjunctive "many" becomes a conjunctive "one" (PR 33, category of explanation II). Creativity is the ultimate of ultimates in Whitehead's system (PR 31e, the category of the ultimate). Actual entities are related by their prehensions of each other. Thus, one actual entity is said to prehend another. The unification of these feelings is the entity's synthetic aspect. Their internal relatedness constitutes an organic entity. Although the actual occasion is a synthesis of other factors of actuality, the way it experiences these factors is entirely private to itself and cannot be shared with other entities (PR 33, category of explanation V).

Prehensions are concrete facts of relatedness, and this is all Whitehead means by feeling. A group of actual entities related in some way is called a nexus (PR 35, category of explanation XIV). The concept of a nexus replaces the concept of an event in the earlier books. "An event is a nexus of actual occasions interrelated in some determinate fashion in some extensive quantum" (PR 124d). The ordinary objects of our experience are usually "*nexūs*." The actual entity prehended is said to be objectified for the actual entity prehending, sometimes called the subject (PR 34, category of explanation VIII). Only actual entities can prehend, but eternal objects, actual entities, and prehensions can be prehended. The *way* in which the subject prehends the datum is the subjective form of the prehending actual entity. The subjective form has a definite character determined by the eternal objects involved in it. Hence every prehension has a subject, a datum, and a subjective form (PR 35, category of explanation XI). The "ultimate facts of immediate actual experience are actual entities, prehensions, and nexūs. All else, is for our experience, derivative abstraction" (PR 30a).

Probably second in importance among the categories of existence are eternal objects (PR 37, category of explanation XIX). These are the specific forms existing in a realm of possibles or "pure potentials for the specific determination of fact" (PR 32). This function for the specific determination of fact is analyzable into "definiteness" and "position," where definiteness relates to what eternal objects are involved, and position means relative status in a nexus of occasions (PR 38, category of explanation XX).

The concrescence of an actual entity is the process whereby it achieves a harmonious unity of many feelings through a process of integration and valuation (PR 39, category of explanation XXVII). The end which directs the unification is called the subjective aim of the actual entity and provides teleological causation for the process. The achievement of the subjective aim is called the satisfaction of the entity; it becomes one of the many actual entities to be felt (prehended) in some new concrescence. Concrescence is sometimes referred to as "microscopic process." On the other hand, "macroscopic process" is the transition from one actual entity to another. Such transitions are brought about by prehensions which are acts of causation or causal feelings.

There are three phases in the process of concrescence (PR 323–26). First, the responsive or receptive phase in which the subject receives by prehensions or feelings the past world of actual entities relevant to its concrescence. Second, the supplemental phase, whereby the many separate prehensions of the responsive phase are integrated and reintegrated with themselves and "conceptual feelings" (PR 39, category of explanation XXVII). Conceptual feelings are prehensions of eternal objects. The presence of an eternal object in an actual occasion is termed the ingression of the eternal object in the actual occasion (PR 34, category of explanation VII).

Ingression is a complex relation. Prehensions of eternal objects which are rejected as not relevant to the achievement of the subjective aim are called negative prehensions (PR 35, category of explanation XII). There can also be prehensions of other prehensions within the actual entity itself. This second phase is directed teleologically by the subjective aim and limited in definite ways by the causal feelings, by the physical prehensions of the responsive phase. Lastly, the "satisfaction" is the final unification of feelings into one single determinate occasion. This satisfaction is a single prehension which includes in one unity all other prehensions (PR 38, category of explanation XXV). When an actual entity achieves its satisfaction it perishes. This perpetual perishing is part of the eternal flux described by Whitehead's system. The "being" of an actual entity is constituted by its "becoming" (PR 34–35, categories of explanation IX and X).

Besides the complex relations realized through prehensions with their special kinds of internality, there is another group of relations called extensive connections. These relations do not depend on the creative character of the actual entity but on the demarcation by the actual entity of a certain minimal region which is their situation. Geometrical properties are derivative from extensive connections between regions as are space-time systems of science (PR 95a, 442d, 443a).[1]

In addition to the categories of existence already described (actual entities, prehensions, nexūs, subjective forms, and eternal objects) there are three others: propositions, multiplicities, and contrasts. A proposition is the datum of an impure prehension arising from the integration of pure conceptual prehensions whose data are eternal objects, and physical prehensions whose data are actual entities (PR 280a). A multiplicity is a pure disjunction of diverse entities such that "its unity is constituted by the fact that all its constituent entities severally satisfy at least one condition which no other entity satisfies" (PR 36b, category of explanation XVI). A contrast is a felt synthesis of the components of a complex datum of prehension (PR 36d, category of explanation XVII). The number of possible contrasts is indefinite; hence there are an indefinite number of categories of existence (entities) in this sense.

There are two more important categories of explanation which have confused some of Whitehead's critics. These are crucial to his theory of perception. For reasons to be made clear later in connection with the discussion of perception in the mode of presentational immediacy, Whitehead accepts a revised form of the subjectivist principle which is "merely an alternative statement of the principle of relativity" (PR 252b).[2] This principle states "that the potentiality for being an element in a real concrescence of many entities into one actuality, is the one general metaphysical character attaching to all entities, actual and *non-actual*; and that every item in its universe is involved in each concrescence" (PR 33, category of explanation IV, my italics).

Blyth has maintained the separation of the principle of relativity from the subjectivist principle in an effort to show that these two principles lead to fundamental contradictions in Whitehead's system.[3] He states the subjectivist principle as follows: "that apart from the experience of real particulars or existents there is nothing, nothing, bare nothing-ness." [4] What Blyth's restatement leaves out is the important group of entities designated as "non-actual" in the definition of the principle of relativity. Consultation of Whitehead's own definition of the subjectivist principle does not reveal the limitation Blyth puts on it (PR 252b, 254a, 288b). Blyth seems to have taken his definition from the following state-ment of Whitehead's: "that apart from the experiences of subjects there is nothing, nothing, nothing, bare nothingness" (PR 254a). Comparing this with Blyth's we can see how he went wrong. He has changed the word "experiences" to "experience" and substituted "real particulars" or "existents" for Whitehead's "subjects." The effect of these changes is considerable. Blyth's emphasis on real particulars tends to restrict what is experienced to entities both actual and particular. But Whitehead's definition clearly allows any kind of experience by the subject whether particular or universal, actual or non-actual, so long as they are experi-ences of some subject, some actual entity. It is just this kind of experience which is allowed by the above definition of the principle of relativity. The two principles clearly amount to the same thing when Whitehead's definitions are used.

The seemingly devastating criticisms and contradictions which Blyth finds in the foundations of Whitehead's metaphysics are, so far as I can discover, completely groundless. The false separation of these two principles achieved by a misinterpretation of one is the pivot for all his criticism. The specific points of his criticism and my answers will be given in the elaboration of the theory of perception.

The second important category of explanation is the ontological prin-ciple. It states "that every condition to which the process of becoming conforms in any particular instance has its reason *either* in the character of some actual entity in the actual world of that concrescence, *or* in the character of the subject which is in process of concrescence" (PR 36, cate-gory of explanation XVIII). Or briefly, "no actual entity, then no reason" (PR 28b). Hence, every reason must be either in the real internal con-stitution of some other actual entity or in the subjective aim condition-ing the process of concrescence. A common mistake in connection with this category has been to limit it to the real internal constitution of actual entities, and thus to forget the subjective aim.

So far we have outlined three of the four groups of basic categories in Whitehead's cosmology: the category of the ultimate, categories of exist-ence, and categories of explanation. We have yet to express the "cate-goreal" obligations. This can be accomplished most fruitfully in connec-tion with our summary of the doctrine of prehensions.

Section II. The Doctrine of Prehensions

Our summary of this doctrine is important because it constitutes one of two ways of analyzing the structure of reality and Whitehead's mature theory of perception is the foundation of this doctrine of prehensions. Hence, the theory of perception is the foundation for the structure of reality and necessary for comprehension of his metaphysical outlook. In the chapters that follow I try to demonstrate this conclusion, just as, in Chapters III, IV, and V, I tried to demonstrate how Whitehead's views on perception were the foundation for his reconstructions in the philosophy of science.

The two modes of analysis for reality are the genetic theory and the morphological theory (PR 334–35). Genetic analysis is concerned with the division of the process of concrescence, through which every actual entity passes from its reception of simple physical feelings to its satisfaction (PR 433–34). It deals with the various kinds of prehensions, their integrations and reintegrations, how the pattern of integration is directed, the rejection of some prehensions, the value component of prehensions, and the role of propositions and contrasts.

Morphological analysis is concerned with the division of the concrete; with the world of actual entities considered from the standpoint of their satisfactions as complete, finished beings (PR 448b, 433a, 336a). Each such complete determinate actual entity marks out the enjoyment of a certain quantum of time, but the process of concrescence is not in time. Rather, it presupposes the whole quantum at any point in the concrescence. Physical time expresses some features of this concrescence (PR 434a,b). This is exactly what is meant by an epochal theory of time. Each entity marks out an epoch.

This quantum marked out by the satisfaction of the actual entity has a spatial as well as a temporal element. The spatial element is called an extensive region (PR 434c). "This region is the determinate basis which the concrescence presupposes" (PR 434c). The extensive division of such regions ignores the unity achieved in the satisfaction. Hence Whitehead has to maintain that regions are potentially divisible, although the satisfaction is never divided (PR 435b).

The method of extensive abstraction, utilizing the whole-part relation among events, was the form of morphological analysis attempted in PNK, CN, and PRel. It led to difficulties with respect to the definition of a point. The method of extensive connection in PR is designed to meet these difficulties (PR 439–40).

The two types of division have been explained. "But this scheme of *external* extensive relationships links itself with the schemes of internal division which are *internal* to the several actual entities. There is, in this way, one basic scheme of extensive connection which expresses, on one uniform plan, (1) the general conditions to which the bonds, uniting the atomic actualities into a nexus, conform, and (2) the general conditions to which the bonds, uniting the infinite number of coordinate subdivisions of the satisfaction of any actual entity, conform" (PR 438–39). If these general conditions could not be specified, then (1) the adherence to a doctrine of internal relatedness would be disastrous for knowledge; (2) the derivation of geometry and space-time on an empirical basis would be hopeless; and (3) the construction of a uniform scheme necessary for the real foundation of induction in science would be lacking.

John Dewey has criticized Whitehead for trying to make co-ordinate the genetic-functional and the intuitional-structural methods of analysis (what Whitehead calls the genetic and morphological methods of division).[5] Dewey maintains that the two methods, which he calls experimental observation and mathematical, cannot be co-ordinate, that is, on the same level, but one "must lead and the other follow." [6] Apparently it is Dewey's contention that when combined on the same level the two methods must clash, but that the two can be consistently combined if one leads the other so that one can correct the assertions of the other when they disagree on some issue. My previous paragraph should make it clear why both methods are equally important with respect to the three crucial philosophic problems mentioned. It was necessary that Dewey solve these problems by taking one method as primary. Whitehead has given his own answer to Dewey but without the precision I have tried to give within his system.[7]

We now turn our attention to a summary sketch of the doctrine of prehensions. The genetic division of an actual entity falls roughly into three stages marked out in the process of concrescence by the prehensions involved: conformal feelings, conceptual feelings, and comparative feelings, which include propositional feelings (PR 249b). A prehension involves three factors: the subject or actual entity which is prehending, the datum which is prehended, and the subjective form, which is how the subject prehends the datum (PR 35c). The origin of the idea of prehension as a generalization of the root element in apprehension and comprehension and as expressing Bacon's use of the term "perception" was discussed in the previous chapter (Chap. VI, Sec. II). Prehensions effect a transition of the objectivity of the datum into the subjectivity of the prehending occasion (PR 65a, 82a). Prehensions are of two kinds, positive and negative (PR 66a, 337b). "A negative prehension is the definite exclusion of that item from positive contribution to the subject's own real internal constitution" (PR 66a). Items are excluded because they may be irrelevant to the subjective aim, or introduce insufficient novelty for the subjective aim (PR 40–1, categoreal obligation VII), or involve incompatibility with the subjective aim (PR 39, categoreal obligation I). Although Whitehead is very unclear on this point, it would seem that there can be negative prehensions of eternal objects only for reasons which relate to his view of causality as involving simple physical feelings between actual entities.[8] Negative prehensions are important because of their subjective forms, which add to the emotional complex of the prehending occasion but not to the objective data (PR 66a). Every actual entity is prehended by some other actual entity.

A positive prehension, also called a feeling, "is the definite inclusion of that item into positive contribution to the subject's own real internal constitution" (PR 66a). A positive prehension consists of five factors: "(1) the 'subject' which feels, (2) the 'initial data' which are felt, (3) the 'elimination' in virtue of negative prehensions, (4) the 'objective datum' which is felt, and (5) the 'subjective form' which is *how* that subject feels that objective datum" (PR 337–38). Compare this with the three factors involved in prehensions in general. The additions are (2) and (3), whereby initial data are distinguished from data actually felt so that negative prehensions have an opportunity to contribute their subjective forms to the emotional complex of the subject. A feeling cannot be separated from its subject, for without the subject the feeling is ambiguous, indefinite, and vague. Hence the relations of prehension are particulars because their subjects (actual entities) are particulars.

There are three categoreal obligations exemplified in the process of concrescence that stand out with a certain ultimacy: subjective unity, objective identity, and objective diversity. The category of subjective unity states that "the many feelings which belong to an incomplete phase in the process of an actual entity, though unintegrated by reason of the incompleteness of the phase, are compatible for integration by reason of the unity of their subject" (PR 39c, 341c). This categoreal obligation provides the way for the achievement of the satisfaction of the entity. The aim guides the integration throughout the concrescence. In order that the aim be present throughout the concrescence there must be a conceptual feeling in the primary phase of concrescence of the subjective aim (PR 342b). In any incomplete phase the actual entity has the unity of a proposition; that is, a limited number of possibilities are envisaged for that particular concrescence (PR 342c). The category of objective identity asserts that "there can be no duplication of any element in the objective datum of the satisfaction of an actual entity, so far as concerns the function of that element in that satisfaction" (PR 344b, 39d). Hence every actual entity is a particular with one single, self-identical satisfaction that can never be realized again in quite the same way. By virtue of this principle there seems to me to be an ultimate privacy of subjective feeling of every actual entity. On the other hand, in another sense, there is an ultimate publicity, since every actual entity is prehended (objectified) in others. The category of objective diversity asserts that there can be no diverse elements exercising an absolute identity of function "in the objective datum of an actual entity, so far as concerns the functions of those elements in that satisfaction" (PR 344d, 39f,g). Hence no two prehensions with the same datum could have the same function in the prehending actual entity. This is another aspect of the particularity of the actual entity.

In the first phase of concrescence, the conformal phase, the most primary kind of feeling is a simple physical feeling whose initial datum is another actual entity and whose objective datum is some feeling belonging to the actual entity which is the initial datum (PR 361a, 375b). Hence, in any simple physical feeling two actual entities are involved, the subject and the initial datum; and two feelings are involved, the feeling of the subject and the feeling belonging to the satisfaction of the initial datum, which is the objective datum. The feeling which is the objective datum has for its subject the actual entity which is the initial datum; that feeling belongs to the objectification of the initial datum. This particular objectification of the initial datum is the "perspective" of the initial datum felt by the subject of the original prehension (PR 361b).

Simple physical feelings provide an ontological basis for the notion of causation. The "cause" is the actual entity which is the initial datum; the "effect" is the simple physical feeling; and the subject of this simple physical feeling is the entity "conditioned" by the "effect" (PR 361c). Simple physical feelings are the most primitive acts of perception and devoid of consciousness. The initial datum is the actual entity perceived; the objective datum is the "perspective" or manner in which the actual entity is perceived; and the subject of the simple physical feeling is the perceiver (PR 361–62).

There are two kinds of simple physical feelings, pure and hybrid. If the objective datum, which is a feeling belonging to the actual entity prehended, be a physical feeling, then we have a pure physical feeling. If the objective datum be a conceptual feeling, then we have a hybrid physical feeling (PR 343b, 375, 376). Two subspecies of hybrid physical feelings can be distinguished: "(1) those which feel the conceptual feelings of temporal actual entities, and (2) those which feel the conceptual feelings of God" (PR 377c). We can now explain how in the primary phase of concrescence the subjective aim of that process is an integral part.

Since God is an actual entity like other actual entities, he can be prehended by them in the early phases of their concrescence by means of a physical feeling. Such a physical feeling may have for its objective datum some conceptual feeling of God. If this conceptual feeling relates to what is immediately relevant to the universe given for that actual entity, then by means of the category of conceptual valuation there is a derivative conceptual feeling for that actual entity which reproduces the aim and value of God's conceptual feeling (PR 343b). Hence the direction of the novelty involved in any concrescence is provided as an integral part during the early phase of concrescence by a hybrid physical feeling of God. Without such a feeling there is mere conformal reproduction of prehended entities. The interlocking functions of God, creativity, and temporal creatures are the backbone of concrescence. Without these three, Whitehead's system would fall apart (PR 344a).

Perhaps the most important characteristic of a simple physical feeling is what Whitehead calls "re-enaction," "reproduction," or "conformation" (PR 364c). In AI this is called the doctrine of the conformation of feeling (AI 235, 236). The thesis of this doctrine is that there is a continuity and limited identity among actual entities according to a certain functioning of eternal objects. This characteristic is very important for science. It provides the metaphysical basis of induction, of continuity in change, of permanence of enduring things, of causation, and of the vector character of energy-transfer (PR 365a,b). There is no complete conformation, nor is every physical feeling a conformal feeling.

One reason for distinguishing the initial datum from the objective datum is to provide the mechanism whereby one actual entity is immanent in another while at the same time transcendent of the other. If the initial datum were the objective datum, then every actual entity would be literally a constitutive part in the other, actually and wholly immanent in it. Privacy and particularity would disappear, contrary to our basic experience. But there is an experience of "within-ness" in respect to other entities, and the objective datum provides this, as will be explained in detail in the next chapter.

The second general type of primary prehension is a conceptual feeling. All other complex feelings arise out of physical and conceptual feelings. The datum of a conceptual feeling is an eternal object (PR 367a). We have already remarked that negative prehensions are restricted to conceptual prehensions, although Whitehead is ambiguous on this point. In a conceptual feeling the initial datum and objective datum can be the same (PR 367a). Conceptual feelings are of two kinds, simple and reverted (PR 380–81). The origination of simple conceptual feelings from physical feelings is guaranteed by the category of conceptual valuation. It states that "from each physical feeling there is the derivation of a purely conceptual feeling whose datum is the eternal object determinant of the definiteness of the actual entity, or of the nexus, physically felt" (PR 39–40). This is Whitehead's technical statement of the empiricist principle that mental experience is derivative from physical (perceptual) experience, but there is also mental experience derivative from mental experience (PR 379e).

There is a value-aspect to the subjective form of a conceptual feeling depending on its relevance to the subjective aim of the subject (PR 367–69, 380b). According to the category of conceptual reversion, reverted conceptual feelings have "data which are partially identical with, and partially diverse from, the eternal objects forming the data in the primary phase of the mental pole; the determination of identity and diversity depending on the subjective aim at attaining depth of intensity by reason of contrast" (PR 380c). But Whitehead's account of where these other eternal objects are derived from is confused. A revised view derives them from hybrid physical feelings of God (PR 382a).[9]

It needs to be emphasized that in neither physical feeling nor conceptual feeling as discussed so far is there any element of consciousness (PR 369–79, 371b). Consciousness arises only in the later phases of concrescence when there is integration of physical and conceptual feelings.

Transmuted physical feelings provide simplification and regularity of the minor differences among actual occasions so there can be highly developed organisms with perception and comprehension in the usual sense. A transmuted physical feeling arises "when (in accordance with category iv, or with categories iv and v) one and the same conceptual feeling is derived impartially by a prehending subject from its analogous, simple physical feelings of various actual entities in its actual world, then, in a subsequent phase of integration of these simple physical feelings together with the derivative conceptual feelings, the prehending subject may transmute the *datum* of this conceptual feeling into a characteristic of some *nexus* containing those prehended actual entities among its members, or of some part of that nexus. In this way the nexus (or its part), thus characterized, is the objective datum of a feeling entertained by this prehending subject" (PR 40d). Thus by reason of the similarities among actual entities they can be grouped together into an enduring thing from some perspective and prehended as a single whole by some other actual entity. The things with which we are familiar are almost entirely nexūs (PR 383–85). The eternal object by which the nexus is qualified as a whole may not always be directly derived from each member of the nexus but sometimes only from a part; and in some cases the eternal object may be the datum of a reverted conceptual feeling, so that the possibility of error occurs (PR 386d–87b).

Our account of physical feelings, conceptual feelings, and transmuted feelings completes the foundation of the theory of prehensions. The basic mechanism of the interplay of prehensions involves several more categoreal obligations. The category of subjective harmony stipulates that "the valuations of conceptual feelings are mutually determined by their adaptation to be joint elements in a satisfaction aimed at by the subject" (PR 389c). This category indicates the connection between value and self-realization. The category of subjective intensity holds that the intensity of feeling belonging to the subjective aim is greatest in the immediate subject and in the relevant future (PR 41c). This relevant future is uncreated, but nevertheless it is a real potential, for it consists of those most intense elements of the present likeliest to be derived from it in the future. Lastly, according to the category of freedom and determination, each actual entity is externally free and internally determined in its concrescence (PR 41e)—externally free in respect to how and by whom it will be prehended and internally determined by its subjective aim.

Section III. The Higher Phases of Experience

We turn next to an outline of the higher phases of experience, which are all derivative complexes of the basic prehensions and categoreal obligations. There are several kinds of propositional feelings which result from the integration of physical and conceptual feelings (PR 393b). This integration, which forms the propositional feeling, requires that the following simple feelings shall have occurred: (1) an "indicative feeling," whose objective datum includes the logical subjects of the proposition; (2) a "physical recognition" feeling, which has some eternal object determinant of the definiteness of its datum; and (3) a "predicative feeling," whose datum is the eternal object involved in the physical recognition of (2). This last feeling may sometimes have as its datum another similar eternal object, according to the category of conceptual reversion (PR 397c–98a). A proposition results from the integration of the indicative feeling with the predicative feeling in a later stage of concrescence (PR 398b). This integration involves a synthesis of the two data such that the individual entities felt by the indicative feeling are bare logical subjects with the potentiality for realizing the character or pattern of the eternal objects felt by the predicative feeling (PR 398b). Such integrations provide two general types of propositional feelings, the perceptive and the imaginative.

Perceptive feelings are authentic or unauthentic. If the eternal object which is the datum of the predicative feeling is acquired by reversion, that is, is similar to but not identical with the eternal object determinant of the definiteness of the physical recognition feeling, then the predicative feeling will not be true to the nexus felt, hence unauthentic (PR 399–400). If the predicative feeling is directly derived from the physical recognition feeling, then we have an authentic perceptive feeling (PR 401b). Authentic perceptive feelings may be direct or indirect, depending on whether or not the indicative feeling which provides the logical subjects is transmuted (PR 410a).

An imaginative propositional feeling occurs when the indicative feeling and the physical recognition feeling differ (PR 401d). That is, when the nexūs which are the objective data of each differ. This can be a matter of degree ranging from practical identity at one end, which gives a perceptive feeling, to greater and greater diversity at the other end, in which the imagination attributes the eternal object to the members of the nexus of the indicative feeling (PR 402a).

Propositional feelings need not involve consciousness or judgment, but they do involve decision for or against the value of the predicative pattern (logical predicate) in their concrescence (PR 399b, 402b). In this sense they are "lures for feeling." Thus the proposition is not important because of its truth or falsity but as a focus of interest involving value (PR 395–96).

Comparative feelings constitute the second major group of complex feelings of the later phase of concrescence. The data of comparative feelings are "generic contrasts" (PR 406a), that is, comparisons of other feelings. There are an indefinite number of variant comparative feelings reflecting the degree of development of the mental pole of the actual entity and the indefinite number of possible contrasts.

"Physical purposes" are comparative feelings of the simplest kind, which have as their data the contrast resulting from the integration of a physical feeling and its correlate conceptual feeling (PR 422a). Since the conceptual feeling may be simple or reverted, two subspecies result (PR 406b). The subjective form of a physical-purpose feeling is either desire (adversion) or rejection (aversion), depending on whether the contrast contributes to the realization of the subjective aim or not (PR 406b, 422b). These feelings serve to intensify the experience of the actual entity (PR 422b). In the case of integration with a reverted conceptual feeling derived from a physical feeling of the primordial nature of God, a novel element is introduced into the concrescence (PR 423–24).

An "intellectual feeling" has as its datum a generic contrast between a nexus of actual entities and a propositional feeling whose logical subject is the nexus of entities (PR 407a). Theoretically, there ought to be at least as many intellectual feelings as there are propositional feelings. All intellectual feelings involve some degree of consciousness, which distinguishes them from all other feelings (PR 406b, 407–08). There is both identity and diversity among the feelings in the integrated datum; an identity of actual entities which are the data of the physical feeling (indicative feeling) and the logical subjects of the propositional feeling; a diversity between the eternal objects constituting the predicative pattern of the propositional feeling (acquired in various ways) and the eternal objects which are the subjective forms (determinants of character) of the physical feelings (PR 407a).

One kind of intellectual feeling is a "conscious perception," whose datum is a contrast involving the integration of a physical feeling with its correlate perceptive feelings (PR 409d). Recall that a perceptive feeling is a propositional feeling having three subspecies: direct authentic, indirect authentic, and unauthentic. Hence conscious perception can produce error when reverted or transmuted feelings are involved, as they are in the unauthentic or indirect forms (PR 409c). A detailed discussion of conscious perceptions will be given in Chapter X, Section III.

Another kind of intellectual feeling is an "intuitive judgment," which has for its datum a contrast between a physical feeling (indicative feeling) of a nexus and an imaginative feeling, which was the second general type of propositional feeling (PR 412c). Three subjective forms of the intuitive judgment are distinguished: "yes-form," "no-form," and "suspense-form" (PR 413a). In the yes-form the predicative pattern of the propositional feeling is the character of the actual entities constituting the nexus physically felt. In the no-form the predicative pattern, due to reversion and/or transmutation, is felt as incompatible with the eternal objects exemplified in the nexus physically felt. In the suspense-form the predicative pattern is wholly or partially irrelevant to the eternal objects in the nexus physically felt (PR 415–16). The distinction between a conscious perception and an intuitive judgment is vague insofar as the origination of the perceptive feelings and imaginative feelings is similar (PR 415b). When considerable reversion or transmutation has occurred the conscious perception appears more like an intuitive judgment. On the other hand, a yes-form of intuitive judgment may be hard to distinguish from a conscious perception based on a direct authentic perceptive propositional feeling (PR 417a).

One of the ways in which the genetic analysis of concrescence provided by the theory of prehensions connects with the morphological analysis of regions defined by the satisfaction is through "strain feelings." A strain feeling is a feeling "in which the forms exemplified in the datum concern geometrical, straight, and flat loci" (PR 472a). The strain feeling is a complex integration of simpler feelings, with attention concentrated on these forms.

This concludes our summary. We now have before us a sufficient framework of fundamental categories and theories to enable us to present a detailed statement of Whitehead's mature theory of perception.

Chapter VIII

THE MATURE THEORY OF PERCEPTION

Section I. The General Nature of Perception

Let there be no illusion about it: Whitehead does not use the term "perception" in its usual meaning (AI 229b). The statement and discussion of Bacon's distinction between sense and perception in Chapter VI should have made this clear. Whitehead was trying to cut beneath the usual discussion to a more basic or generic meaning, true for the whole metaphysical situation.

But why, apart from philosophical difficulties, would one become suspicious of some accounts of perception? Suppose we see a certain colored shape before us and conclude "there is a chair." We may account for our probable conclusion by means of a chain of inferences dealing with our past experiences of certain shapes and colors. Thus we might suppose that the passage from sense-data to chair required a high level of mentality. But for an artist, say, to remain aware primarily of the colors and shapes, mental discipline is required: he must block the inference from sense-data to chair. Suppose a dog sees the shapes and colors. He may react by leaping onto the chair for a quiet nap. If he is highly trained he may refrain. Thus it seems that the transition from shapes and colors to the chair is a basic, natural one and not dependent on special training or the function of intellect (S 3–4).

Another sign of the derivative or complex nature of sense-perception as reflected in human experience is that sense-experience is fallible while direct experience is infallible (MT 99c, 181a, S 6c). The transition from sense-data to chair may be wrong.

Whitehead's theory of perception claims attention because of his repudiation of the dogma, almost uncontroverted in modern philosophy, of the primacy of immediate sensation in our experience (PR 173–74, MT 152c,d). In AI this dogma or erroneous presupposition of modern thought is stated in another way; namely, "that the sole way of examining experience is by acts of conscious introspective analysis" (AI 290b). On the contrary, each actual entity lifts some components of experience into primacy and forces others into the background, but the attitude of introspection serves to lift the "clear-cut data of sensation into primacy, and cloaks the vague compulsions and derivations which form the main stuff of experience" (AI 290b).

This dogma of perception by itself gives no information of past or future (AI 232b). To provide such information has been the unsuccessful task of modern philosophy. Recognizing its failure, Whitehead returns afresh to Hume's analysis of perception, which laid the clear foundation for the sensationalist doctrine of immediate sensation as primary. He finds that Hume's analysis is incompatible with Hume's asserted doctrine of only immediate sensation. For since Hume holds that all our knowledge is derived from experience and our experience is made up only of immediate sensations, then, as Hume's analysis shows, we can have no knowledge of cause and effect as necessary connection. But it is clear to most of us, and Hume agrees, that we do have scientific knowledge of cause and effect (PR 203c). From whence? (1) We can say, as Hume and logical empiricists do, that such necessary connections do not exist; that all we have are associations according to habit and depending on repetition. But Santayana has made it clear that this position ultimately leads to "solipsism of the present moment," and I agree (S 31–37, PR 125d). (2) We can say with Kant that causality as a category of the understanding is a necessary presupposition for experience, but then we have given up real causal connection in experience, for all that experience gives us is particular facts, and causality is a category of the understanding. In any such dualism it seems that we can never get causality over the bridge back into experience as an element therein (S 37–39). (3) We can maintain that Hume's analysis of experience was incomplete and go on to complete it so as to put causality back into experience. Two general paths have been followed in the re-analysis: we can (a) join the objective idealists in belief in an absolute with its necessary internal relations or (b) follow Whitehead in his doctrine of prehensions or causal feelings. Except for divergence of orientation, procedure, and terminology, with emphasis on different ultimate principles, (a) and (b) tend eventually to converge toward the same view with minor differences (PR 254b, AI 296d–99a).

Whitehead agrees with Hume that all of our knowledge begins in experience but rejects Hume's second premise, that such experience yields only simple, discrete, immediate sensations. He rejects it in the light of Hume's own analysis, wherein he finds clear evidence of more than immediate sensation, namely, of process.[1] According to Whitehead,

Hume recognizes the following process in perception: "first, impressions of sensations, of unknown origin; then, ideas of such impressions 'derived from' the impressions; then, impressions of reflection 'derived from' the antecedent ideas; and then, ideas of impressions of reflection. Somewhere in this process there is to be found repetition of impressions and thence by 'habit'—by which we may suppose that a particular mode of derivation is meant—by habit, a repetition of the correlate ideas; and thence expectancy of the repetition of the correlate impressions. . . . It is difficult to understand why Hume exempts 'habit' from the same criticism as that applied to the notion of cause. We have no 'impression of habit,' just as we have no 'impression of cause'" (PR 213b). The implicit dependence on the fact of "derived from" in this process points to the fact that there is more in perception than mere sensation.

Again Hume says, "if it be perceived *by the eyes*, it must be a color," [2] and so on with the other senses. But "by the eyes" is a perceptual recognition of the efficacious part played by the eyes in our supposed immediate perception, and by the body in general (PR 125c, 180b). What we see in immediate perception is causally dependent upon the nature of our eyes unless all physiology is to be denied (AI 274b). Therefore, in addition to immediate perception we have perception of causal efficacy, perception of a certain eye strain in our immediate visual perception, and awareness of the antecedent functioning of the body (PR 125c). Whitehead calls these two kinds of perception: (1) perception in the mode of presentational immediacy and (2) perception in the mode of causal efficacy. These two pure modes of perception are related by perception in the mode of symbolic reference. Thus far, we have seen how a re-analysis of one basic presupposition of modern philosophy shared by Hume and Kant leads to Whitehead's theory.

A second presupposition has infected modern philosophy. It is "the assumption of a few definite avenues of communication with the external world, the five sense organs" (AI 289b). But even the recognition of the bodily efficacity of the five senses is not enough. To restrict ourselves to these five is to inflict on our perceptions an abstract character instead of a concrete contact with experience. We have many other feelings and emotions which are avenues of information, not so neatly analyzable, but providing information and molding our experience. Any theory of perception must take account of these avenues as well as the usual ones.

In accordance with the last presupposition, if we use the term "prehension" for any form of perception in Bacon's sense of "taking account of," recalling our discussion of SMW, then we can say that sense-perception via the five senses is only a limited part of perception in its new broad meaning (AI 279e, 231–32). Sense-perceptions have been singled out by reason of their clear and distinct exhibition in consciousness (MT 100a), with the result that "all attempts at an exact systematic doctrine of the nature of things seeks its most obvious verification in the conformity of its theory with sense-perception" (AI 278–79). The effect of this has been to identify direct observation with sense-perception. This identification again leads to the neglect of those other avenues of "taking account of" which are significant for our experience (AI 279b). An example of such direct perception is that of the infant nursing at his mother's breast and directly perceiving her emotional moods of love, gaiety, depression, or irritation (AI 316a).

Whitehead holds that any representative theory of perception creates an insoluble epistemological problem as to how the representation is related to what it represents and how the representation can be guaranteed as representing the fact (PR 85a). Ultimately, any representative theory must resort to some belief like Santayana's "animal faith" or to some doctrine of illusion like F. H. Bradley's "appearance." There might appear to be some inconsistency between this thesis and the doctrine of appearance in AI, wherein a sort of correspondence or representative theory of truth is given (AI 270c, 309b). The two theses become compatible in virtue of the fact that Whitehead denies the primacy of the sensationalist principle of mere sensation upon which representative theories are based (PR 173b). The doctrine of prehensions provides the explanation of how appearance and reality are connected.

The rejection of representative theories of perception leads us to a general presupposition of the philosophy of organism, and in fact of any realistic philosophy, "that in perception there is a disclosure of objectified data, which are known as having a community with the immediate experience for which they are data" (PR 123c). There is not representation but immanence. If we interpret the notion of "power" as the way in which one entity is objectified (immanent) in another, then power and perception are the same (PR 91a).

We have canvassed thus far a number of reasons, both theoretical and practical, pointing to the conclusion that perception is a complex process having several parts. Although perception in the mode of presentational immediacy is more familiar to us and it is the fallacy of much modern philosophy to take it as fundamental, it is Whitehead's contention that perception in the mode of causal efficacy is fundamental and constitutes a basis for much of the former (PR 260–61). That this is so is not clear from our own common-sense experience, because consciousness itself is the result of a developed stage of concrescence involving complex integrations of feelings in a highly developed organism. Certain aspects of common-sense experience which indicate the underlying role of causal efficacy have been pointed out. It will become clear when we discuss presentational immediacy just how causal efficacy aids it. Ignoring familiarity, let us begin at the beginning with causal efficacy.

Section II. Arguments from Experience for Causal Efficacy

Causal efficacy is described as follows. It "produces percepts which are vague, not to be controlled, heavy with emotion: it produces the sense of derivation from the immediate past, and of passage to an immediate future; a sense of emotional feeling, belonging to oneself in the past, passing into oneself in the present, and passing from oneself in the present towards oneself in the future; a sense of influx of influence from other vaguer presences in the past, localized and yet evading local definition, such influence modifying, enhancing, inhibiting, diverting, the stream of feeling which we are receiving, unifying, enjoying, and transmitting. This is our general sense of existing, as one item among others, in an efficacious actual world" (PR 271b; *cf.* S 53b–54a). What arguments are there from common-sense experience to convince us that we have such perceptions of causal efficacy?

If we go along with Hume or Kant and maintain that causality is imported into the data of immediate perception by some way of thinking, called by Hume a habit of thought (S 39b) or by Kant a category of the understanding (S 37b), then we ought to find that our apprehension of causality depends upon the vividness of thought or of the impressions of sensation. "For an apprehension which is the product of thought should sink in importance when thought is in the background" (S 40b). And this thought, we must remember, is about immediate sense-data. On superficial consideration, complex causal relations seem to call for just such clear thought and vivid sense-data. But throughout any such causal reasoning there is the presupposition that the immediate present is conforming itself to the settled environment of the immediate past (S 41b, 58b). Unless such conformation existed from moment to moment, causal thought or habit would have no ground whatsoever. We require an assumption of conformation. It is just this assumption which is provided by the notion of objectification in a simple physical feeling, whereby the determinate character of a past actual entity is reiterated in the prehending actual entity. Hume and Kant could deny such conformation because of their false conception of time as merely the generic notion of pure succession (S 40c). Smw has already provided a satisfactory substitute theory of time in terms of concrete epochal durations. The belief in such conformation and action taken in accord with it are a daily experience.

The whole point of Whitehead's argument is that when sense-data are most vague and thought is hardly present, we act or design our action because we feel that the immediate future will conform to the immediate past (S 42–43); that is, we directly feel this causal efficacy of past to future (AI 233a). If the opposite were true, then clear thought and vivid sense-data should compel us to act as if conformation of future to past were the case, but it is just in this clarity and vividness that we find ourselves left in great indecision (S 42b). "The present fact is luminously the outcome from its predecessors, one quarter of a second ago" (S 46b). Thus Whitehead's argument on the common-sense level appeals to a basic feeling in us of the conformation of the immediate future to the immediate past (AI 233a). This immediate feeling of conformation is perception in the mode of causal efficacy.

Several common-sense examples are in order. Some speaker utters the words "United States." There are several syllables here, each respectively occupying the immediate present, then the past; a series of impressions of sensations. Hume's explanation is that the particular sequence of impressions is guided by habit, by frequent association. Whitehead's explanation is that the first syllables are connected with the later ones through the conformation of the intention of the speaker from moment to moment. Suppose that after uttering the term "United" the speaker had gone on to add the terms "Fruit Company." Surely, on Hume's theory, if the speaker were president of the Company and uttering the name for the first time, there would be no ground (habit of association) whatsoever for the speaker to complete the series of syllables as he did, since each syllable is an immediate impression of sensation without reference to past or future. But Whitehead's explanation on the ground of causal efficacy is adequate. The doctrine of the conformation of feeling insists that each syllable uttered by the speaker be in accord with a single intention conformal from past to future guiding the procession of syllables (AI 233–35).

Suppose I have a baby fifteen months old and I decide it is time to begin to discipline him. As he prepares to pull all the books out of the bookcase I say in a very stern voice "No! No!" This may be the first time I have expressed a command to him in this tone of voice, and he does not yet understand language. At the command he turns round to look at me and lets go of the books. The subjective form or quality of my voice exercises an influence on him. There is a conformation of feeling-tone passing between the two of us.

Similarly, the flower which has been thriving in the sunlight continues as long as possible to turn itself toward the changing position of the sun. There is a conformation of feeling the sunlight from moment to moment.

The conditions from moment to moment surrounding the existence of inanimate enduring things like a stone show an even greater degree of conformation (S 42a). Isn't it the case, when we stop to examine our experience, that the feeling of immediate conformation is just as strong and present and given as our feeling of the awareness of some sense-data "here-now" in presentational immediacy?

But this argument from experience needs restatement. If Hume's thesis be true, that is, the primacy of immediate sensation with no causality revealed, then certain conclusions as to behavior ought to follow. "According to Hume, our behavior presupposing causation is due to the repetition of associated presentational experience" (PR 264d). Hence, the vivid presence of certain sensations should cause by association certain consequences in our behavior through the subjective transition from the former to the latter. This subjective response to immediately present data is the whole of causation, according to Hume. The consequent action is itself just another diverse immediate presentation (PR 264-65). Consider this example: "In the dark, the electric light is suddenly turned on and the man's eyes blink" (PR 265a). First, there is a physical and physiological explanation in terms of causal efficacy, based on scientific reasoning. It involves the transmission of light from the source to the eye; the impingement on the eye, exciting certain nerves which set off an impulse to some center and a return impulse to the eyelids, setting off the blink (PR 265b). This is surely not an explanation in terms of presentational immediacy, in terms of immediate sense-data. But, second, dismissing this explanation, what is the man's own experience? There is the following sequence of perceptions which are immediate impressions: (1) flash of light, (2) feeling of eye closure, and (3) instant of darkness. They are practically simultaneous although the flash maintains a certain priority. Ask the man why he experiences the flash as prior and he will answer "because it made me blink." This is nothing but a recognition of causal efficacy, and if some Humean positivist asks him how he knows this, he will answer "because I feel it" (PR 265-66). Whitehead accepts the man's testimony as supporting his theory of prehensions. But Hume says "now wait; all the man really had was the impression of sensation 'flash' followed by the impression 'blink,' with no impression 'making him.'" The man protests his feeling but Hume asserts his dogma, "nothing but immediate impressions." Press Hume and he resorts to an explanation in terms of association-forming habits. Apply his principle to himself. Is there any immediate impression of habit, of association? No! Then how can habit and association fare any better than causation? They cannot (PR 266b).

Consider another illustration: since according to Hume the causal feeling is due to a long association of presentations of sensa, it would seem to follow that, if there is an inhibition of sensa, then there will be a corresponding absence of causal feeling, of associated movement. The contrary seems closer to our experience. "An inhibition of familiar sensa is very apt to leave us prey to vague terrors respecting a circumambient world of causal operations" (PR 267a; *cf.* 355b). In darkness vague presences are felt, feared, and "in the dim consciousness of half-sleep, the presentations of sense fade away and we are left with the vague feeling of influences from vague things around us" (PR 267a).

Again, the awarenesses of our various bodily parts are primarily perceptions of them as efficacious in our immediate perceptions of projected sensa. We feel *with our hands*; we see *with our eyes*. The eye is the agent for our immediate presentations of sight. This experience indicates that the feeling of causal (bodily) efficacy is primary to our feelings of presentational immediacy, of sense-data (S 51a). Hume inverts this order in experience and enunciates the sensationalist principle, which has infected modern philosophy (PR 267b).

Section III. The Theoretic Argument for Causal Efficacy

Besides these arguments from common-sense experience, Whitehead's theory of prehensions, central to his whole cosmology, provides indirect support for this view of perception in the mode of causal efficacy. I say indirect, because of the way in which Whitehead constructs his system. By analysis of certain areas of experience or of particular sciences we discover certain general principles. Some of these principles are capable of further generalization (PR 8c). We can then select different sets of principles, generalize them for a complete metaphysical system, and proceed to draw out the consequences of these principles for all aspects of experience. The aim is toward an interrelated set of principles which are internally coherent and logical and externally applicable and adequate (PR 4b). Such systems are open to the same kinds of tests as scientific systems. Consequences which can be tested (applicable) and which are sufficient for interpretation (adequate) for all relevant realms of our experience must be deducible. In the case of a metaphysical system, they must be relevant for all realms of experience. Although one aims at a necessary system of ideas (PR 4b), such systems are tentative (PR x). If the theory of prehensions, drawn from a certain aspect of our feelings, can provide a theoretical foundation for an adequate, applicable interpretation of the other realms of experience and science, then we have an indirect justification for belief in the theory. Our present task is an explanation of the theoretic account of causal efficacy, with some references to its adequacy and applicability.

Common-sense experience and Whitehead's analysis of Hume point to a primitive type of experience which Whitehead calls perception in the mode of causal efficacy. The opening paragraph of this chapter roughly characterized this mode. This type of perception is "feeling the body as functioning . . . feeling of the world in the past . . . the inheritance of the world as a complex of feeling" (PR 125d). But the boundaries of the body are vague, and our feelings of the past are feelings of the past world as efficacious in us. "The primitive form of physical experience is emotional—blind emotion—received as felt elsewhere in another occasion and conformally appropriated as a subjective passion" (PR 246c). Simple physical feelings are the technical means by which we have these direct emotional feelings of other actual entities in the past actual world (PR 361d).

A simple physical feeling or primitive act of perception is a feeling entertained by one actual entity of some other actual entity in its past. The past actual entity felt is called the initial datum of the feeling (PR 361b), but this entity is not felt as a complete, determinate unique whole, since these feelings are literally the stuff out of which the prehending entity is constituted, and thus we would end up with a complete immanence of actual entities in any subsequent entity, a collapse of the universe into a single entity, a position denied by Whitehead's pluralistic system. This was the error of absolute idealism. Rather, the past actual entity is felt by means of some feeling which was a part of its own concrescence. This feeling, which belongs to the initial datum, is taken up into the concrescence of the prehending actual entity but not with the same subjective immediacy it enjoyed in the felt entity. The prehended feeling is called the objective datum of a simple physical feeling (PR 361b). This feeling, which is the objective datum, has for its subject the actual entity that is the initial datum, and it is in this sense that there is a direct experience by one actual entity of another. Manifestly there are many feelings belonging to the concrescence of the felt entity which could function in the role of an objective datum. These various possible objective data of a given felt actual entity constitute different "perspectives" of the initial datum (PR 361b). Any one such perspective of the initial datum constitutes a particular "objectification" of the initial datum for the prehending actual entity.

The notion of objectification calls for careful analysis.[3] Whitehead speaks in many passages of an immanence of one actual entity in another, a transfer of feeling, a vector flow of energy (PR 363–64, 374, 177, AI 242, 233), and also of a separateness or transcendence among actual entities (PR 72d). W. A. Christian finds that there are three senses in which past actual occasions are exclusive (transcendent) of some present actual occasion feeling them. First, the locus of feeling for the past actual entity cannot be present in the locus of feeling of the present actual entity. The past actual entity cannot be present in the present actual entity as "an experiencing subject here-now," but it can be present as "an experiencing subject there-then." [4] This exclusiveness is guaranteed by two conditions which "must be fulfilled in order that an entity may function as an object in a process of experiencing: (1) the entity must be *antecedent,* and (2) the entity must be experienced in virtue of its antecedence; it must be *given*" (AI 229c).

Second, the past actual entity is not present in the present actual entity in its complete internal constitution. [5] The complete immanence and collapse of the pluralism in a single absolute are why objectification must have the above character (PR 230, 97). Those aspects which are included define the objective datum of the simple physical feeling.

Third, the past actual entity is separate from the present actual entity insofar as no aspect of the past entity is felt in the present entity with the same subjective immediacy which it had as a factor in the concrescence of the past entity. [6] The principal reason for this sense of separateness springs from the internal relatedness of feelings in the concrescence of any actual entity. No two actual entities could possess the same set of feelings; hence no feeling could enjoy the same subjective immediacy in two actual entities (PR 35, 247). The subjective immediacy arises with the origination of any actual entity and passes with its satisfaction and perishing. Three senses have now been stated in which a past actual entity is not present in a present actual entity.

But then just what is present in a present actual entity from the past; just how is one occasion present in another? For the whole theory of prehensions is designed to explain this fact. The particular feeling which constitutes the objective datum had a certain subjective form when it was an element in the concrescence of the initial datum. This subjective form was an eternal object or group of eternal objects constituting a contrast or a multiplicity. Further, the feeling belonging to the present actual entity of the past actual entity has a certain subjective form dependent upon how it prehends that past actual entity via the particular objective datum which constitutes the perspective of that feeling. This subjective form is some eternal object or group of eternal objects. What is present in the present actual entity and also present in the past actual entity is "partial equivalence of subjective form" (PR 363a, 497c). That is to say, there is a repetition or re-enactment of eternal objects rather than any simple reflection or copying or literal inclusion of one actual entity in another (PR 100b).

In objectification there is thus a two-way relational functioning of the eternal objects (sensa) which constitute the respective subjective forms (PR 249a). The solidarity of the universe depends upon this relational functioning of eternal objects. One of the essential properties of eternal objects is that they can function in many ingressions at the same time; this is the case because the relation between an eternal object and an actual entity is external on the side of the eternal object and internal on the side of the actual entity. Hence the same eternal object can be literally constitutive of the concrescence of many actual entities. Whitehead in discussing the notion of objectification frequently sacrifices precision to vividness of language. Now that we have discovered just what is present in or passed along from past occasion to present occasion, we must consider how eternal objects function in perception.

"Sensa constitute the lowest category of eternal objects," and "do not express a manner of relatedness between other eternal objects" (PR 174b). Hence they are not contrasts or patterns. They are necessary components in any actual entity relevant to its realization of higher grades of eternal objects in contrasts or patterns (PR 174b). In this sense they are "simples," but insofar as any sensum can enjoy many ingressions it is complex. Examples of such sensa (simple eternal objects) are colors, tastes, and sounds. Sensa combine in patterns which are themselves sometimes taken to be sensa (PR 175b,d), although the pattern is abstracted from particular contrasts which illustrate the pattern (PR 176a).

This development of the notion of a pattern as abstracted from particular contrasts of eternal objects that illustrate it provides an explanation for the generic character of the relational essence of an eternal object, which we found was essential to the possession of finite truths in our discussion of the internal relatedness of eternal objects in Chapter VI, Section IV (PR 175–76). The relational essence of an eternal object is the pattern of the network of relations sustained by that determinate eternal object to other determinate eternal objects. An instance of the pattern is called a contrast, which is in itself another complex eternal object. The pattern is abstract and can be illustrated by other contrasts. These generic patterns are an essential part of any eternal object, hence internal, and provide finite knowledge about particular groups of eternal objects.

Some actual entities experience only a few sensa with a minimum of complexity in their contrasts. Further, reintegration in the concrescence of such actual entities may only increase the intensity of feeling of these sensa in the final satisfaction, with the result that the process of concrescence lacks originative development, and is thus dominated by only a few sensa (PR 176b). Subsequent actual entities feeling this type of simple actual entities are severely limited in the choice of a feeling for the objective datum of the prehension, since the felt actual entity had few feelings in its concrescence. When this situation occurs there is the greatest conformation of feeling from past to present, and we have causal efficacy at its clearest (PR 479c).

Whitehead neatly sums up his detailed account of causal efficacy as follows: "Occasion B prehends occasion A as an antecedent subject experiencing a sensum with emotional intensity. Also B's subjective form of emotion is conformed to A's subjective form. Thus there is a vector transmission of emotional feeling of a sensum from A to B. In this way B feels the sensum as derived from A and feels it with an emotional form also derived from A" (PR 479–80; *cf.* 176–77, 183b).

We can now state how causal efficacy operates through a connected chain of objectifications from one actual entity to another (PR 183–84). We begin with some simple actual entity A. A has a certain feeling F with a subjective form which is a sensum, say S (an eternal object). A is now prehended by B. A is the initial datum; F is the objective datum; and S is the subjective form of the feeling F, which is re-enacted in the subjective form of B's feeling of A. Similarly B is felt by C and again there is a re-enaction of the sensum S as the subjective form of C's feeling of B. Now in B and C there may be increased intensity of relevance of S for the respective satisfactions or relegation to irrelevance. C is then prehended by M. M may prehend A directly or through B and C and so on with the other actual entities B and C, except that C can only be prehended directly by M because of the order of antecedence. Thus M may have present in its concrescence two sets of eternal objects (sensa) with the same members but with difference in emotional tone due to whether or not the sensa gained intensity of relevance or lost intensity with respect to different satisfactions. M itself will select, according to its subjective aim, one set rather than another. In many cases the distinction among A, B, and C will be vague. This gain or loss of intensity in reenaction is important to the energy transactions of physics and the value side of reality.

Section IV. The Theoretic Argument for Complex Causal Efficacy

In different contexts Whitehead appears to contradict himself, for he claims that there can be no error in either of the pure modes of perception, causal efficacy or presentational immediacy (S 6c, 19a,b), and that errors can arise in causal efficacy (PR 387b, 390e, 410b). The confusion arises because Whitehead fails to distinguish what we may call simple causal efficacy and complex causal efficacy, although he hints at such a distinction (PR 411a). The two technical examples given thus far in the previous section are cases of simple causal efficacy which involve only simple physical feelings, pure or hybrid. Simple conceptual feelings, which have for their data eternal objects constitutive of the subjective forms of the simple physical feeling, may be involved in the increase or decrease of intensity of emotion. Cases of complex causal efficacy which may involve error have yet to be considered. They involve reverted conceptual feelings and/or transmuted physical feelings. Before we explain complex causal efficacy, we have to give a case of simple causal efficacy involving hybrid feelings.

A hybrid physical feeling has for its initial datum either some past actual entity or God, who is also an actual entity. It differs from a pure physical feeling in that its objective datum is a conceptual rather than a physical feeling. This leads to the following difference. If the objective datum is a pure physical feeling, its subjective form is some eternal object or contrast of eternal objects characteristic of that actual entity which is the initial datum. If the objective datum is a conceptual feeling, its subjective form is some valuation. The valuation determines (1) in what status the eternal object, which is the datum of the conceptual feeling, has ingression in that concrescence or, to put it in another way, how the eternal object is to be utilized; and (2) the intensive importance of that eternal object to the subjective aim (PR 368–69).

In the case of a hybrid physical feeling wherein the initial datum is the primordial nature of God, which involves "the unconditional conceptual valuation of the entire multiplicity of eternal objects" (PR 46a), the objective datum of the hybrid physical feeling is some particular conceptual feeling belonging to God. The datum of this conceptual feeling is an eternal object. The subjective form of that conceptual feeling which belongs to God is a value. It is to be remembered that the original feeling of God by the subject is a physical feeling involving as its objective datum this feeling, which is one of God's conceptual feelings. Then there arises in the original subject a conceptual feeling derivative from this physical feeling according to categoreal obligation IV. This derivative conceptual feeling has for its datum the contrast of eternal objects and their value. The datum of this derived conceptual feeling becomes the subjective aim of that original concrescent actual entity. This explanation of the origin of the subjective aim shows how the subject is inherent in the very process of concrescence before the character of the subject is completely and determinately finished in the satisfaction (PR 342b, 343b).

There is no way around this technical vocabulary. Attempts to explain Whitehead's position in ordinary philosophical language are impossible, because that language is based on a subject-predicate type of statement which can never hope to express a process philosophy. This explanation is also an answer to the various criticisms of Gentry and Miller, who discern the following contradiction in Whitehead: that in order for there to be prehensions by an actual entity there must already be a definite subject, but in order for there to be a subject there must be prehensions. They suppose that this contradiction explodes Whitehead's entire system. Instead it merely shows how far they are from understanding the system, for I have just explained why this contradiction does not exist. The real reason for the misunderstanding is that Miller and Gentry are unable to emancipate their thinking from subject-predicate categories. They have stated this criticism in various ways in various articles, but they all boil down to the same point.[7] Although A. H. Johnson has correctly criticized Miller and Gentry on this point it seems to me that his own explanations suffer from vagueness.[8] The reason for his vagueness becomes clear upon reading his footnote on the theory of objectification.[9] He holds that there is a literal inclusion of the content of one actual entity in another. My reasons for not accepting this viewpoint have been stated and the more technical and detailed explanation already provided.

There is a kind of error which may take place in complex causal efficacy wherein reverted conceptual feelings and transmuted physical feelings are involved. Both these species of feeling still belong to the simple phases of experience (concrescence), in which consciousness is not yet involved. Hence error in this special sense can occur without consciousness; it is not dependent on thinking.

The effect of reverted conceptual feelings can be technically stated as follows. An actual entity A has a physical prehension of actual entity B. If the prehension is a pure physical feeling, the feeling which is the objective datum is a physical feeling belonging to the concrescence of B. According to categoreal obligation IV there will be a conceptual feeling by A derived from this physical feeling. The datum of this conceptual feeling is an eternal object or contrast of eternal objects. In the case of a simple conceptual feeling the eternal object which is the datum is the same as the eternal object, which is the subjective form of the physical feeling from which the conceptual feeling was derived. Error arises when, according to the category of conceptual reversion, the eternal object which is the datum of the derived conceptual feeling is partially diverse from the eternal object constituting the definiteness of the subjective form of the physical feeling (PR 380, 381). This relevant diversity is determined by the subjective aim of the actual entity which is the subject of this feeling and introduces novelty into the concrescence so that there is not complete conformation of feeling.

But where did this partially diverse eternal object come from, for according to the ontological principle we must be able to specify some actual entity as a reason for the ingression of this eternal object? The answer is that it is derived from a previous hybrid physical feeling of God, who is an actual entity. As previously explained, if an actual entity A has a hybrid physical feeling of God, then the objective datum for A is a conceptual feeling belonging to God. The datum of this conceptual feeling is the partially diverse eternal object which becomes substituted in a reverted conceptual feeling (PR 381–82). While Whitehead remains an empiricist adhering to Hume's principle that all knowledge is derived from experience, he provides an empirical account of the introduction of genuine novelty into the world and forges a system of empiricism linked with a theology. This is certainly a solution to a philosophical problem which plagues empiricists and naturalists: how to account for the origination of novel ideas, purposes, and the status and function of God.

Transmuted physical feelings provide the means for one actual entity feeling a group of actual entities forming a nexus as a group and not individually (PR 382b). The genesis of a transmuted physical feeling involves a number of stages. First, there is a group of actual entities each of which prehends some of the others with pure physical feelings so that there is a conformation of feeling among them. There may of course be many other kinds of feelings among them. Second, there is a subsequent actual entity which prehends each and every member of the group singly as a multiplicity of initial data. Third, it may happen, though not necessarily, that the objective datum of each of these pure physical prehensions of the multiplicity of actual entities has the same subjective form so long as it was previously the case, though again not necessarily, that, among the multiplicity of feelings belonging to the group of entities, there was at least one pure physical feeling between each two entities that had the same subjective form. We now have an identity between the eternal objects constituting the subjective forms of the objective data of several diverse prehensions of diverse initial data. Fourth, there is the derivation in the subsequent actual entity of a single conceptual feeling from each of these pure physical feelings. The datum of the conceptual feeling is the eternal object identical in the subjective forms of the physical feeling, although the identical eternal objects need not be felt in the same way. If instead, reverted conceptual feelings arise, a species of error is introduced. Fifth, a further derivative conceptual feeling arises in the subsequent actual entity, which has as its datum this one eternal object without particular reference to any one of the group of actual entities. This integration of data of different conceptual feelings is allowed by category of explanation XXVII. Finally, in a subsequent phase of integration there originates a transmuted physical feeling which has for its datum the group of actual entities as a single unified group characterized by that particular eternal object, which has been derived by the above process (PR 384, 385). It must be remembered that the eternal object need not have the same mode of ingression in each member of the group; consequently, in a transmuted feeling minor differences in mode of ingression have been eliminated. (PR 383b).

If the nexus prehended by a transmuted physical feeling should contain some members which are contemporary with the actual entity that prehends the nexus, a number of special problems arise which we must explain, for they have led to serious confusions among some of Whitehead's critics.

First of all, we must make clear what is meant by "contemporaries." The doctrine of prehensions enables us to define three different loci with respect to any actual entity (PR 486–87). First, there is the "causal past" of a given actual entity M, which is made up of all the actual entities felt as data of simple physical feelings of M. Second, the "causal future" of M consists of all the actual entities which can prehend M as the datum of simple physical feelings. What is objectified for an actual entity constitutes its past, and that for which it is an object constitutes its future. Between the causal past and causal future are those actual entities for which M has no causal feelings—for which it functions as neither subject nor object. These actual entities are causally independent of M. Actual entities belonging to this class are M's contemporaries. In this manner each actual entity defines its own private time system. Two actual entities contemporary with M need not be contemporary with each other. The relativity of time is the consequence of this principle.

Before we say how a transmuted physical feeling can prehend a nexus containing some actual entities contemporary with the subject of the transmuted feeling, we must state how future actual entities are immanent in the present. In the last two phases of concrescence there is a continual integration and reintegration of feelings according to the subjective aim. Propositional feelings originate which concern the constitution of the immediate subject occasion. Finally, in the last phase constituting the satisfaction there "is a propositional realization of the essence of the present-subject, in respect to the necessities which it lays upon the future to embody it and to re-enact it so far as compatibility may permit" (AI 248c). This is the one determinate feeling which constitutes the final and complete unification of all feelings of the concrescence into a single organic whole. The subject then perishes into objective immortality, which is to say it is objectified in later actual entities which prehend it. Hence any future actual entity which has a simple physical feeling of this completed actual entity must conform to the determinate character achieved by this completed entity because of the doctrine of conformation with respect to simple physical feelings. But these future actual entities are not yet existent when the actual entity reaches its satisfaction. The future is immanent in the present in the special sense that certain general relationships are embodied in the satisfaction of the present actual entity: (1) that the future must involve objectification of this satisfaction and (2) that the future is determined in certain general patterns to which particular future actual entities must conform if they prehend the present satisfaction (AI 250b, 251a). This much about the character of the future is present in the subjective immediacy of the actual entity in its satisfaction. It knows this much about the general metaphysical character of the universe.

We can now say how contemporary actual entities are immanent in each other.[10] "If A and B be contemporaries, and C be in the past of both of them, then A and B are each in a sense immanent in C, *in the way in which the future can be immanent in its past*. But C is objectively immortal in both A and B. Thus, in this *indirect* sense, A is immanent in B, and B is immanent in A" (AI 252c, my italics). But A and B do not causally prehend each other. It must be admitted that A causally prehends its past in a slightly different way than B causally prehends the same common past, because they enjoy that past under a different private perspective dependent upon the subjective forms of their feelings.

A transmuted physical feeling of a nexus involving contemporaries can now be explained. I need not repeat how a transmuted physical feeling originates. There is no restriction to prohibit the group of actual entities forming the nexus, according to some re-enacted eternal object, from including contemporary entities. These entities are not causally felt, but, as long as some members of the nexus from which a transmuted feeling can be derived are causally felt, the subject of the transmuted feeling may also conclude that conditions embodied in the causally felt part of the nexus will be objectified in the future; that is, in actual entities which are its contemporaries. This indirect perception of contemporaries can be more fully explained after we have expounded the notion of projection in presentational immediacy.

The immanence of the past in the present by means of objectification, the immanence of the future in the present, and the indirect immanence of the present in the present constitute the doctrine of mutual immanence in AI. In PR nothing is said about the immanence of the future in the present, and this omission left certain unsolved problems in connection with perception. The doctrine of prehensions in PR concerns the immanence of the past in the present.

We witness once again a development in Whitehead's thinking, with both continuity and extension of ideas. The doctrine of internal relatedness in SMW is expanded into the doctrine of prehensions, and that in turn into the doctrine of mutual immanence. The great-grandfather of all of these was the early doctrine of significance. The criticism of the assumption of simple location in science and the sensationalist principle in philosophy were the stimulants for these doctrines. In this way perception is linked to science and metaphysics.

For example, perception in the mode of causal efficacy provides a foundation for certain basic notions in physics. In our analysis of the prehension of one actual entity by another we could distinguish a direction of transfer or re-enaction between actual entities, a definite intensity of feeling according to the category of subjective intensity (PR 41c,d), and specific kinds of prehensions. "The experience has a vector character, a common measure of intensity, and specific forms of feeling conveying that intensity. If we substitute the term 'energy' for the concept of quantitative emotional intensity, and the term 'form of energy' for the concept of 'specific form of feeling,' and remember that in physics 'vector' means definite transmission from elsewhere, we see that this metaphysical description of the simplest elements in the constitution of actual occasions agrees absolutely with the general principles according to which the notions of modern physics are framed" (PR 177b). Thus we see that the datum in metaphysics is the basis of the vector theory, that the satisfaction terminating a process of concrescence is the basis of the scalar localization of energy in physics, and that eternal objects are the basis of the diversity of specific forms of energy. It is one of the difficulties of modern epistemologists following Hume or Kant that they cannot provide a metaphysical basis for physics.

For two reasons I have refrained from trying to give in this section any examples of perception in the mode of causal efficacy: (1) "consciousness only dimly illuminates the prehensions in the mode of causal efficacy," and (2) "these prehensions are the primitive elements in our experience" (PR 246a). Consciousness only arises in the developed phases of concrescence of highly complex organisms in connection with the vividness of the data of presentational immediacy in symbolic reference. Hence to give examples of causal efficacy is nearly impossible in our ordinary perceptual experience, because this is so highly refined and derivative. Examples will be given in connection with presentational immediacy and symbolic reference.

In connection with causal efficacy Blyth criticizes Whitehead on the following points. How can there be a "simple perception of a group of contemporary entities which together constitute the surface of a book," [11] that is, of a nexus of contemporaries? Clearly Whitehead would not claim such a perception to be simple because the perception of such a group would require a transmuted feeling which involves complex integrations of feelings. Second, it seems to me a complete misunderstanding of Whitehead to suppose that he holds that there can be direct perception of actual contemporaries. In AI he explicitly asserts that for contemporary occasions "the mutual immanence between the occasions of the nexus will be of the *indirect* type . . ." (AI 259a, my italics). It is true that some assertions in S made in connection with presentational immediacy seem to suggest the direct perception of contemporaries, but this seeming inconsistency with the technical discussions of PR and AI can be interpreted as the result of a loose form of expression. All this will be explained in the next chapter. Whitehead never maintained that there was direct information about contemporaries. The sense in which there can be indirect perception of contemporaries belonging to a nexus, some of whose members are antecedent and thus causally felt, has been explained. Perception of contemporaries is possible in no other way. Blyth's hazy view of objectification also leads him to this erroneous criticism. If the nexus consists purely of mutual contemporaries, it is true that there cannot be a transmuted feeling of such a nexus in its actuality and, so far as I can discover, Whitehead never asserted that there was. Blyth traces the source of these difficulties to the conjunction of the subjectivist principle and the principle of relativity.[12] But I have already shown that this separation is completely false (Chap. VII, Sec. I). A resolution of Blyth's difficulties lies in Whitehead's doctrine of mutual immanence, which he neglects to discuss.

Chapter IX

PERCEPTION IN THE MODE
OF PRESENTATIONAL IMMEDIACY

Section I. The Definition of Presentational Immediacy

The immediate awareness of data in consciousness, which seems such a simple primitive source of knowledge to empiricists who hold this sensationalistic principle, turns out under Whitehead's analysis to be complex and difficult. In S perception in the mode of presentational immediacy is defined as "our immediate perception of the contemporary external world, appearing as an element constitutive of our own experience. In this appearance the world discloses itself to be a community of actual things, which are actual in the same sense as we are" (S 21c). Or presentational immediacy is "the familiar immediate presentation of the contemporary world, by means of our projection of our immediate sensation, determining for us characteristics of contemporary physical entities" (S 13–14).

In PR we find the following definitions: presentational immediacy is "distinct, definite, controllable, apt for immediate enjoyment, and with a minimum of reference to past, or to future" (PR 271d). It reveals that "the contemporary world is consciously prehended as a continuum of extensive relations" (PR 95a). It is a "perception which merely, by means of a sensum, rescues from vagueness a contemporary spatial region, in respect to its spatial shape and its spatial perspective from the percipient . . ." (PR 185b; cf. AI 277b).

PR and AI explicitly assert that we do not have direct perception of contemporaries, while some of the statements in S seem to assert that we do (PR 188a, 257a, AI 251b, 252, S 21c). There is a possible contradiction here, which might indicate a change in Whitehead's position from S to PR. On the other hand, it seems to me that this confusion arises because in S Whitehead is trying to discuss the nature of perception in philosophical categories foreign to his position. At least in some places in S he mentions the theory of the projection of sensa (S 13–14), which is the technical device in PR that accounts for our supposed direct experience of contemporaries. Further, there is an aspect of presentational immediacy which presents an aspect of the contemporary world in terms of the "presented locus"; but this aspect does not contain actual entities as actual. Also against this possible contradiction of views there is the fact that SMW had already enunciated the theory of prehensions and the principle of relativity, which enforce the conclusion that we do not have a direct perception of contemporaries. These are the reasons why I do not think Whitehead changed his position from S to PR.

From the previous quotations it is clear that Whitehead finds two main parts of perception in the mode of presentational immediacy. First, there is a direct perception of the presented locus as directly illustrated by the sensa of our experience (PR 96b). We cannot say from this direct perception alone where or how the actual occasions of the contemporary world are. Discussion of this direct aspect involves the nature of the extensive continuum and of strain loci. Second, there is an indirect aspect of presentational immediacy involving the sensa inherited from causal efficacy that are projected on the presented locus as characteristics belonging to contemporary actual entities.

Although the sensa are derived from causal efficacy and projected in presentational immediacy, Whitehead holds that "there are no bare sensations which are first experienced and then projected. . . . The projection is an integral part of the situation, quite as original as the sense data" (S 14c). Two reasons can be given for the first sentence quoted. First, the process of concrescence of an actual entity is not in time. We cannot speak significantly about one phase happening in time before another (PR 434a). Second, those feelings, namely perceptive propositional feelings, wherein projection occurs do not convey to us an awareness of recognition of inheritance and then of projection; rather, each feeling is a unified whole. The second sentence of the quotation emphasizes that the area of projection given directly in the presented locus is as primitive as the awareness of sensa inherited from causal efficacy. Either aspect of presentational immediacy is impossible without the other (S 15). In contrast with those epistemologists who take sense data as simple primitive elements of awareness characterizing objects, what Whitehead is concerned to emphasize is the complexity of presentational immediacy.

This point serves to distinguish clearly Whitehead's empiricism from the sensationalistic empiricisms derivative from Hume. Contrary to the sensationalistic empiricists Whitehead holds that "in the immediate subject, the presentational immediacy is to be conceived as originated in a late phase, by the synthesis of the feeling of bodily efficacity with other feelings" (PR 475a). "The whole point of the connection between the two feelings [presentational immediacy and causal efficacy] is that presentational immediacy is derivative from the bodily efficacity" (PR 475b; *cf.* 96b). We turn first to a consideration of the direct aspect of presentational immediacy dealing with the extensive continuum and strains.

Section II. Direct Aspect of Presentational Immediacy

"Our direct perception of the contemporary world is thus reduced to extension, defining (1) our own geometrical perspectives, and (2) possibilities of mutual perspectives for other contemporary entities *inter se,* and (3) possibilities of division" (PR 96b; *cf.* 188a). The possibilities of division of extension reveal it as a continuum, but so far as the contemporary world is composed of actual entities it is atomic. Thus the direct aspect gives no information about the actual atomic division but only about potential extensive division (PR 96b, 188a). This is the case because there can be no actual causal objectifications among contemporaries according to the condition regulating prehensions that the entity prehended must be antecedent (AI 229, 251). This condition is a fundamental aspect of Einstein's formula for the physical continuum (PR 95, footnote).

If no contemporary actual entities are directly perceived in presentational immediacy in their actuality, then what is the datum of this mode of perception? This datum is a complex affair. What is "thus objectified, is the objectification of a contemporary nexus of actual entities in its unity as a nexus. This nexus is illustrated as to its constitution by the spatial region, with its perspective relations" (PR 98a). This nexus of contemporaries is provided by the datum of a perceptive propositional feeling wherein, by transmutation of content provided by past physical feelings, a group of entities is perceived as a unity. The character of the unity derived from the past is projected upon an extensive region as characterizing contemporary entities which for that subject are potential, not actual, and are called an "image" in contrast to an "object" in causal efficacy (PR 98a, 386d). The exact mechanism of projection we shall consider later. What we want to focus on is the notion of a region, for this seems to be the really actual part of the datum of presentational immediacy (PR 484b).

The exact status of the notion of a region is uncertain. Some persons have suggested that a region is an additional primitive notion in PR to be included in the categories of existence. What does Whitehead say about regions? In AI a region seems to be a derivative notion, a particular kind of nexus (AI 254b). "By the aid of the notion of contiguity, the notion of a region can be defined as denoting a nexus in which certain conditions of contiguity are preserved" (AI 260b). And spatial and temporal contiguity is definable in terms of mutual immanence (AI 259b–60a). Nexūs of this kind "are discriminated by differences of bare extensive pattern" (AI 260c). But unfortunately Whitehead does not specify what the "certain conditions of contiguity" are.

On the other hand, PR seems to make the region primitive. "This region is the determinate basis which the concrescence presupposes" (PR 434c). The objectifications of presentational immediacy are controlled by this region presupposed by the concrescence. The divisibility of this extensive region ignores the subjective unity of the satisfaction. Thus the divisions of such regions are potential and not actual, for what is actual belongs to some actual entity or its feelings. Regions are divisible but not divided (PR 435a,b). In contrast to the definitions of spatial and temporal contiguity in AI, contiguity in PR is defined in terms of regions externally connected (PR 468). Another difference between AI and PR with respect to regions is that in AI regions are always nexūs, while in PR each actual entity presupposes in its concrescence a basic region. By restricting regions to nexūs Whitehead found it possible to define them in AI by using certain conditions of contiguity.

It seems that Whitehead saw some confusion about the status of a region in PR and later found a way around it in AI, but AI unfortunately does not give the technical definitions. One hopes that some logician-geometer will.[1] It would iron out a rough spot in the system. But it is unlikely that Whitehead would assert such a definition to be possible without having thought through how it could be done, so I shall assume that AI settles the status of a region as a derivative notion defined as a certain kind of nexus. Some statements in PR seem to support this view. I shall now try to give an account of regions which renders PR and AI consistent with one another.

Regions are a special kind of nexus. Nexūs are the data of transmuted physical feelings which are originated in virtue of some characteristic (eternal object) which is held to characterize the members of the nexus. This characteristic belongs to the subjective form of the separate prehensions of some or all of the members of the nexus. In the case of a regional nexus, there are, first, separate physical feelings of some of the actual entities forming a nexus with the subjective form of "extensiveness." Second, conceptual feelings are originated which have as their data eternal objects expressing extensiveness in its most general form

(PR 448a). This characteristic (eternal object) of extensiveness is the common element possessed by some of the numbers of the nexus. By means of transmutation, this characteristic is supposed to characterize other members of the nexus as well. Some of these other members may be contemporaries of the original prehending occasion. When certain conditions of contiguity hold for these other contemporary members of the nexus that are supposed to possess this common characteristic of extensiveness, the nexus is a regional nexus. Perhaps this clarifies what is meant in PR when it is said that the concrescence presupposes a region; that is, presupposes the characteristic of extensiveness which is essential to the definition of a region (regional nexus). This interpretation of the status of a region renders it a derivative notion derived from the basic extensiveness (an eternal object) of actual entities and from the category of transmutation.

What we have before us is another instance of Whitehead's philosophical development, a new concept adumbrated in one book (PR), worked over, and settled without details in the next (AI), since his interest has moved on to other topics. The significance of AI with respect to Whitehead's systematic philosophy is that it completes the doctrine of prehensions in the doctrine of mutual immanence and clarifies the status of regions without details.

Regions are the relata of the relation of extensive connection (PR 449c). Extensive connection "is probably an ultimate metaphysical character, persistent in every cosmic epoch of physical occasions" (PR 441c), from which definable notions like regions can be derived, expressing the morphological structure of the cosmic epoch. The relation of extensive connection results from the co-ordinate division of the satisfaction of an actual entity (PR 433a). This is a division of the concrete, complete, finished entity to be contrasted with the division of the concrescence into prehensions, which is genetic division. The satisfaction presupposes a certain extensiveness (quantum) which constitutes a "standpoint in the extensive continuum which is consonant with the subjective aim in its original derivation from God" (PR 434b). Thus the process of concrescence is not in physical time, because it presupposes the satisfaction in its subjective aim and hence presupposes the entire quantum (extensiveness). Physical time and space are derivative from aspects of the process of concrescence; specifically, from the nature of prehending as relating actual entities (PR 434a,b). According to the category of subjective unity the satisfaction cannot be actually divided; hence the co-ordinate division of the extensive quantum is only potential (PR 434–35). Thus co-ordinate division of the satisfaction reveals feelings which *might* have been separate but are not actually separate (PR 435b).

Further, there are extensive connections among diverse actual entities which express the most general conditions of orderly arrangement of diverse objectifications of entities in other entities (PR 438e). These two schemes of extensive connections (internal co-ordinate division of the satisfaction and external extensive connection of actual entities) form "one basic scheme of extensive connection which expresses on one uniform plan, (1) the general conditions to which the bonds, uniting the atomic actualities into a nexus, conform, and (2) the general conditions to which the bonds, uniting the infinite number of coordinate subdivisions of the satisfaction of any actual entity, conform" (PR 438–39). The general scheme of extensive connections is derived in Part IV, Chapter II, of PR, leading to the general definition of a point via abstractive sets, from which the particulars of various geometries can be derived. This scheme of extensive connection constitutes the extensive continuum which replaces the continuum of events in PNK, CN, and PReL. Since the conditions of orderly arrangement partly depend upon the nature of objectification, this extensive continuum is limited to this cosmic epoch if the character of objectification is peculiar to this cosmic epoch. Whitehead does not say whether the conditions of objectification are so restricted.

The early view of PNK, CN, and PReL was limited to the co-ordinate subdivision of an actual entity (event) according to the notions of whole and part or extending over, and led to certain limitations and defects regarding the definition of a point (PR 439–40). These are corrected in the expanded view of PR, eliminating certain criticisms of the method made by other philosophers. (*Cf.* Chap. V, Sect. I).

What is the character of this extensive continuum which is the datum of the direct aspect of presentational immediacy? It is potential, for "actuality is incurably atomic" (PR 95b). Two reasons have been given for its potential nature: (1) since it is indefinitely divisible it forms a continuum and "continuity concerns what is potential . . ." (PR 95b), for otherwise we are caught in Zeno's paradoxes (PR 53a); and (2) since it involves division of the satisfaction, which is atomic, it must be potential (PR 435b).[2]

It is a metaphysical assumption of the direct aspect of presentational immediacy "that the real potentialities relative to all standpoints are coordinated as diverse determinations of one extensive continuum" (PR 103a). By "real potentialities" Whitehead means some segment of the general potentiality which includes all possibilities that are limited by their relevance to some particular actual entity which conditions the possibilities of the future (PR 101c). Any potential objectification must have a place in the relational complex of this extensive continuum. The properties of this general extensive continuum are few and concern the relations of whole and part, and overlapping. They do not include metrical geometry, for it depends upon the particular conditions of this cosmic epoch (PR 103a). Thus metaphysics is more general than cosmology. Metaphysics expresses those conditions which every cosmological system must exemplify. Additional restrictive empirical conditions single out one cosmological epoch from another. These different cosmologies correspond to the different cosmic epochs which Whitehead talks about in PR. PR is mainly about our particular cosmic epoch.

The continuum is indefinitely divisible and has unbounded extension (PR 103a); hence the solidarity of the world. The continuum is the first and most general determination of order in metaphysics and does not involve shapes, dimensions, or measurability—all of which determine specific cosmic epochs. Since the continuum is real it must be interpreted in terms of the relatedness of prehensions. This is the role of strain feelings which reveal the direct aspect of presentational immediacy.

Our direct perception of the extensive continuum is "of an immediate extensive shape, in a certain geometrical perspective to ourselves, and in certain geometrical relations to the contemporary world . . ." (PR 97d). This extensive continuum belongs to our cosmic epoch and has certain limitations dependent upon the doctrine of objectification (PR 118c).

Whitehead's use of the term "extensive continuum" is ambiguous, for in some contexts it refers to the most general conditions of extensiveness holding for any cosmic epoch, conditions I attempted to state above, and in other contexts it refers to the particular conditions of extensiveness holding in our cosmic epoch, wherein objectification has a particular character (PR 148a,b).[3] But these two uses of the term are not logically incompatible; the one is included in the other as a special case. This particular extensive continuum characterizing our cosmic epoch "provides the general scheme of extensive perspectives which is exhibited in all the mutual objectifications by which actual entities prehend each other. Thus in itself, the extensive continuum [of this cosmic epoch] is a scheme of real potentiality which must find exemplification in the mutual prehensions of all actual entities. It also finds exemplification in each actual entity considered 'formally'" (PR 118c).

This last sentence provides an answer to part of Blyth's criticism of the extensive continuum. Blyth claims that Whitehead uses the term "extensive continuum" in two incompatible senses: (1) "to denote the one set of relations which unites all possible standpoints in one comprehensive system," and (2) to denote "the most general conditions to which any set of relations between actual entities must conform."[4] This ambiguity is based on the following alleged contradiction. According to Blyth's account of the subjectivist principle, "any real fact about the universe must be found in the analysis of the experience of an actual entity." [5] But the experience of an actual entity is limited and does not encompass the entire world. Therefore the extensive continuum which applies to the entire world cannot be experienced by an actual entity.[6] Each actual entity only experiences a limited continuum of the entire world. On the other hand, Whitehead claims that the extensive continuum as an element in the experience of an actual entity is not limited but encompasses the entire world (PR 118c). This is the supposed contradiction.

First of all, we must recall our account of Blyth's misinterpretation of the subjectivist principle and its false separation from the principle of relativity (*cf.* Chap. VII, Sect. I). The incompatibilities which he finds, insofar as they are based on this false separation, simply do not follow. Second, Whitehead does not claim that the extensive continuum is experienced by an actual entity but only that it "finds exemplification in each actual entity considered 'formally'" (PR 118c). The question now is what is meant by "exemplification" and "formally." By exemplification Whitehead means that some abstract pattern of eternal objects is re-enacted in a particular contrast of eternal objects ingredient in some particular actual entity. The contrast is derivative from causal efficacy of the past actual world of that actual entity, but it exemplifies a pattern belonging to the past actual worlds of all actual entities. By formally Whitehead means that not only is this pattern exemplified in those standpoints which are actually realized, but that it would also belong to all potential standpoints involved in the co-ordinate division of the satisfaction of any actual entity. Hence this pattern holds not only for those actual entities which are realized but for all the potentially realizable standpoints.

We turn now to an account of how particular shapes and perspectives belong to the extensive continuum of this cosmic epoch (PR 94d). The extensive continuum of a cosmic epoch is sometimes called the "geometrical society" of that epoch (PR 148c). This geometrical society specifies some special relations which enable us to define straight lines and hence a systematic geometry. Further, the systematic geometry leads to a definition of congruence and then to a theory of measurement contrary to the usual view (PR 148–49). Finally, the geometrical society contains the "electromagnetic society," which further restricts the alternative metrical geometries and congruence definitions to a single metrical system and congruence definition (PR 149b).

"The geometrical facts concerning straight and flat loci are public facts characterizing the feelings of actual entities" (PR 472a). Feelings in which the forms exemplified in the datum are such geometrical facts are called strain feelings (PR 472a). In such strain feelings the other qualitative elements involved are sensa supplied by causal efficacy. They illustrate the geometrical form of the extensive continuum and will be discussed under the indirect aspect of presentational immediacy. Strain feelings are complex integrations of simpler feelings.[7] Every strain feeling has a "seat," which is the volume of points "defining the standpoint of the experient subject" (PR 472b). The seat defines certain sets of straight lines similar to a "station" in PNK (PNK 78a). A subset of these straight lines marks out a focal region which "is a region of dense concurrence of straight lines defined by the 'seat'" (PR 476a; *cf.* 492a). The subset of straight lines marking out a focal region is called the "projectors" (PR 492a). The projection of sensa is upon this focal region. A given focal region is a part of the extensive continuum and can be potentially the focal region defined for various seats which are standpoints of actual entities. Each such standpoint with respect to that focal region is a perspective of that region. The various potential perspectives of a given focal region are marked out by the bodily strains involved in the feelings of bodily efficacity. Of course there are intermediary regions connecting the focal region to the seat in the extensive continuum.

Let us consider some complex feeling of presentational immediacy. The objective datum of this complex propositional feeling involves a nexus of contemporary entities. The nexus has two parts: one part is a regional nexus which is the contemporary focal region (PR 494a); the other part is the sensa which illustrate this focal region so that we recognize it. Let us now consider the genetic origin of the former part, the focal region.

First of all, some actual entity M has a number of separate simple physical feelings. From these simple physical feelings, simple conceptual feelings are derived whose data (eternal objects) are geometrical facts about regions. In each of these conceptual feelings the geometrical facts concern "the feeling as relating its subject (which includes the 'seat' in its volume) to a definite spatial region (the focal region) external to itself" (PR 476b). Other related conceptual feelings are also being derived from other related simple physical feelings of the same original initial data, whose objective data are certain qualitative eternal objects (colors, sounds, etc.), but we are not tracing this genetic history at the moment. Many sets of feelings of these two sorts are involved in the concrescence of the actual entity M. In the supplemental phase of concrescence there arise transmuted feelings involving these simple feelings.

By a double act of transmutation the following result is achieved (PR 477a). First, there is an identity of exemplification of geometrical facts concerning some focal regions of each simple feeling. By virtue of the category of transmutation this set of geometrical facts is transferred so as also to characterize other actual entities which are contemporary with M (PR 479a, 386d). Thus a geometrical characteristic common to the past members of a nexus which also involves contemporaries is transferred so as to characterize the contemporary members of the nexus (PR 484b).

Second, there is involved in each of the simple feelings by M of the other actual entities a "seat" which is the volume of points constituting the standpoint of the percipient actual entity with respect to the various initial data (PR 492a). By virtue of the category of transmutation these identical seats are transmuted into a single seat with respect to the perception of the actual entities as forming a single nexus. Here again contemporaries may be involved.

Finally, by means of this double act of transmutation, there arises a transmuted physical feeling which involves the focal-region-nexus and the common seat (PR 477a). This transmuted feeling of the nexus involves a certain definite geometrical strain. The resultant strain, which belongs to the direct aspect of a perception in the mode of presentational immediacy, thus defines: (1) a bare focal region of the extensive continuum, (2) a seat which is the standpoint of the percipient actual entity and constitutes its personal perspective of the focal region, (3) a group of intermediate regions of the extensive continuum connecting the seat and the focal region, and (4) a vaguely discerned whole "presented space" which contains the focal region (PR 477a).

This account explains in detail what was asserted at the beginning of this discussion of the direct aspect of presentational immediacy: that "our direct perception of the contemporary world is thus reduced to extension, defining (1) our own geometrical perspectives, and (2) possibilities of mutual perspectives for other contemporary entities *inter se,* and (3) possibilities of division" (PR 96b).

In the last chapter we were able to define three loci with respect to causal efficacy for any one actual entity: the causal past, the causal future, and its contemporaries. Among the contemporaries, say A and B, of some actual entity M, it is not necessary for A and B to be contemporaries of each other. Either one may be in the causal past of the other. This is so because it is the character of objectification that only certain actual entities are prehended by others. This characteristic of the contemporaries of M allows us to define another set of loci.

A duration is a locus of actual entities, such that any two members of the locus are contemporaries (PR 487a). It follows that any "actual occasion, not belonging to the duration, is in the causal past or causal future of some members of the duration" (PR 487a). Such a locus of actual entities is said to be in "unison of becoming" and constitutes the notion of the present in classical physics (PR 189–90). It follows that the locus of M's contemporaries contains an indefinite number of durations (PR 191c). Each of these durations serves to define two more loci. The "durational past" of any given duration is composed of those actual entities which belong to the causal past of every actual entity in the duration. This durational past will contain some actual entities which are contemporaries of M (PR 488b). Similarly, the "durational future" of any duration is composed of those actual entities which lie in the causal future of every actual entity in the duration—to those actual entities for which any and every member of the duration functions as a datum in objectifications. Again, this durational future will include some contemporaries of M (PR 488b). So much is a necessary prolegomenon to understanding the following locus defined by the direct aspect of presentational immediacy.

The "presented duration" of an actual entity M is that unique duration of the many durations associated with M which is the datum of a perception in the mode of presentational immediacy for M (PR 488d). Or we can say the presented duration is that unique duration which includes all M's immediate present, which is usually a duration in unison of becoming (PR 191c, 192g). We must distinguish the locus constituting the presented duration from the "strain locus" of M (PR 488d, 491a), although the two are closely related in conscious perception (PR 492–93). M has various perceptions in the mode of presentational immediacy, each of which involves a particular strain defining geometrical facts. Each such strain defines a certain focal region. All these focal regions lie in the contemporary world of M and, being regions, they are interrelated in a single locus of the extensive continuum. This unified locus is the strain locus of M, composed of the various focal regions (PR 485–86, 492a). Whitehead in another place calls it the "presented locus" of M (PR 192a, 195f–96a).

The definitions of the strain locus, the presented duration, and the focal region of the strain locus marked out by the projectors (straight lines defined by the seat) provide the background for the discussion of the projection of sensa in presentational immediacy.

Section III. Indirect Aspect of Presentational Immediacy

The indirect aspect of presentational immediacy supplies the content in the form of sensa by means of which we discriminate the regions contributed by the direct aspect of presentational immediacy (PR 97b). For the purpose of analysis we have separated these two aspects, but they are not separated in any concrete case of preception in this mode. We could not discriminate the regions unless they were characterized, nor could we project our sensa unless there were regions on which to project them (S 14–15). The two aspects are abstractions from the concrete. To take the sensa as primitive and construct space-time systems from them, as Russell did at one stage, is to misplace concreteness.

The concrete perception of "presentational immediacy arises from the integration of a strain feeling and a 'physical purpose,' so that by the category of transmutation, the sensum involved in the 'physical purpose' is projected onto some external focal region defined by projectors" (PR 493b; *cf.* 474b).

The sensa such as colors, sounds, bodily feelings, tastes, and smells are eternal objects supplied by antecedent states of our own bodies by means of causal efficacy (PR 96b, 97b). Let us recall, also, that the geometrical facts contributed by strain feelings are eternal objects (PR 485a). These two groups of eternal objects are the relational elements which make possible our perception of a contemporary world of independent actual entities (PR 475c).

Sensa are provided for presentational immediacy by means of physical purpose feelings belonging to causal efficacy (PR 482b, 493b). A physical purpose feeling has as its datum the contrast between a physical feeling and its correlate conceptual feeling. This contrast is a synthesis of two entities: a particular actual entity which was the initial datum of the physical feeling and a particular eternal object which was a characteristic ingredient in that actual entity. The contrast is of a character belonging to an object in a complex manner.

Suppose you prehend a chair in the mode of causal efficacy. This is no simple affair. The chair is a society of actual entities. A society is a special kind of nexus in which (1) there is a defining characteristic shared by each member and (2) the defining characteristic is due to the environment provided by the society (PR 137b). Thus, the prehending actual entity M has many simple physical feelings of the individual members of the society (PR 179c). Various sets of these have correlate derivative conceptual feelings which have some eternal object in common (PR 476b). These eternal objects are the so-called secondary qualities, whose origin is made perfectly clear in this system, although for Hume they are given "from unknown causes" (PR 99c). One set, for example, gives some color, another set, some geometrical properties, and another set, some tactile quality. From each one of these sets a transmuted physical feeling arises which attributes that common characteristic to the society as a whole (PR 386c). In the case of transmuted physical feelings which later function in presentational immediacy, "only part of the original nexus may be objectified [for presentational immediacy], and the eternal object may have been derived from members of the other part of the original nexus" (PR 386d). The carry-over of the nexus from past to present is a necessary assumption of the system (PR 101c). There may then be a complex integration of these various transmuted feelings so as to form a complex contrast of a group of characteristics, which is a society. This complex integration constitutes a prehension of the "past-chair" in causal efficacy. For the objects we ordinarily perceive, this is a very complex physical purpose prehension (PR 100b, 420c–23b).

Besides the many sets of feelings that are contributing data that are sensa, other sets of feelings are contributing geometrical facts from strain feelings which define, by means of projectors, some focal region (PR 100b). All of these simple feelings and transmuted feelings of sets belong to the process of concrescence of the original prehending actual entity *M*. Thus far, they all belong to the mode of causal efficacy. This society of past actual entities causally felt constitutes a past-chair.

We now consider how these sensa inherited through causal efficacy are projected on to a focal region in presentational immediacy. I need not repeat here how the focal region is defined by the straight lines connected with the seat of the percipient actual entity. The sensa are projected onto the focal region by virtue of a propositional feeling (PR 477b). The following complex elements are involved in that propositional feeling. First, there is a set of characteristics (eternal objects) which are associated with some society of past actual entities constituting the datum of a complex physical purpose feeling, as explained in the last paragraph. This complex physical purpose feeling plays the role of the predicative feeling belonging to a propositional feeling which provides the definite characteristics (sensa). Second, the indicative feeling of a propositional feeling indicates the logical subject of the proposition. In this case, the indicative feeling has the focal region as its datum. Third, the physical recognition feeling of a propositional feeling provides the character of the particular perspective of the focal region of the indicative feeling. The propositional feeling is an integration of these three feelings such that the sensa of the predicative feeling are associated with the focal region of the indicative feeling according to the particular perspective provided by the physical recognition feeling. This linkage of the sensa with the focal region is the projection of the sensa on that focal region. In the case of the perception of the past-chair in the mode of causal efficacy, the projection of the inherited sensa upon the focal region constitutes the chair-image. The image is *there,* away from us, on some extensive region. Since transmuted physical feelings are involved in the projection, the possibility of error is introduced because of reverted conceptual feelings or illegitimate transmutations (PR 387b). But the introduction of error does not yet manifest itself in the process of concrescence. For the chair-image is just the chair-image out there (PR 99d). It is not until we attempt to correlate this chair-image with the past-chair into the perception of a chair that the error can occur, and this correlation does not take place until there is perception in the mixed mode of symbolic reference. We have not yet perceived a chair.[8]

It is not always the case that the sensa are projected (associated) in the propositional feeling upon the focal region although this is usually the case with visual sensa. The indicative feeling may provide as a logical subject of the proposition the region constituting the seat of the percipient entity. In this case, the sensa are associated with the seat-region (PR 478a). This is often the case with sound sensa. Further, the sensa may be projected in some or all of the intermediate regions linking the focal region and the seat as in the case of other sound sensa. Again, the sensa, if they consist of some vague emotional feelings like tenderness, may be diffused throughout the correlated strain locus of the percipient (PR 473a).

This discussion of presentational immediacy, whereby data objectified from the past provide content for perception in the present, required the following metaphysical assumption: "that the actual world, in so far as it is a community of entities which are settled, actual, and already become, conditions and limits the potentiality for creativeness beyond itself" (PR 101c). This presupposition guarantees the indirect aspect of presentational immediacy. Simple physical feelings express this principle of conditioning and limitation.

Chapter X

SYMBOLIC REFERENCE AND CONSCIOUS PERCEPTIONS

Thus far we have seen (1) how causal efficacy contributes direct information about antecedent actual entities to actual entities in process of concrescence; and (2) how presentational immediacy has two aspects, (a) a direct aspect in which we have direct perception of a potential extensive continuum capable of division from many possible perspectives, and (b) an indirect aspect in which sensa inherited through causal efficacy are projected upon regions of the extensive continuum. Presentational immediacy is barren insofar as it reveals no connections between contemporary actual entities, even though it is vivid, controllable at will, clear, and prominent in our consciousness (S 43–44). On the other hand, causal efficacy is extremely vague, unmanageable, primitive, hardly present in our refined consciousness, and weighted with the significance of the past for us, but it contains the valuable specific information necessary to perception and knowledge (S 43–44).

Section I. Symbolic Reference

Symbolic reference results from the integration or fusion of the two pure modes of perception (S 18b). Paralleling the case of presentational immediacy, we distinguish in our analysis two main parts, causal efficacy and presentational immediacy, but these parts are fused together in any concrete case of perception in the mixed mode of symbolic reference. Sometimes in S Whitehead gives the impression that the two pure modes are distinguished as being either "symbol" or "meaning" of the other: "the former set of components are the 'symbols,' and the latter set constitute the 'meaning' of the symbols" (S 8a). Either pure mode may function as symbol for the meaning of the other (S 8b). The reference of symbol to meaning is contributed by the nature of the percipient. On the other hand PR emphasizes the synthetic organic character of symbolic reference. Thus, "in the transition to a higher phase of experience, there is a concrescence in which prehensions in the two modes are brought into a unity of feeling . . ." (PR 255b). "The result of symbolic reference is what the actual world is for us, as that datum in our experience productive of feelings, emotions, satisfactions, actions, and finally as the topic for conscious recognition when our mentality intervenes with its conceptual analysis" (S 18–19; *cf.* 19c). Hence consciousness is not necessary for symbolic reference (PR 274a). This is why we discuss conscious perception separately after symbolic reference.

If the two pure modes are fused in a synthetic feeling there must be some common ground in virtue of which they can be joined (S 49c, PR 255b). There are two such common grounds, (1) the presented locus and (2) eternal objects (S 49b, PR 256b, 259b). With respect to each common ground we must explain how it is a part of each of the two pure modes.

First, consider the presented locus. Its derivation and function in presentational immediacy were explained in the last chapter. The presented locus is made up of the various focal regions defined by the seat and certain sets of projectors; that is, all the various perspectives of an actual entity mesh together by extensive connections to constitute this locus. The perspectives defined by the projectors and seat obtain their geometrical elements from the strain feelings. This presented locus does not reveal any actual contemporary entities but only potential divisions of the continuum by possible actual entities. In many cases, it seems likely that the common element is some specific focal region of the presented locus rather than the whole locus. Hence the common ground provided by the presented locus is directly contributed by the direct aspect of presentational immediacy.

The presented locus is present in causal efficacy in the following manner. Certainly it cannot be claimed that the presented locus is directly present in causal efficacy, because causal efficacy deals with the past actual world while the presented locus belongs to the contemporary world. It must then be present indirectly in causal efficacy (PR 256b). The indirect presence depends upon the conformation of feelings to the immediate past. In a route of causal inheritance through a nexus of actual entities leading up to the percipient actual entity, each of the members of this route has a certain strain feeling whose data are geometrical facts. These data in connection with the seats of the actual entities define for each a presented locus. These presented loci are related in the extensive continuum. There may be another route of causal inheritance leading up to actual entities contemporary with the previous percipient and occupying its presented locus. But these contemporary actual entities are not actually perceived as dividing that presented locus. The metaphysical character of the universe only renders it potentially divisible. For each of the supposed actual entities in this second route of inheritance there is an associated presented locus. These loci are also linked in the extensive continuum. In those cases where there is some actual entity in the immediate past common to both routes of inheritance of causal feeling, this actual entity has its presented locus, which is common in both routes of inheritance. But this presented locus is a part of the satisfaction of that common past actual entity, and it lays its limitations upon the character of the future. Therefore, the two continua formed by these two routes of inheritance intersect and by virtue of a common element they are linked into a single larger continuum which spreads in this manner both spatially and temporally. Insofar as the presented locus of that past actual entity, with the various perspectives of it and its geometrical character, is efficacious in the contemporary members of the two routes of inheritance by means of conformation of present to past, the past presented locus is indirectly present in the perceptions in the mode of causal efficacy for those contemporary actual entities. Thus, the presented locus given directly in presentational immediacy "enters subordinately into the perceptive mode of causal efficacy, vaguely exemplifying its participation in the general scheme of extensive interconnection, involved in the real potentiality" (PR 256b). This presented locus, or focal regions in it, can be present under different perspectives for different percipient actual entities. Since some of these different percipients may be antecedent to others, there may be causal feelings of these antecedent members which have as their data the character of this presented locus from another perspective. "The percipient therefore, under the limitation of its own perspective, prehends the causal influences to which the presented locus in its important regions is subjected" (PR 256b). This amounts to an indirect perception of this locus in causal efficacy.

The best example of the common role of the presented locus is in the animal body, for it "is the great central ground underlying all symbolic reference" (PR 258b). In the case of visual perception in symbolic reference we are aware of a focal region as the result of the eye strain in that perception. But we correlate this region defined by the eye strain with the sensa inherited in causal efficacy because of our feeling of the bodily efficacy of the eyes. This correlation of presentational immediacy and causal efficacy is possible because we correlate the region of eye strain with the region of eye efficacy (PR 258b, S 55–56). The same holds true with the other senses.

Eternal objects constitute the second common ground for symbolic reference (PR 259b). This common ground can occur in two ways, depending upon whether the eternal objects are sensa or geometrical characters, but usually the two occur together. How sensa originate in causal efficacy has previously been explained. From a simple physical feeling whose initial datum is a past actual entity and whose objective datum is some feeling belonging to the concrescence of the initial datum, there is derived a conceptual feeling whose datum is an eternal object. This eternal object is the subjective form of the feeling which is the objective datum and is now able to play a part in the concrescence of the prehending actual entity. The complexities arising from reverted conceptual feelings and transmuted physical feelings have been discussed. The point is that causal efficacy contains eternal objects which are sensa (PR 260b).

How sensa are present in presentational immediacy has also been explained. They are present indirectly, having been inherited from causal efficacy and are now associated with certain regions directly discriminated (PR 260–61).

In a strictly analogous manner there are other eternal objects common to both pure modes of perception: the geometrical facts determinant of the definiteness of past actual entities and determinant of the shape and perspective of the regions perceived in presentational immediacy (PR 260b).

When the same eternal object is common to the two pure modes of perception, there arises the possibility of a perception in the mixed mode of symbolic reference (S 50). This perception is a complex propositional feeling containing the following elements. The indicative feeling is a transmuted physical feeling of a nexus some of whose members are past actual entities, originally felt separately by simple physical feelings, and other members which are contemporaries not directly felt but assumed to embody the same common character found among the past members of the nexus (PR 261a). For example, this sheet of paper on which I am writing is such a nexus, containing past members that are felt causally and containing present members assumed to have the same character. Second, it contains a physical recognition feeling which is also a transmuted physical feeling whose subjective form is the determinate characteristic constituting the way the actual entities of the indicative feeling are felt. Third, it contains a predicative feeling, again transmuted, whose datum is the eternal object which constitutes the subjective form of the physical recognition feeling; for example, the feeling of the eternal object (sensum) whiteness as constituting this subjective form of the physical recognition.

Correlated with these sets of feelings there are others whereby certain geometrical facts causally felt, say of the rectangularity of this sheet of paper, are transmuted so as to give character to regions directly discriminated by the strain of a feeling of presentational immediacy. Further sets of feelings belonging to presentational immediacy, and previously explained, associate (project) the inherited sensa with these regions, say whiteness with the rectangular region marked out by the sheet of paper (PR 262a). Finally there is the complex propositional feeling, which associates the feeling of presentational immediacy, with its characterized regions, with the feeling of causal efficacy, and with its discriminated nexus. That is, the sheet of paper as a past nexus continuing into the present is linked with the contemporary whiteness-on-a-rectangular-region to form a perception of a white sheet of paper.

There is a tendency to confuse the genetic process involved in perception in the pure mode of presentational immediacy whereby the sensa and geometrical facts are obtained, and the genetic process whereby symbolic reference arises, which involves presentational immediacy (PR 262–63). The first provides an explanation of the source of the sensa and geometrical facts associated with the regions directly perceived, but in *no* case is there any awareness of past actual entities in the pure mode of presentational immediacy. For this reason, if we restrict ourselves to this pure mode in the manner of Hume and the sensationalists, we have to say that the impressions of sensation arise from unknown causes. The second genetic process involves the integration of feelings of presentational immediacy with other types of feelings into complex feelings of symbolic reference. The confusion arises because in any concrete instance all these feelings are taking place together in the concrescence.

Section II. How Errors Occur in Symbolic Reference

Perception in the mixed mode of symbolic reference can be erroneous even though consciousness is not involved (PR 274a, S 19b). In Whitehead's system the most fundamental source of error does not arise from a mistaken judgment, which would be an intellectual feeling involving consciousness, but from an integration of causal efficacy and presentational immediacy in which the supposed common ground is not present. Errors can arise at several points in the complex integration of various feelings required for symbolic reference. We shall now indicate some of these points.

With respect to the common ground of eternal objects there are a number of places at which errors may arise in causal efficacy because of the category of conceptual reversion or the category of transmutation.

A reverted feeling has as its datum an eternal object relevant to, but not identical with, the eternal object determinant of the definiteness of some actual entity felt. At any point in the process of causal efficacy where a conceptual feeling is derived from some physical feeling a reversion may occur with the substitution of the relevant eternal object. But this substitution may falsify the character of the actual entity from which it is supposed to be derivative (PR 387b). This may happen to sensa as well as to geometrical facts. We may suppose we perceive in symbolic reference a circular copper penny on the table when our actual prehensions in causal efficacy are of an elliptical shape and another shade of brownness.

Transmuted feelings in causal efficacy lead to errors in the following way. An eternal object derived from parts of a nexus may be taken to characterize the whole or other parts of the nexus when in fact it does not characterize the nexus in exactly the same way (PR 386d). This type of error is especially likely to happen in presentational immediacy when an eternal object derived from one part of a nexus causally felt is supposed to characterize another part of the nexus contemporaneous with the perceiver. Before a perception in the mixed mode can occur, many transmuted feelings must have occurred, each one of which may be subject to this fault. For example, some perceiver may derive from some past causally felt members of a nexus certain geometrical facts dependent upon the perceiver's perspective of these actual entities. These geometrical facts attributed to other members of the nexus, some of which may be contemporaries, may falsify the geometrical facts really belonging to these other members because of changes in perspectives although there may be sufficient relevance to permit the error.

In the case of presentational immediacy errors may arise with respect to eternal objects as follows. Eternal objects inherited from causal efficacy may be projected on a region potentially divisible into actual entities which the eternal objects do not characterize. For example, a perceiver may inherit certain visual sensa which he wrongly attributes to a region behind a mirror, or he may inherit certain sound sensa which he wrongly attributes to some focal region, as in the case of an echo. It must be emphasized that so far as the pure modes of perception are concerned these sensa are exactly where they are and what they are. The error arises in the integration of the two modes (PR 255b), in the integration of the source of the sound in causal efficacy with the focal region of sound in presentational immediacy.

With respect to the common ground of the presented locus error can arise in the following manner. The degree of conformation of the presented locus of some present actual entity to a past actual entity varies according to the complexity of concrescence of that present actual entity. If this degree of conformation is sufficiently weak, then the indirect perception of the presented locus will be affected by considerable distortion. An actual entity *A* may have a certain presented locus potentially divided by a contemporary actual entity *C*. Further, another actual entity *B* may have a presented locus also potentially divided by *C*. Thus the two presented loci have regions in common belonging to the extensive continuum. Further, *B* may be in the causal past of *A*. Hence *A* can causally prehend *B* by means of the feeling belonging to *B* which has as its datum *B*'s presented locus potentially involving *C*. Finally, there is an indirect perception of the presented locus of *A* in causal efficacy, but this indirect perception may involve characteristics not belonging to *A*'s direct presented locus potentially involving *C*. The differences between these form the basis for the introduction of error.

These different examples conclude our account of error in perception in the mixed mode of symbolic reference. Such errors are often called delusive perceptions and are of various degrees of seriousness (PR 100a).

Section III. Conscious Perceptions

A conscious perception can be defined as an intellectual feeling whose datum is a contrast involving the integration of a nexus of actual entities with a perceptive propositional feeling (PR 409d). Or one can say, a conscious perception arises from "the contrast between a 'theory' [proposition] which may be erroneous and the 'fact' [nexus] which is 'given'" (PR 245c). The subjective form of such a feeling is consciousness, hence its name. Consciousness seems to be increased by greater lack of conformation between the nexus and proposition; otherwise there is mere physical reproduction, re-enaction (PR 407a). Thus consciousness may be said to arise from the feeling of difference, of "negation" (PR 245b). Intellectual feelings involving judgment require this principle of "negation." To judge that *A* is not *B* is the negative contrast at the root of conscious thought. The greater the contrast the more consciousness is freed for the imaginative flights of creative art and science.

Whitehead discusses only conscious perceptions and intuitive judgments as species of intellectual feelings involving consciousness. It seems to me that a proper place is not provided for conscious memories, so I suggest that intellectual feelings be divided into intuitive judgments, inferential judgments, and conscious recognitions. Conscious recognitions include conscious perceptions and conscious memories. The distinction between them depends upon whether or not presentational immediacy is involved, and different varieties of each arise depending upon (1) how the nexus physically felt is formed and (2) the kinds of perceptive propositional feelings involved (direct or indirect authentic, and unauthentic). Conscious perceptions involve symbolic reference and thus may be erroneous like intuitive and inferential judgments (PR 409c), but the recognition of errors of memory is a matter of coherence among memories, and no single memory is recognizable as erroneous.

All that we have discussed thus far concerning perception in the process of concrescence is genetically prior to consciousness so that it was difficult to suggest any specific examples, but now that we have arrived at the stage of consciousness in our discussion we shall proceed by the analysis of some specific examples, discussing in each the necessary stages leading up to the conscious perception.

First, let us consider an example of conscious memory, say a memory that yesterday I saw and heard my first red-wing blackbird of the season. This memory belongs to my present conscious awareness (PR 372a). But I cannot rest content as did Hume and hold that it came "from unknown causes." We have a theory based on certain primitive concepts, from which the conscious awareness should follow as a derivative notion. One important warrant for the truth of the theory is that it does explain this and other facts. How do I remember my red-wing?

According to the theory, at some time in my past I had some simple physical feelings of certain actual entities. From these feelings certain correlate conceptual feelings were derived whose data were eternal objects: some sensa, some geometrical facts, and many other eternal objects. Among these many conceptual feelings there were some with the same datum; for example, of red, of black, of wing shape, of flight pattern, and of musical notes. These were grouped into relevant sets. By means of the category of transmutation, these separate feelings were integrated into a single transmuted feeling of that group of entities as a unit, a nexus. Also, each one of these conceptual feelings had for its subjective form some value. This value is a fusion of a certain qualitative pattern and a quantitative intensity (PR 356b). The red is important because of its qualitative relations to other color sensa that were prehended and because it was felt with a certain intensity. Both facts contribute to the determination of its relevance in the concrescence. There was an adjustment of these separate values according to the subjective aim of the prehending subject.

Suppose I had prehended a female red-wing (itself a nexus of actual entities) whose red shoulder-patches, if any, were hardly observable. Then it is possible, according to the category of conceptual reversion, that I should have substituted red sensa as the data of the conceptual feelings. Perhaps I wanted to see a bright colored male, because of the mood of springtime which was pervading my concrescence at that time. Such a relevant substitution provides the novel introduction necessary to my having later an unauthentic perceptive propositional feeling.

To consider another possibility, suppose I prehended only a series of musical notes borne down to me upon the morning breeze. The prehension of each one of these notes (eternal objects) has a subjective form with its related qualitative pattern. The pattern formed in an integration via transmutation of these sounds constitutes the song of the bird. But the song is a nexus not found in any one of the single conceptual feelings. Hence my perceptive propositional feeling of the song is an indirect yet authentic propositional feeling of the song. In this way an indirect authentic propositional feeling can introduce error in the sense that in the transmuted feeling the eternal object characterizing the nexus as a whole does not characterize each of the parts as physically felt (PR 410b).

If the eternal object which characterizes the nexus of a transmuted feeling is a character of each of the actual entities constituting the nexus, we have the basis for the origination of a direct authentic perceptive propositional feeling which has as its datum the integration of that eternal object—the predicate—with those actual entities—the logical subject (PR 410a). This stage of the genetic account of memory took place yesterday when I had these simple physical and conceptual feelings. The propositional feelings become part of the process of concrescence of certain past actual entities belonging to the personal society nexus which is myself, the perceiver, and may have some relevance to the subjective aim dominating this personal society as well as provide for further complex feelings in the satisfaction of actual entities in that personal society.

Today it is cold and wintry again, a sharp breeze penetrating the cracks around the window by my desk in the library where I am writing. I have been trying to find an example of a conscious memory while I recall the spring-like weather of yesterday. Suddenly I remember my perception of the red-wing. How can I account for this memory? Yesterday the perceptive propositional feeling was an element in the complex satisfaction of some actual entity in the personal society constituting me. This satisfaction is objectified in the succeeding actual entities under different perspectives with varying degrees of relevance. Finally, there originates today an actual entity in the personal society constituting me that has for its subjective aim the discovery of a memory to serve as an illustration. With respect to this subjective aim there is an intense relevance of the objectification of that satisfaction constituted by the perceptive propositional feeling of the red-wing. There is now in the specious present an integration of these two: the objectified satisfaction of the perceptive proposition about the bird and the actual entity which is a member of the specious present of my personal society. This integration originates a conscious memory.

A conscious memory differs from what Whitehead calls a conscious perception in that the perceptive propositional feeling has a double reference, or a double integration: (1) a direct reference to some member of the personal society constituting the remembering self and (2) an indirect reference to those actual entities which the proposition describes, the causally felt red-wing. This double reference might lead some persons to think that we were dealing with the integration of an imaginative feeling (instead of a perceptive feeling) and some nexus physically felt. But it seems to me that the essential component of an imaginative feeling, namely, the difference between the indicative feeling (nexus physically felt) and the physical recognition (character attributed to the nexus), is not present in a conscious memory, for the character does belong indirectly to the nexus felt in the past. Whitehead does not name or discuss conscious memories as such, but they are an easy extension of the theory of prehensions.

It seems that presentational immediacy is not involved in conscious memories for the following reasons. There is no projection of content on a contemporary region. There is not even association of the content with the seat-region but only with some past region. On the other hand there is a sense in which the content (eternal objects) is immediately present to our awareness, but this need only be an awareness of an actual entity in our personal society and not of any contemporaries. We might call this "subjective immediacy" in contrast to presentational immediacy, which involves a reference to contemporaries. Conscious memories seem to involve only causal efficacy. If this is the case the possible errors introduced by reverted and transmuted feelings cannot be recognized in any single conscious memory. The conscious memory is what it is. The errors would only be recognized when an incoherence with other memories developed; the problem of deciding between conflicting memories seems to be one of greater or lesser coherence.

What happens, according to the theory of prehensions, when we have a conscious perception which involves presentational immediacy and thus symbolic reference (PR 410–11)? Let us consider as an example the conscious perception of a friend approaching across the campus. A personal society S consisting of many interrelated actual entities will have by means of some of its actual entities many simple physical feelings of other actual entities belonging to another personal society F, our friend. Various types of nexūs are formed, as has been explained many times, involving sensa and geometrical characteristics.

Errors may be introduced by reverted or transmuted feelings. For example, when our friend is at some distance, we may have a transmuted physical feeling whose datum is a brownish object that we take to be his leather brief case, only to discover, later on, as the result of another transmuted feeling, that it is not his usual brief case but a slightly different-colored brown paper package. Thus instead of the proper derivative eternal object, a relevant eternal object is substituted, which had its source in a hybrid physical feeling of some other actual entity. Thus a reverted conceptual feeling occurs which leads to an unauthentic perceptive propositional feeling in the next stage of integration. Or we might have a transmuted physical feeling whose datum is a hand waving to us. But the various single physical feelings involved are of an eternal object (shape) in a particular position (region). The waving hand is a nexus whose characteristics do not belong to each member of the nexus but only to certain members. This type of transmuted physical feeling leads to the formation of an indirect authentic perceptive propositional feeling which is a simplification of the actual state of affairs and in this sense is erroneous.

In the concrete case of our approaching friend many perceptive propositional feelings of all three types (direct, indirect, and unauthentic) are formed, integrated, eliminated, and modified according to the various categoreal obligations. Some of the propositional feelings are also in the mode of presentational immediacy whereby inherited sensa and geometrical characteristics are projected upon regions defined by the strain of the feeling.

The next stage in this concrescence of feelings is the formation of perceptions in the mixed mode of symbolic reference by the integration of the datum of each of the pure modes in virtue of the double functioning (common ground) of the presented locus and/or various sensa. The various presented loci determined by the strain of the feelings of various past actual entities in the personal society S form an interrelated segment of the extensive continuum characterized by certain geometrical characteristics. These loci are also related to the presented locus determined by the strain of the propositional feeling in the mode of presentational immediacy. This is one way in which the feelings of causal efficacy can be integrated with presentational immediacy. Secondly, integration occurs in virtue of sensa which are projected on the regions of presentational immediacy and are identical with sensa felt in causal efficacy. When such integrations result in incompatibilities among some aspects of the complex eternal objects functioning as common elements, we have the first indication that error has occurred.

The discord here experienced is the source of the awakening of consciousness in concrescence, for the conscious perception is a contrast between a nexus of actual entities physically felt and a perceptive propositional feeling—in the above case belonging to symbolic reference (PR 406b). The subjective form of this feeling is consciousness; that is, the recognition of incompatibility, of difference, of "negation" (PR 245a, 372a). This definition of consciousness leads to the conclusion that the more primitive types of prehensions are illuminated only insofar as they are still elements in the developed stage of concrescence when consciousness arises (PR 245b). This explains why we are not conscious of causal efficacy. To take the clear and distinct elements marked out in consciousness as basic is to invert the concrete situation (PR 246a).

Because of the similarity between a conscious perception involving a perceptive propositional feeling and an affirmative intuitive judgment involving an imaginative propositional feeling, we should distinguish them clearly (PR 417a). The origin of these two feelings is different although the final results are about the same. An affirmative (yes-form) intuitive judgment has for its datum a generic contrast between the physical feeling of a nexus (indicative feeling of an objectified nexus) and an imaginative propositional feeling. The conscious perception under consideration involves in its datum the contrast between an indicative feeling and a perceptive propositional feeling.

A propositional feeling involves the following feelings: first, an indicative feeling of a nexus of actual entities which is the logical subject of the proposition, second, a physical recollection feeling whose datum is a nexus of actual entities with respect to their exemplification of some common eternal object (PR 413c), and third, a predicative feeling whose datum is the eternal object involved in the physical recognition (recollection). When the nexus of the indicative feeling is identical with the nexus of the physical recognition, a perceptive propositional feeling results. In the special case of an unauthentic perceptive propositional feeling, some relevant but different eternal object is substituted for the eternal object belonging to the nexus according to conceptual reversion. Hence in this case the final integration of predicative feeling and indicative feeling into a propositional feeling involves a slight relevant error in the characterization of the nexus physically felt; otherwise there is an identity of eternal objects. On the other hand, when the nexus of the indicative feeling differs from the nexus of the physical recognition feeling, an imaginative propositional feeling results. But the eternal object involved in the physical recognition feeling may be relevant or identical to the eternal object in the nexus of the indicative feeling. Hence the imaginative characterization of the nexus of the indicative feeling is correct or not far off. The steps in the origination of these two propositional feelings should indicate how, in their parallel comparative feelings, specifically conscious perceptions and intuitive judgments, the same result can be achieved in two different ways: through the conscious characterization of a nexus physically felt by a pattern of eternal objects identical with the nexus physically felt or merely relevant to the nexus (PR 413c, 414b, 415b, 417).

This concludes our discussion of the mature theory of perception. It involves four fairly distinct parts: (1) causal efficacy, (2) presentational immediacy, (3) symbolic reference, and (4) conscious perception. The last two involve the antecedent functioning of the first two. A further sort of justification of the theory can be found in its explanation of and application to certain concepts and problems in science and metaphysics. We turn to this topic in the next chapter.

Chapter XI

APPLICATIONS TO SCIENCE
AND METAPHYSICS

The intimate connection between science and perception was clearly apparent in our discussion of the earlier theory of perception in PNK, CN, and PRel. This intimacy is also true of the mature theory of perception and involves metaphysics in addition. The purpose of this chapter is to demonstrate this intimate connection by means of citing certain key concepts and problems of science and metaphysics for which it provides a solution. According to Whitehead's characterization of the method of speculative philosophy, these applications serve as a test of the adequacy and applicability of the theory (PR 4b.)

Section I. Applications to Science Provided by Simple
Physical Feelings

Although some modern scientists have denied that causality is a concept of modern science, especially physics, some kind of connection of matters of fact seems necessary for science. There is a sense in which Russell's career epitomizes the modern outlook, for he begins with the denial of causality and finally returns to it as a basic postulate for science.[1] Whitehead's theory of perception provides an ontological explanation for connections of matters of fact (actual entities) in terms of prehensions. "A simple physical feeling is an act of causation. The actual entity which is the initial datum is the 'cause,' the simple physical feeling is the 'effect,' and the subject entertaining the simple physical feeling is the actual entity 'conditioned' by the effect. . . . All complex causal action can be reduced to a complex of such primary components" (PR 361c).

Causal connections are usually held to involve a contiguity of events; that is, science generally denies the possibility of action at a distance (PR 469a). This means that the objectification of a past actual entity in the simple physical feeling of a present actual entity involves the contiguity of the two entities. Two actual entities are contiguous "when the regions constituting their 'standpoints' are externally connected" (PR 468c). Causal objectifications between noncontiguous actual entities require intermediate contiguous entities to link them. Thus we can recognize the atomic character of actual entities and maintain a view of continuous transmission in science (PR 468b). But this contiguity of objectification is an empirical discovery maintained at present in science with no ultimate metaphysical basis; it may be merely a characteristic of this particular cosmic epoch (PR 469a).

A simple physical feeling also provides the basis for the concept of a vector in physics. "Feelings are 'vectors'; for they feel what is *there* and transform it into what is *here*" (PR 133b). Every simple physical feeling has the directional character of a vector. It is "a definite transmission from elsewhere . . ." (PR 177b) conditioning the concrescence of some actual entity. The directional connection of the datum of a feeling to the feeler, defined by means of the geometrical character of the strain locus, is the metaphysical or generic basis of the concept of a vector in physics. The datum is determinate and so is the direction of connection (PR 247a). The vector character of a simple physical feeling provides a metaphysical basis for the view "that all fundamental physical quantities are *vector* and not *scalar*" (PR 268c, 324a). In Newtonian physics the dominance of the scalar physical quantity, inertia, obscured this fact.

Simple physical feelings belonging to the experience of some actual entity M provide the basis for the concept of energy (PR 177b, 178b). Actual entity M may have a set of simple physical feelings of actual entities A, B, C, directly or indirectly, depending upon the order of antecedence, each with its specific emotional intensity. The contribution of (re-enaction of) sensa from A, B, and C proportionately conformed to by M determines a quantitative emotional intensity in the satisfaction of M (PR 177a,b). This is the quantitative generic notion underlying the concept of energy in physics. These definite quantities are the basic quanta of quantum physics (PR 179a, 389a). Since any actual entity has many simple physical feelings, the quantitative measure of its energy, as manifested in its satisfaction, is a multiple of the basic quanta involved, but the basic quanta as such are not perceived (PR 178b).

The intensity of the re-enacted sensa vary according to the way in which they were objectified. Thus in the co-ordinate division of the satisfaction of M a given sensum has a fluctuating emotional intensity. There are definite limits to the range of fluctuation and periods of recurrence. These fluctuations and periods manifested quantitatively in the co-ordinate division of the satisfaction serve to define for each sensum felt a definite wave length and frequency of vibration (PR 247a). "In physics, such transmission can be conceived as corpuscular or undulatory, according to the special importance of particular features in the instance considered" (PR 247a). Hence the philosophy of organism provides a basis for the compatibility of wave and particle phenomena, depending upon the way in which the co-ordinate division of the satisfaction occurs. Division with respect to other potential seats of feelings yields a particle view while division according to fluctuating emotional intensity yields a wave view.

The application of the philosophy of organism to quantum theory in SMW (Chap. VIII) should not be omitted, for the vocabulary of the discussion can be translated easily into the technical vocabulary of PR. In SMW two forms of vibration are distinguished: vibratory locomotion, which involves a pattern as a whole, and vibratory organic deformation, which involves change of pattern. The "primates" in the discussion are the actual entities of PR considered only in respect to spatio-temporal characters (SMW 191c). Each primate defines its own space-time system. "If two primates do not continue either mutually at rest, or mutually in uniform relative motion, at least one of them is changing its intrinsic space-time system" (SMW 192a). The conditions of change of space-time systems express the laws of motion. Conditions for vibratory locomotion depend upon these laws of motion.

Further, the re-enaction (reiteration) of a pattern throughout a series of primates need not occur with undifferentiated sameness. "The pattern may be essentially one of aesthetic contrasts requiring a lapse of time for its unfolding" (SMW 193a). The reiteration of such a complex pattern provides a generic notion for vibration in physics. But this type of vibration reflects in the satisfaction internal changes of intensity in the concrescence; hence it is called vibratory deformation. In PR, as previously explained, Whitehead enlarges this notion to include simple sensa as well as contrasts.

A simple physical feeling provides a basis for the specific kinds of energies found in physics (PR 177b). These specific forms of energy result from the particular way in which the eternal objects give definiteness to the subjective form of the simple physical feeling. Whitehead does not hold that we can deduce from the metaphysical scheme involving simple physical feelings what the specific kinds of energy are. This is a matter for the experimental side of science. Science must provide the specific content, but metaphysics can frame a coherent system in which this content has a place (PR 178a). Thus the "metaphysical description of the simplest elements in the constitution of actual entities agrees absolutely with the general principles according to which the notions of modern physics are framed" (PR 177b). Physical science can now be defined as the study of the spatio-temporal and quantitative characteristics of simple physical feeling (PR 364d). One of the defects of modern philosophy has been that it did not illuminate and systematize basic scientific principles.

Simple physical feelings are the basis for the doctrine of the conformation of feelings elaborated in AI. This doctrine provides a metaphysical groundwork for the theory of induction in science. The problem of induction has tormented logicians because they asked too much of it. They wanted general principles from particular cases (SMW 65b). In SMW, Whitehead maintains that "inductive reasoning proceeds from particular occasion to the particular community of occasions, and from the particular community to relations between particular occasions within that community" (SMW 65b). Some members of the community may be in the future. Besides the conformation of feelings (PR 310b), a doctrine of internal relations is also required as a necessary foundation for induction (SMW 64a). This requirement is satisfied by Whitehead's doctrine of internal relatedness. In PR Whitehead merely repeats this view (PR 310c). These two doctrines provide the metaphysical "basis of all probability and induction [in] . . . , the fact of analogy between an environment presupposed and an environment directly experienced" (PR 314e).

Section II. Additional Applications to Science

Besides providing a basis for the quantum side of nature revealed in quantum physics, the philosophy of organism constitutes a foundation for relativity physics. In fact there is a sense in which the theory of actual entities is a philosophical generalization of the principle of relativity in physics (PR 102c). The influence of relativity is apparent throughout Whitehead's thinking. Each actual entity by means of its prehensions of other entities determines a causal past and by its objectification in other actual entities determines a causal future, while those actual entities not so related are contemporary (PR 486–87). The most general characteristics of all objectifications constitute a spatio-temporal extensive continuum wherein each actual entity has its own space-time system. The Lorentz transformations are the connections between these different space-time systems. The classical system of an absolute space-and-time system is a special case of this more general approach involving a duration whose actual entities are in unison of becoming (PR 102c). The same sort of account of the relativity theory is given in SMW with changes in vocabulary and omissions (SMW 177).

With respect to the objectification of actual entities three more loci can be defined with reference to a duration. A duration is a locus of contemporary actual entities such that any two are contemporaries of each other (PR 487a). All actual entities antecedent to the duration belong to the durational past and all subsequent actual entities belong to the durational future. But with respect to any single actual entity there are many durations which include it. This is a consequence of the relativity of space-time systems not allowed by the Newtonian system (PR 487c, 191c). Of these different possible durations including some actual entity M, there is only one which constitutes M's immediate present as subjectively felt. It is called the presented duration and is determined by the nexus of the datum of a perception in presentational immediacy (PR 192e).

The notion of the presented duration provides a metaphysical basis for the notions of rest, motion, velocity, acceleration, and simultaneity in physics. An actual entity is "at rest" only in its presented duration. Thus, the awareness of rest to an actual entity in its presented duration seems like an absolute concept (PR 488d). An actual entity without perceptions in the mode of presentational immediacy has no unique presented duration and cannot be said to be at rest (PR 486b). Hence the notion of rest is relative to actual entities. Motion does not apply to a single actual entity (PR 113b), for that actual entity is what it is where it is in its presented duration. But a nexus of actual entities may be so connected as to form an enduring object or physical object, each member of which has an associated presented duration (PR 489a). The motion of a physical object "is nothing else than the difference between the successive occasions of its life-history in respect to the extensive quanta from which they arise . . ." (PR 124d). Thus motion is relative to physical objects. Shortly we shall provide a basis for the notion of distance from whence the notion of velocity can be defined. Whitehead says that " 'acceleration' is nothing else than a mode of estimating the shift from one family of 'presented loci' [belonging to a physical object] to another such family [belonging to some other physical object]" (PR 155a). Finally, the presented duration itself defines what is meant by simultaneity. Any other actual entity potentially included in the locus of the presented duration is simultaneous with the actual entity defining that presented duration. The sensed simultaneity appears as absolute to the actual entity defining the presented duration but as relative when viewed from the standpoint of any other actual entity.

The method of extensive connection enabled Whitehead to provide a metaphysical foundation for pure geometry, physical geometry, and hence of congruence and a theory of measurement. Regions are related by extensive connections to form the extensive continuum. By means of extensive connections among regions, pure abstract points and segments can be defined (PR 456, 457). The strain loci of this particular cosmic epoch define conditions such that a particular systematic geometry with its specific definition of straight lines (segments) is determined (PR 457–58, 504a). Such a particular systematic geometry embodies a homology of relations throughout all its regions (PR 196b). Other cosmic epochs may embody alternative systematic geometries (PR 503–04). Each such systematic geometry will have its own definition of congruence (PR 148c, 506a) such that "two segments are congruent when there is a certain analogy between their functions in a systematic pattern of straight lines, which includes them both" (PR 505c). Once a specific definition of congruence is chosen, a theory of measurement and metrical geometry can be developed (PR 506–07). One of Whitehead's criticisms of Einstein's development of the relativity theory is that Einstein thinks that congruence has to be defined operationally in terms of actual physical happenings (PR 194d). Thus the fundamental equations of physics involved in the metrical geometry of some cosmic epoch are consequent upon the ordering of strains in that epoch (PR 474a). Since the strains belong to presentational immediacy, all scientific measurement belongs to the potential extensive continuum revealed in presentational immediacy.

The applications presented thus far all belong to physical science, but Whitehead means to provide metaphysical notions for biological sciences as well. The whole theory of prehensions is a description of the most generic elements applicable to growth or evolution of any kind. But, more specifically, definitions are given for various kinds of societies that are biological entities of various types. Again we must remember that Whitehead does not claim that metaphysics can predict the specific organic structure of a biological entity; this calls for experimentation. But metaphysics can state the generic conditions of connection for different types of societies. The metaphysical foundations of sociology are also a part of the discussion about societies.

W. E. Agar, a zoologist, has written for biologists an article descriptive of Whitehead's metaphysics, and in another article dealing with the concept of purpose in biology he uses Whitehead's metaphysics as a generic account of how there is purpose in an organism.[2] H. Hermann has provided a brief but excellent discussion of the application of the category of actual entities to the problem of structure and function in biological organisms.[3]

A nexus which is a society, either organic or inorganic, (1) has a "defining characteristic" (eternal object) shared by its members and

(2) the presence of the defining characteristic is due to the environment provided by the society (PR 137b). An atom, a molecule, a stone, a turbine, a cell, a plant, an animal, and a solar system are examples of societies. A society is a living society if it contains living occasions (PR 156e). A living occasion is one in which reversion and transmutation introduce novel elements into the satisfaction (PR 156e). In an "entirely living" nexus, each member actual entity will have original (novel) reactions and the entirely living nexus, if it is to survive, requires the "protection" (environment) of the rest of the living society of which it is a part. (PR 157b).

These distinctions may sound like rather naive generalizations to a biologist, for they provide no new information; but the point is that this hierarchy of societies is the consequence of the cosmological system. Insofar as it coheres with scientific findings, the cosmological system is supported.

Section III. Applications to Metaphysics

That the mature theory of perception is the foundation for a cosmological system, with its epistemology, ontology, logic, ethics, and aesthetics, is clearly apparent. I intend at this point only to indicate some of these foundations, many of which have already been discussed.

Concerning epistemology, a theory of perception has been stated and reference made as to how this issues in a theory of judgment with intellectual feelings. The theory of perception in relation to propositional feelings has provided the basis for certain logical concepts. A discussion of the concept of validity is lacking.

Insofar as we have described the structure and function of actual entities, the basis of Whitehead's ontology is presented. In addition, the value aspect of the subjective form of conceptual prehensions forms the basis for his ethics and aesthetics, although no details are stated.

Solutions are provided for the following traditional problems in philosophy, explicitly in this book or easily by inference from what has been said. The problem of relations is solved by a new theory of internal relatedness first adumbrated in PREL as the doctrine of significance, altered and expanded in SMW, applied concretely in PR in the doctrine of prehensions, and completed in AI with the doctrine of mutual immanence. The problem of universals and particulars is solved by the relations of actual entities, eternal objects, prehensions, and subjective forms in the relations of ingression and objectification. Whitehead finds the usual notions of universals and particulars to be abstractions from concrete elements in experience (PR 76b). Actual entities, although similar to particulars, enter into the constitution of other actual entities; and eternal objects, although like universals, are particular entities, in the sense of being just what they are, diverse from everything else (PR 76b).

The mind-body problem is explained by the theory of prehensions, which offers an account of each and of how they are related. A theory of efficient causation is provided by the doctrine of the objectification of actual entities in simple physical feelings and a theory of final causation, by the doctrine of the subjective aim controlling the concrescence. The empiricism of Hume with its insistence on the derivation of knowledge from experience is accepted and elaborated in the theory of prehensions although the primacy of the sensationalist principle is denied (PR 382a). But also, the rationalism of Plato with his doctrine of reminiscence (Plato's way of explaining a priori knowledge) is accepted and explained by means of hybrid physical feelings of God (PR 381a).

A doctrine of potentiality is developed in the relation of eternal objects to actual entities. The relation of actuality to potentiality is expounded in the connection of the extensive continuum revealed in presentational immediacy to the actual past revealed in causal efficacy. The status of subjectivity and objectivity is clarified by their roles in the doctrine of prehensions. The perishing of any actual entity constitutes its objective functioning in the world succeeding it, while the subjective aim controls the subjective privacy of each concrescence with its own immediacy of experience.

These indications are sufficient to show how the mature theory of perception provides a foundation for the cosmological system. Many of the details for some of these topics have already been worked out in earlier chapters; implications for the others may be readily worked out.

Chapter XII

A BACKWARD GLANCE—
SUMMARY AND CONCLUSIONS

This study of Whitehead was designed (1) to expound his views on the nature of perception at various stages in his development; (2) to indicate how these particular views on perception are the result of (a) his analysis and criticism of the foundations of science and (b) his analysis and criticism of certain key issues in philosophy; (3) to show the continuity and change in his development; and (4) to indicate how the different theories of perception provide the foundation for (a) his philosophy of science and (b) his cosmological system. Our findings in connection with each of these points will now be reviewed.

Section I. The View of Perception in OT

Three different views of perception have been discussed in the course of this book. The first was expounded in Chapter II, and was extracted from a group of essays occurring in OT. This view was characterized by its employment of the class theory and by its use of the method of logical constructions for inferred entities. Both of these principles were typical of British empiricism. The fundamental entities which form the basis for this theory of perception are sense-objects. Sense-objects are roughly the same as sense-data or sensa. But there is a difference which serves to constitute a novel aspect in this view of perception marking it off from traditional lines. Thought-objects of perception and thought-objects of science, which are constructed out of sense-objects by means of the class theory and logical constructions, have a hypothetical aspect. They are not just the immediate given awarenesses of sensation. Inference is involved. This is why thought and fact are said to be the same.

A second point of novelty in this view of perception occurs in connection with the distinction between science and metaphysics. The separation is achieved in virtue of the fact that science and metaphysics have a common root in perception, and proceed in the main in diverse directions. Nevertheless, Whitehead insists that metaphysics is necessary for a complete understanding of science. There is nothing about this view which entails the ultimate divorce of science and metaphysics. The door is left open for the later investigations of smw, pr, and ai.

The class theory and the method of logical construction are the means of operation for two key principles: the principle of convergence and the principle of aggregation. These two principles provide a way for defining certain scientific and geometrical notions like points of space, instants of time, and particles of matter, yielding a relational theory of space and time. The whole structure is founded upon an empirical basis of sense-objects.

The criticism of previous ways of defining points, instants, and particles was initiated in the 1905 memoir. The criticism (hence the 1905 memoir) is important because it indicates the way in which these entities are to be defined in a sound philosophy of natural science. In the 1905 memoir this criticism was based on Occam's Razor. In the essays in ot the criticism was based on the view that we do not directly perceive points, instants, and particles, but rather durations and extensions. Ot provides an empirical justification for Occam's Razor.

Section II. The View of Perception in PNK, CN, and PRel

In Chapter III the exposition of Whitehead's criticism of scientific concepts is continued. The difficulties for science resulting from the assumption of points, instants, and particles as fundamental entities are made more explicit. In fact much of the difficulty is seen to flow from the assumption that extension in space and in time expresses disconnection. Besides the criticism of these classical notions, Whitehead cannot agree with the way in which Einstein develops his relativity theory. In addition to the criticism of scientific concepts, Whitehead presents in cn a philosophical criticism of a certain epistemological viewpoint which he calls the bifurcation of nature. This scientific and philosophical criticism paves the way for the second major view of perception by indicating along what lines a sound foundation for the philosophy of natural science can be built.

There is continuity with the earlier view in three major respects. First, the two principles of convergence and aggregation are combined into one, the principle of extensive abstraction. Second, the notion of objects as fundamental entities is carried over. The analysis of objects is more detailed. Terminology changes: sense-objects remain sense-objects;

thought-objects of perception become perceptual objects; and thought-objects of science become scientific objects. Some new objects are distinguished: percipient objects and physical objects. Third, the hypothetical aspect of objects is retained. This point is most clearly expressed in the definition of perception in PREL as including both awareness and cogitation.

Two major novel elements are introduced in the second view of perception: events are added as a second fundamental entity; and the doctrine of significance provides a new theory of relatedness. Events are introduced as a result of the philosophical criticism of those epistemological views which involve the bifurcation of nature. In a sense, events replace the traditional notion of substance, but their character is quite different. Whitehead holds that subject-predicate logic and substance-attribute metaphysics are instances of the fallacy of misplaced concreteness.

The doctrine of significance is Whitehead's answer to the false assumption that extension expresses disconnection, which led classical physics into difficulty. This doctrine has three important functions. First, it explains how events are internally related to each other, and hence how a uniform structure of space-time is possible. Second, it explains how objects are related to events in the relation of ingression. Third, it explains how objects are significant of each other. This last function provides a basis for the notion of causality.

The details of the second view of perception are provided in Chapter IV. The fundamental entities are events and objects. Their relations are explained by significance. Applications to science leading to the definition of scientific concepts are achieved by the principle of extensive abstraction.

I have shown in Chapter V how this view of perception provides a foundation for the philosophy of natural science expounded in PNK, CN, and PREL. A relational theory of space-time can be derived from the notion of events and their internal relations. Points of space, instants of time, and particles of matter are defined by the method of extensive abstraction. The status and function of scientific objects are explained. Significance provides an explanation of causality. The theory of events and objects provides a way to avoid the bifurcation of nature in the construction of a philosophy of science.

Section III. The Mature Theory of Perception

A third view of perception is presented by Whitehead in SMW, PR, and AI. SMW is mainly devoted to a final statement of his criticism of modern science. I discussed this in Chapter VI. Modern science, according to Whitehead, has assumed simple location with respect to its fundamental entities. It is this assumption which has led to the various difficulties concerning the relations of points, instants, and particles when they are taken as primitive notions. This disconnection among fundamental entities is the ruin of scientific materialism, the label he applies to the position of modern science. In general the same criticisms are made of classical physics and of Einstein as in the previous view, but the whole discussion is much more generalized in SMW. The assumption of simple location is another instance of the fallacy of misplaced concreteness.

Criticism of philosophical notions has a greater role in SMW. The notion of substance is attacked along with Aristotelian logic. The subjectivist-objectivist controversy is discussed. A new theory of internal relatedness is presented. The problem of God is scrutinized. Whitehead's attitude towards each of these helps to mold the third view of perception.

The following lines of continuity can be traced between the second and third views of perception. The notion of an event becomes a prehensive unity or an actual occasion in SMW, and an actual entity or actual occasion in PR. The prehensive unity has a more complex character than an event, but the two entities play about the same role. Both are concrete, organic wholes internally related. But prehensive unities are basic not only to scientific foundations but to metaphysical foundations. In PR actual entities have ethical, aesthetic, emotional, and rational aspects which were not attributed to events. The addition of these aspects increases their complexity manyfold and makes them seem like full-blooded ontological entities. In SMW prehensive unities are said to be a synthesis of modes or aspects, while in PR actual entities go through stages of concrescence. They are creative. Such a concrescence was clearly not possessed by events, so these entities are in this sense different.

Objects become eternal objects in SMW and PR. In contrast to the actuality of objects, eternal objects are potential. The notion of potentiality is introduced in order to clarify how they can ingress in many actual entities at the same time. Further, they must be potential in order to explain the teleological character of concrescence whereby there can be a determination of an uncreated future. The essence of an eternal object is analyzed into a relational essence and an individual essence, and a new theory of internal relations between them is developed.

The doctrine of significance is expanded into a doctrine of internal relatedness in SMW, then into the doctrine of prehensions in PR, and finally into the doctrine of mutual immanence in AI. I have contended in Chapter VI, Section IV, that the doctrine of internal relatedness in SMW makes explicit what the doctrine of significance really involved in PRel. There is a rough similarity between cogitation as a part of perception in PRel and the individual essence of an eternal object in SMW, and between awareness of a factor of fact in PRel and the relational essence of an eternal object in SMW. This distinction of the individual essence and the relational essence enables Whitehead to answer the objection to a theory of internal relations that any knowledge requires knowledge of everything.

The doctrine of prehensions in PR provides an elaborate analysis of the process of concrescence of an actual entity, whereby its relations to (prehensions of) other actual entities, prehensions, or eternal objects form a constitutive part of its character. Such an analysis is lacking in the earlier expression of a doctrine of relatedness.

The doctrine of mutual immanence in AI deals with how contemporary actual entities are related to each other and with how the future is related to the present and past. Each of these doctrines directs its attention to only a part of the total problem of relatedness. All of them must be considered together in order to achieve a full view of Whitehead's theory of relations.

The major novel element introduced in the third view of perception is the analysis of perception into the two pure modes of causal efficacy and presentational immediacy, and the mixed mode of symbolic reference. This analysis is the result of Whitehead's discovery of a third instance of the fallacy of misplaced concreteness: the assumption that sense-data are immediately given elements in perception from unknown sources. This assumption he calls the sensationalist principle. He had held this assumption in his two earlier views on perception, for sense-objects are taken as primitive givens. In PR sense-data which are eternal objects are primitive entities, but how they are derivative factors in perception is explained. Causal efficacy explains the source of sense-data in perception, and presentational immediacy explains their apparent given immediacy.

Chapter XI contains an account of the applications of the third view of perception to science and metaphysics. In the realm of science the third view of perception provides (1) an ontological basis for causal connections, (2) a basis for vectors in physics, (3) a foundation for the notion of energy, (4) an interpretation of the quantum character of nature, (5) an interpretation of vibration and frequency, (6) a foundation for induction, (7) a relational theory of space-time, (8) a basis for the notions of rest, motion, acceleration, velocity, and simultaneity, (9) an explanation of the relation of geometry to experience, and (10) a foundation for the biological notion of an organism and the sociological notion of a society. In the realm of metaphysics, this view provides (1) a new theory of relations, (2) an account of universals and particulars, (3) a solution to the mind-body problem, (4) a synthesis of empiricism and rationalism, (5) a new doctrine of potentiality, and (6) clarification of the role of subjectivity and objectivity.

In conclusion, it seems to me that Whitehead's entire philosophical development can be illuminated by the following generalization. Each of the three views of perception which provide the bases for his scientific and philosophical insights can be taken as an answer to one of three instances of the fallacy of misplaced concreteness. The first instance of the fallacy is the assumption that subject-predicate propositions (Aristotelian logic) are the most accurate explication of the structure of reality. *Principia Mathematica* provides a logical system with far-ranging modes of application vastly superior to the Aristotelian system. The 1905 memoir is an example of the fruitful application of this logical system to the foundations of physics. An important notion in this logical system is that of a class. The first view of perception in OT is based on a class theory utilizing sense-objects as primitive entities. The second instance of the fallacy is the assumption that the primitive entities of science and philosophy can be simply located. The doctrine of significance in the second view of perception is the first answer to this erroneous assumption. Events and objects cannot be understood or defined without specification of their internal relatedness to other events and objects. The second view of perception in PNK, CN, and PRel provides Whitehead's answer to the assumption of simple location although the name is not coined until SMW. It also takes over the solution to the first instance of the fallacy in its attack on substance-attribute philosophies. The third instance of the fallacy is the assumption of the sensationalist principle. This is explicitly dealt with in PR by means of the third view on perception. This erroneous assumption is made in the two earlier instances of the fallacy. I conclude that the development of Whitehead's philosophy depends upon the interaction of his views of perception with theories of science and metaphysics.

NOTES

CHAPTER I

1. *Philosophical Transactions of the Royal Society of London,* Series A, 205 (1906), 465–525, hereafter referred to as M or the 1905 memoir. The entire essay is reprinted in *Alfred North Whitehead: An Anthology,* ed. F. S. C. Northrop and Mason W. Gross (New York: Macmillan Co., 1953).
2. Another more extended summary of this paper (M) emphasizing its relations to previous and later work of Whitehead's is given by Victor Lowe in his admirable essay "The Development of Whitehead's Philosophy" in *The Philosophy of A. N. Whitehead,* ed. Paul A. Schilpp (Evanston & Chicago: Northwestern University Press, 1941), pp. 33–46. I am much indebted to this essay. It appears revised as Chapter 7 of his *Understanding Whitehead* (Baltimore: Johns Hopkins University Press, 1962). A third summary by Wolfe Mays, "The Relevance of 'On Mathematical Concepts of the Material World' to Whitehead's Philosophy" is in *The Relevance of Whitehead,* ed. I. Leclerc (New York: The Macmillan Co., 1961).
3. Bertrand Russell, *Principles of Mathematics* (London: George Allen and Unwin, Ltd., 1903), p. 445.
4. *Mind,* 10 (1901), 293–317.
5. *Cf.* especially Chapter III of *An Enquiry Concerning the Principles of Natural Knowledge* (New York: The Macmillan Co., 1919) and also F. S. C. Northrop, "Whitehead's Philosophy of Science," in Schilpp, *op. cit.,* pp. 167–207.
6. These two theories are developed in their logical details in M, pp. 484–88 and 492–505, respectively.
7. Another fascinating discussion of the relation of some of Whitehead's ideas in logic and mathematics prior to the 1905 memoir to later ideas in his philosophy is contained in David Harrah, "The Influence of Logic and Mathematics on Whitehead," *Journal of the History of Ideas,* XX (1959), 420–30.

CHAPTER II

1. All contained in *The Organization of Thought* (London: Williams and Norgate, 1917), and reprinted with omissions in *The Aims of Education* (New York: The Macmillan Co., 1927).
2. *Encyclopaedia Britannica,* 11th ed., XVII, 878–83; reprinted in A. N. Whitehead, *Essays in Science and Philosophy* (New York: Philosophical Library, 1947), under the title "Mathematics," pp. 269–88.

3. *Encyclopaedia Britannica,* 11th ed., XI, 730–36, 724–30, respectively; reprinted with the same titles in *Essays in Science and Philosophy,* pp. 243–68 and 289–312, respectively.

4. A. N. Whitehead, *Introduction to Mathematics* (London: Williams and Norgate, 1911).

5. *Revue de Métaphysique et de Morale,* 23 (1916), 423–54.

6. A rough explanation of the principle occurs in ot 164–78 with respect to points.

7. See Chapter IV, Section III, on perceptual objects.

8. F. S. C. Northrop, "Whitehead's Philosophy of Science," in *The Philosophy of A. N. Whitehead,* ed. Paul A. Schilpp (Evanston & Chicago: Northwestern University Press, 1941), pp. 191, 205c.

9. F. S. C. Northrop, *The Logic of the Sciences and the Humanities* (New York: The Macmillan Co., 1947), p. 94.

10. N. Lawrence, "Whitehead's Method of Extensive Abstraction," *Philosophy of Science,* 17 (1950), 143c, 163b. Lawrence continues to hold this mistaken view in his book *Whitehead's Philosophical Development* (Berkeley: University of California Press, 1956), wherein he calls the two strands "conceptual" and "realistic." This is one of the main theses of his work and is, I think, shown false by reference to the above passages.

11. See A. N. Whitehead, *Introduction to Mathematics* (London: Thornton Butterworth Ltd., 1911), pp. 225–35, for a beautiful explanation of this essential point in Whitehead's method. The definition is given on p. 229d.

Chapter III

1. Pr 143–45, ai 144c–47, 156–59, especially ai 144c.

2. Whitehead's own answer to this *reductio* is given in Chapter IV, pp. 121–124.

3. A. Einstein, "Physics and Reality," *Journal of the Franklin Institute,* 221 (1936), 355–57. This paper presents his views from a philosophical angle.

4. *Ibid.,* p. 350c.

5. The large amount of agreement between Einstein and Whitehead is revealed throughout pnk, cn, and prel, but see especially pnk, Chapter III.

6. Einstein, *op. cit.,* p. 350d.

7. Einstein and others, *Principle of Relativity* (New York: Dover, 1923), p. 39, and A. d'Abro, *Evolution of Scientific Thought* (New York: Dover, 1950), p. 170.

8. Another discussion of the Einstein-Whitehead differences on the definition of simultaneity in favor of Einstein can be found in F. S. C. Northrop, "Whitehead's Philosophy of Science," in *The Philosophy of A. N. Whitehead,* ed. Paul A. Schilpp (Evanston and Chicago: Northwestern University Press, 1941), pp. 167–207.

9. E. B. McGilvary, "Space-Time, Simple Location, and Prehension," in Schilpp, *op. cit.,* pp. 215–29, wherein McGilvary attempts a careful statement of this and other seeming misunderstandings on Whitehead's part.

10. On this point see the discussion in A. d'Abro, *Evolution of Scientific Thought* (New York: Dover, 1950), pp. 105, 110.

11. Concerning doubts about the empirical verification of Einstein's theory with respect to spectral lines, see the review of *Albert Einstein: Philos-*

opher-Scientist, ed. Paul A. Schilpp, in *Scientific American,* May 1950, p. 58, by Sir Edmund Whittaker.

12. Quoted from E. A. Burtt, *The Metaphysical Foundations of Modern Physical Science* (London: Routledge & Kegan Paul Ltd., 1949), p. 75.

13. See the discussion in Burtt, *op. cit.,* pp. 243–54.

Chapter IV

1. A. E. Murphy, "What is an Event?" *Philosophical Review,* 37 (1928), 578–79.

2. L. S. Stebbing, "Professor Whitehead's 'Perceptual Object,'" *Journal of Philosophy,* 23 (1926), 197–213. L. S. Stebbing, "Universals and Professor Whitehead's Theory of Objects," *Proceedings of the Aristotelian Society,* 25 (1924–25), 305–30.

3. The latter half of the sentence anticipates the ontological principle of PR; namely, "no actual entity, then no reason."

4. A. E. Murphy, "Objective Relativism in Dewey and Whitehead," *Philosophical Review,* 36 (1927), gives an account of objective relativism based on SMW and John Dewey's *Experience and Nature.*

5. Another discussion of this difficulty and the two definitions can be found in L. S. Stebbing, "Professor Whitehead's 'Perceptual Object,'" *Journal of Philosophy,* 23 (1926), 197–213.

6. L. S. Stebbing, "Mind and Nature in Whitehead's Philosophy," *Mind,* 33 (1924), 289–97.

7. UC 2d, quoting Hume, Essay VII, "Of the Idea of Necessary Connection."

8. UC 14b, quoting Hume, Essay VII, "Of the Idea of Necessary Connection."

Chapter V

1. Victor Lowe, "Whitehead's Philosophy of Science," in Lowe, Hartshorne, and Johnson, *Whitehead and the Modern World* (Boston: Beacon Press, 1950), pp. 7–8 for this list. Whitehead's own technical statement of these properties is in PNK 101; see also CN 58–60, 75–77.

2. V. F. Lenzen, "Scientific Ideas and Experience," *University of California Publications in Philosophy* 8 (1926), 184–85.

3. A. Grünbaum, "The Philosophy of Continuity" (Doctoral Dissertation, Yale University, 1951), 158–60.

4. W. W. Hammerschmidt, *Whitehead's Philosophy of Time* (New York: King's Crown Press, 1947), p. 46.

5. A. N. Whitehead, "La Théorie Relationniste de l'Espace," *Revue de Métaphysique et de Morale* 23 (1916), 452–54.

6. N. Lawrence, "Locke and Whitehead on Individual Entities," *Review of Metaphysics* 4 (1950), 235, wherein Lawrence seems to suggest the same solution of the demarcation problem for Whitehead.

7. A. E. Murphy, "Ideas and Nature," *University of California Publications in Philosophy* 8 (1926), 204–05.

8. Lowe, *op. cit.,* p. 8, footnote. This point is also discussed in Victor Lowe, *Understanding Whitehead* (Baltimore: The Johns Hopkins Press, 1962), pp. 80–81.

9. Hammerschmidt, *op. cit.,* p. 44a. (See also PR 417, 450–51.)

10. Lenzen, *op. cit.,* pp. 184–85.

11. Grünbaum, *op. cit.*, pp. 160–65.
12. A. P. Ushenko, "Einstein's Influence on Philosophy," *Albert Einstein: Philosopher-Scientist*, ed. by P. A. Schilpp (Evanston: Northwestern University Press, 1949), p. 634b, footnote.
13. R. M. Palter, *Whitehead's Philosophy of Science* (Chicago: University of Chicago Press, 1960), Chap. V. This work contains the most detailed and technical account of the method of extensive abstraction.
14. 1) On the derivation of time, see PNK 110–20; CN 60–65. 2) On the derivation of space, see PNK 128–38; CN 79–83. 3) See also N. Lawrence, "Whitehead's Method of Extensive Abstraction," *Philosophy of Science*, 17 (1950), for a detailed discussion and criticism of the method. 4) See also W. W. Hammerschmidt, *op. cit.*, Chapter III, for a summary which includes the distinction between extension (PNK) and extensive connection (PR).
15. Palter, *op. cit.*
16. Albert Einstein, *Relativity* (New York: Henry Holt & Co., 1920), pp. 135a, 136b.
17. E. B. McGilvary, "Space-Time, Simple Location, and Prehension," *The Philosophy of A. N. Whitehead*, ed. by P. A. Schilpp (Evanston and Chicago: Northwestern University Press, 1941), p. 219a.

Chapter VI

1. The same point is made by W. P. Alston, "Whitehead's Denial of Simple Location," *Journal of Philosophy*, 48 (1951), 715.
2. R. B. Braithwaite, "Is the 'Fallacy of Simple Location' a Fallacy?" *Aristotelian Society: Supplement*, 7 (1924), 224–36; see also his review of SMW in *Mind*, 35 (1926), 489–500.
3. L. S. Stebbing, "Is the 'Fallacy of Simple Location' a Fallacy?" *Aristotelian Society: Supplement*, 7 (1924), 207a; *cf.* SMW 74–75.
4. *Cf.* N. Lawrence, "Single Location, Simple Location and Misplaced Concreteness," *Review of Metaphysics*, 7 (1953–54), 227 ff.
5. Stebbing, *op. cit.*, p. 208b.
6. Excerpted from a quotation in SMW 60–61. The whole original passage is of interest. See *The Works of Francis Bacon*, ed. by Spedding, Ellis, and Heath (Boston: Brown and Taggard, 1862), 5, 63–65.
7. A discussion of this point, with which I agree, can be found in M. W. Gross, "Whitehead's Answer to Hume," *Journal of Philosophy*, 38 (1941), 95–102.
8. In fact it seems to me possible that SMW was composed in separate parts, one done in England, as announced by the notes to the second edition of PNK in 1925, and one in America, delivered as Lowell Lectures in February, 1925. Chapters 10 and 12 on 'Abstraction' and 'God' constitute an even later period in his development. Their later composition is asserted by John Cobb, *A Christian Natural Theology* (Philadelphia: The Westminster Press, 1965), pp. 136–39. I have been able to find no detailed facts or dates which would serve to support this theory. It would be interesting to know whether the theory is correct.
9. See V. M. Root, "A. N. Whitehead's Theory of Eternal Objects" (Doctoral Dissertation, Yale University, 1950), Chapter III, for a detailed discussion of these differences.

10. L. S. Stebbing, *op. cit.*, p. 219b, asserts that it is a misnomer to call this relation an internal relation.
11. *Ibid.*, pp. 215–16.
12. Brand Blanshard, *The Nature of Thought* (London: George Allen & Unwin, Ltd., 1948), Chapter XXXII.
13. Stebbing, *op. cit.*, p. 219.
14. *Ibid.*, p. 219b.
15. *Ibid.*, p. 218a.
16. *Ibid.*, pp. 218–19; *cf.* also SMW 180a.

CHAPTER VII

1. It may be that the notion of a region is an additional primitive in the system of PR. This will be discussed later in connection with presentational immediacy.
2. The reader is reminded not to confuse what Whitehead calls the principle of relativity with the principle of relativity in modern physics, although Whitehead thinks his is a philosophical generalization of this physical principle.
3. J. W. Blyth, *Whitehead's Theory of Knowledge* (Providence, R. I.: Brown University Press, 1941), Brown University Studies, Vol. VII, 42–43, 28a.
4. *Ibid.*, p. 8.
5. J. Dewey, "Whitehead's Philosophy," *Philosophical Review*, 46 (1937), 174d, 175a, b.
6. *Ibid.*, p. 174a.
7. A. N. Whitehead, "Remarks," *Philosophical Review*, 46 (1937), 178–86.
8. For a discussion of this point see V. Root, "A. N. Whitehead's Theory of Eternal Objects" (Doctoral Dissertation, Yale University, 1950), pp. 181b–84b.
9. V. Root, *op. cit.*, pp. 196b–98a contains an elaboration of an alternative account of the origin of reverted conceptual feelings in line with White-head's suggested revision.

CHAPTER VIII

1. For Whitehead's analysis of Hume see PR, Part II, Chapter V; also PR 264–66, 180–81; S 50–51.
2. David Hume, *Treatise*, Book I, Part 1, Section vi, cited in PR 181a.
3. Such a careful analysis has been given by W. A. Christian, "The Mutual Exclusiveness of Whitehead's Actual Occasions," *Review of Metaphysics*, II (1949), 58–68. Also consult Christian's treatment in his book, *An Interpretation of Whitehead's Metaphysics* (New Haven: Yale University Press, 1959), Part I, Chapters 2, 3, 7.
4. Christian, "The Mutual Exclusiveness of Whitehead's Actual Occasions," p. 58c.
5. *Ibid.*, p. 61 ff.
6. *Ibid.*, p. 62c ff.
7. G. V. Gentry, "Prehension as an Explanatory Principle," *Journal of Philosophy*, 35 (1938), 518–19. G. V. Gentry, "The Subject in Whitehead's Philosophy," *Philosophy of Science*, 11 (1944), 222–26. G. V. Gentry, "Eternal Objects and the Philosophy of Organism," *Philosophy of Science*,

13 (1946), 252–60. D. L. Miller, "Whitehead's Extensive Continuum," *Philosophy of Science*, 13 (1946), 144–49. D. L. Miller and G. V. Gentry, *The Philosophy of A. N. Whitehead* (Minneapolis: Burgess Publishing Co., 1938); *cf.* Parts IV and V.

8. A. H. Johnson, "The Psychology of A. N. Whitehead," *Journal of General Psychology*, 32 (1945), 179, 180.

9. *Ibid.*, p. 181, footnote.

10. I cannot agree with W. P. Alston's view that there is a fundamental contradiction in Whitehead because of this principle of mutual immanence and pluralism. Alston's error comes from not distinguishing present and future immanence from past. *Cf.* his article, "Internal Relatedness and Pluralism in Whitehead," *Review of Metaphysics*, 5 (1951–52), 535–58.

11. J. W. Blyth, *Whitehead's Theory of Knowledge* (Providence, R.I.: Brown University Press, 1941), p. 27c.

12. *Ibid.*, p. 28c.

Chapter IX

1. Work in this direction is found in Robert Palter, ed., *Whitehead's Philosophy of Science* (Chicago: University of Chicago Press, 1960) and in Palter's "The Place of Mathematics in Whitehead's Philosophy," *Journal of Philosophy*, 53 (1961), 565–76. Revised version in George L. Kline, ed., *Alfred North Whitehead: Essays on his Philosophy* (Englewood Cliffs, N.J.: Prentice-Hall, 1963), pp. 41–52, esp. p. 49.

2. The dependence of continuity on potentiality is argued by Ivor Leclerc in "Whitehead and the Problem of Extension," *Journal of Philosophy*, 58 (1961), 561 ff. Reprinted in Kline, *op. cit.*, pp. 117–23.

3. This ambiguity is not to be confused with another alleged ambiguity Blyth uses for his criticism, which I will discuss shortly. (*Cf.* J. W. Blyth, *Whitehead's Theory of Knowledge* (Providence, R.I.: Brown University Press, 1941), pp. 35–36.)

4. Blyth, *op. cit.*, pp. 35–36.

5. *Ibid.*, 33c.

6. *Ibid.*, 33c–34a.

7. Further details of "strains" have been worked out by Lucio Chiaraviglio, "Whitehead's Theory of Prehensions," *Journal of Philosophy*, 58 (1961), 518–34. Revised and expanded in Kline, *op. cit.*, pp. 81–92, esp. Part I.

8. For Whitehead's brief account of presentational immediacy see PR 100–01, 260–61.

Chapter XI

1. Bertrand Russell, *Human Knowledge* (New York: Simon and Schuster, 1948), Part 6, Chapter 5.

2. W. E. Agar, "Whitehead's Philosophy of Organism: An Introduction for Biologists," *Quarterly Review of Biology*, 11 (1936), 16–34. W. E. Agar, "The Concept of Purpose in Biology," *Quarterly Review of Biology*, 13 (1938), 225 ff.

3. H. Hermann, "Aspects of Living Matter and Whitehead's Category of Actual Occasions," *Philosophy of Science*, 14 (1947), 254–60.

SELECTED BIBLIOGRAPHY

Whitehead's Books

Whitehead, A. N., *Adventures of Ideas* (New York: The Macmillan Co., 1933).
———, *The Aims of Education* (London: Williams and Norgate, 1950).
———, *Alfred North Whitehead: An Anthology*, ed. F. S. C. Northrop and Mason W. Gross (New York: The Macmillan Co., 1953).
———, *The Concept of Nature* (Cambridge: Cambridge University Press, 1920).
———, *Essays in Science and Philosophy* (New York: Philosophical Library, 1947).
———, *The Function of Reason* (Princeton: Princeton University Press, 1929).
———, *An Introduction to Mathematics* (London: Williams and Norgate, 1911).
———, *Modes of Thought* (New York: The Macmillan Co., 1938).
———, *The Organization of Thought* (London: Williams and Norgate, 1917).
———, *Principia Mathematica* (Cambridge: Cambridge University Press, 1910–13). With B. Russell.
———, *The Principle of Relativity* (Cambridge: Cambridge University Press, 1922).
———, *The Principles of Natural Knowledge* (Cambridge: Cambridge University Press, 1919).
———, *Process and Reality* (New York: The Macmillan Co., 1929).
———, *Religion in the Making* (New York: The Macmillan Co., 1926).
———, *Science and the Modern World* (New York: The Macmillan Co., 1925).
———, *Symbolism* (New York: The Macmillan Co., 1927).

Whitehead's Relevant Articles

Whitehead, A. N., "Axioms of Geometry," *Encyclopaedia Britannica*, 11th ed., XI, 730–36.
———, "The Idealistic Interpretation of Einstein's Theory," *Proceedings of the Aristotelian Society*, N.S. 22 (1921–22), 130–34.
———, "Mathematics," *Encyclopaedia Britannica*, 11th ed., XVII, 878–83.
———, "On Mathematical Concepts of the Material World," *Philosophical Transactions, Royal Society of London*, Series A, 205 (1906), 465–525.
———, "Non-Euclidean Geometry," *Encyclopaedia Britannica*, 11th ed., XI, 724–30. With B. Russell.

Whitehead, A. N., "The Philosophical Aspects of the Principle of Relativity," *Proceedings of the Aristotelian Society,* N.S. 22 (1921–22), 215–23.

———, "The Problem of Simultaneity," *Aristotelian Society: Supplement,* 3 (1923), 34–41.

———, "Remarks," *Philosophical Review,* 46 (1937), 178–86.

———, "La Théorie Relationniste de l'Espace," *Revue de Métaphysique et de Morale,* 23 (1916), 423–54.

———, "Time," *Proceedings: Sixth International Congress of Philosophy,* New York (1927), pp. 59–64.

———, "Time, Space, and Material," *Aristotelian Society: Supplement,* 2 (1919), 44–57.

———, "Uniformity and Contingency," *Proceedings of the Aristotelian Society,* 23 (1922–23), 1–18.

Commentaries

Books

Blyth, John W., *Whitehead's Theory of Knowledge* (Providence: Brown University Press, 1941).

Bowman, A. A., *A Sacramental Universe* (Princeton: Princeton University Press, 1939).

Bright, Lawrence, *Whitehead's Philosophy of Physics* (London & New York: Sheed and Ward, 1958), pp. 9–46.

Christian, William A., *An Interpretation of Whitehead's Metaphysics* (New Haven: Yale University Press, 1959).

Das, R., *The Philosophy of Whitehead* (London: James Clarke & Co., 1938).

Ely, Stephen L., *The Religious Availability of Whitehead's God* (Madison: University of Wisconsin Press, 1942).

Emmet, Dorothy M., *Whitehead's Philosophy of Organism* (London: Macmillan & Co., Ltd., 1932).

Hammerschmidt, W. W., *Whitehead's Philosophy of Time* (New York: King's Crown Press, 1947).

Johnson, A. H., *Whitehead's Theory of Reality* (Boston: Beacon Press, 1952).

Kline, George L., ed., *Alfred North Whitehead: Essays on his Philosophy* (Englewood Cliffs, N.J.: Prentice-Hall, 1963).

Lawrence, Nathaniel, *Whitehead's Philosophical Development* (Berkeley and Los Angeles: University of California Press, 1956), pp. 1–366.

Leclerc, Ivor, ed., *The Relevance of Whitehead* (London: Allen and Unwin, Ltd., 1961).

Lillie, Ralph S., *General Biology and the Philosophy of Organism* (Chicago: University of Chicago Press, 1945).

Lovejoy, Arthur O., *The Revolt Against Dualism* (Chicago: Open Court Publishing Co., 1930).

Lowe, Victor, *Understanding Whitehead* (Baltimore: Johns Hopkins Press, 1962).

Lowe, Victor, Hartshorne, Charles, and Johnson, A. H., *Whitehead and the Modern World* (Boston: Beacon Press, 1950).

Mack, R. D., *The Appeal to Immediate Experience* (New York: King's Crown Press, 1945).

Mays, Wolfe, *The Philosophy of Whitehead* (London: Allen & Unwin, 1959).

Miller, David L., and Gentry, G. V., *The Philosophy of A. N. Whitehead* (Minneapolis: Burgess Publishing Co., 1938).

Morris, Charles W., *Six Theories of Mind* (Chicago: University of Chicago Press, 1932).

Palter, Robert M., *Whitehead's Philosophy of Science* (Chicago: University of Chicago Press, 1960).

Russell, Bertrand, *The Principles of Mathematics* (London: George Allen & Unwin, Ltd., 1937).

Schilpp, Paul A., ed., *The Philosophy of A. N. Whitehead* (Evanston & Chicago: Northwestern University Press, 1941).

Shahan, Ewing P., *Whitehead's Theory of Experience* (New York: King's Crown Press, 1950).

Sherburne, Donald W., *A Whiteheadian Aesthetic* (New Haven: Yale University Press, 1961).

Ushenko, A. P., *The Logic of Events.* University of California Publications in Philosophy, Vol. 12 (1929).

Wells, Harry K., *Process and Unreality* (New York: King's Crown Press, 1950).

ARTICLES

Agar, W. E., "The Concept of Purpose in Biology," *Quarterly Review of Biology,* 13 (1938), 255–73.

———, "Whitehead's Philosophy of Organism: An Introduction for Biologists," *Quarterly Review of Biology,* 11 (1936), 16–34.

Alston, William P., "Whitehead Denial of Simple Location," *Journal of Philosophy,* 48 (1951), 713–21.

———, "Internal Relatedness and Pluralism in Whitehead," *Review of Metaphysics,* 5 (1951–52), 535–58.

Balz, A. G. A., "Matter and Scientific Efficacy," *Journal of Philosophy,* 41 (1944), 645–64, 673–85.

———, "Whitehead, Descartes and the Bifurcation of Nature," *Journal of Philosophy,* 31 (1934), 281–97.

Bar-On, Zvie A., "Whitehead and the Heritage of Modern Philosophy," *International Philosophical Quarterly,* 4 (1964), 48–67.

Bidney, D., "The Problem of Substance in Spinoza and Whitehead," *Philosophical Review,* 45 (1936), 574–92.

Blyth, J. W., "Discussion: On Mr. Hartshorne's Understanding of Whitehead's Philosophy," *Philosophical Review,* 46 (1937), 523–28.

Braham, E. G., "Place of God in Whitehead's Philosophy," *London Quarterly Review,* 1964 (1939), 63–69.

Broad, C. D., "Review of *The Principles of Natural Knowledge,*" *Mind,* 29 (1920), 216–31.

Browning, D., "Whitehead's Theory of Human Agency," *Dialogue,* 2 (1963–64), 424–41.

Carr, H. W., "Professor Whitehead's World Building," *Personalist,* 11 (1930), 157–63.

Cesselin, F., "La Bifurcation de la Nature," *Revue de Métaphysique et de Morale,* 57 (1950), 30–49.

Chappell, Vere, "Whitehead's Theory of Becoming," *Journal of Philosophy,* 58 (1961), 516–27. Reprinted in Kline, *op. cit.,* pp. 70–80.

Chiaraviglio, Lucio, "Strains," *Journal of Philosophy*, 58 (1961), 528–33. Reprinted and expanded in Kline, *op. cit.*, pp. 81–92.

Christian, W. A., "The Mutual Exclusiveness of Whitehead's Actual Occasions," *Review of Metaphysics*, 2 (1949), 45–75.

———, "Whitehead's Explanation of the Past," *Journal of Philosophy*, 58 (1961), 534–43. Reprinted in Kline, *op. cit.*, pp. 93–101.

Cory, D., "Dr. Whitehead on Perception," *Journal of Philosophy*, 30 (1933), 29–43.

Creegan, R. F., "Actual Occasions and Actual History," *Journal of Philosophy*, 39 (1942), 268–73.

DeBurgh, W. V., "Professor Whitehead's *Modes of Thought*," *Philosophy*, 14 (1939), 205–11.

Dewey, J., "Whitehead's Philosophy," *Philosophical Review*, 46 (1937), 170–77.

Dean, Frank M., "On the Construction of Whitehead's Metaphysical Language," *Review of Metaphysics*, 13 (1959–60), 605–22.

Dunham, A. M., "Animism and Materialism in Whitehead's Organic Philosophy," *Journal of Philosophy*, 29 (1932), 41–47.

Eddington, A. S., "Comparison of Whitehead's and Einstein's Formulae," *Nature*, 113 (1924), 192.

Einstein, A., "Physics and Reality," *Journal of the Franklin Institute*, 221 (1936), 349–82.

Frick, Ivan, "A. N. Whitehead and the 'Ordinary Language' Philosophers," *Indian Journal of Philosophy*, IV (1964), 69–84.

Fries, H. S., "The Functions of Whitehead's God," *Monist*, 46 (1936), 25–58.

Gentry, G. V., "Eternal Objects and the Philosophy of Organism," *Philosophy of Science*, 13 (1946), 252–60.

———, "Prehension as an Explanatory Principle," *Journal of Philosophy*, 35 (1938), 517–22.

———, "The Subject in Whitehead's Philosophy," *Philosophy of Science*, 11 (1944), 222–26.

Gross, M. W., "Whitehead's Answer to Hume," *Journal of Philosophy*, 38 (1941), 95–102. Reprinted in Kline, *op. cit.*, pp. 63–69.

Grünbaum, Adolf, "Whitehead's Method of Extensive Abstraction," *British Journal for Philosophy of Science*, 4 (1953–54), 215–26.

Gustafson, D. F., "Christian on Causal Objectification in Whitehead," *International Philosophical Quarterly*, I (1961), 683–96.

Hall, E. W., "Of What Use Are Whitehead's Eternal Objects?" *Journal of Philosophy*, 27 (1930), 29–44. Reprinted in Kline, *op. cit.*, pp. 102–16.

Harrah, David, "The Influence of Logic and Mathematics on Whitehead," *Journal of the History of Ideas*, XX (1959), 420–30.

Hartshorne, C., "Discussion: The Interpretation of Whitehead," *Philosophical Review*, 48 (1939), 415–23.

———, "Is Whitehead's God the God of Religion?" *International Journal of Ethics*, 53 (1943), 219–27.

Hartshorne, C., "Le Principe de Relativité Philosophique chez Whitehead," *Revue de Métaphysique et de Morale*, 57 (1950), 16–29.

———, "Some Criticisms of Whitehead's Philosophy," *Philosophical Review*, 44 (1935), 323–44.

Hélal, Georges, "Le Sens du Développement Philosophique de Whitehead," *Dialogue,* 2 (1963–64), 398–423.

Herrmann, H., "Aspects of Living Matter and Whitehead's Category of Actual Occasions," *Philosophy of Science,* 14 (1947), 254–60.

Hintz, Howard W., "A. N. Whitehead and the Philosophical Synthesis," *Journal of Philosophy,* 52 (1955), 225–43.

Hocking, William E., "Whitehead as I Knew Him," *Journal of Philosophy,* 58 (1961), 505–13. Reprinted in Kline, *op. cit.,* pp. 7–17.

Hooper, S. E., "Professor Whitehead's *Adventures of Ideas,*" *Philosophy,* 8 (1933), 326–44.

——, "Professor Whitehead's *Nature and Life,*" *Philosophy,* 9 (1934), 465–72.

——, "A Reasonable Theory of Morality (Alexander and Whitehead)," *Philosophy,* 25 (1950), 54–67.

——, "Telepathy in the Light of Whitehead's Philosophy," *Hibbert Journal,* 42 (1944), 248–53.

——, "Whitehead's Philosophy: Actual Entities," *Philosophy,* 16 (1941), 285–305.

——, "Whitehead's Philosophy: Eternal Objects and God," *Philosophy,* 17 (1942), 47–68.

——, "Whitehead's Philosophy: The Higher Phases of Experience," *Philosophy,* 21 (1946), 57–78.

——, "Whitehead's Philosophy: Propositions and Consciousness," *Philosophy,* 20 (1945), 59–75.

——, "Whitehead's Philosophy: Space, Time, and Things," *Philosophy,* 18 (1943), 204–30.

——, "Whitehead's Philosophy: Theory of Perception," *Philosophy,* 19 (1944), 136–58.

——, "Whitehead's Philosophy: The World as Process," *Philosophy,* 23–24 (1948–49), 140–61.

Johnson, A. H., "A. N. Whitehead's Theory of Intuition," *Journal of General Psychology,* 37 (1947), 61–66.

——, "A Criticism of Dr. Bidney's 'Spinoza and Whitehead,'" *Philosophical Review,* 47 (1938), 410–14.

——, "Intelligibility in Whitehead's Philosophy," *Philosophy of Science,* 10 (1943), 47–55.

——, "Leibniz and Whitehead," *Philosophy and Phenomenological Research,* 19 (1958–59), 285–305.

——, "The Psychology of A. N. Whitehead," *Journal of General Psychology,* 32 (1945), 175–212.

——, "Reply to Urban's 'Elements of Unintelligibility in Whitehead's Philosophy,'" *Journal of Philosophy,* 36 (1939), 103–05.

——, "Social Philosophy of A. N. Whitehead," *Journal of Philosophy,* 40 (1943), 261–71.

——, "Some Aspects of Whitehead's Social Philosophy," *Philosophy and Phenomenological Research,* 24 (1963–64), 61–72.

——, "Truth, Beauty, and Goodness in the Philosophy of A.N. Whitehead," *Philosophy of Science,* 11 (1944), 9–29.

——, "Wit and Wisdom of Whitehead," *Philosophy of Science,* 13 (1946), 223–51.

Johnson, A. H., "Whitehead's Philosophy of History," *Journal of the History of Ideas,* 7 (1946), 234–49.

——, "Whitehead's Theory of Actual Entities," *Philosophy of Science,* 12 (1945), 237–95.

King, H. R., "A. N. Whitehead and the Concept of Metaphysics," *Philosophy of Science,* 14 (1947), 132–51.

——, "Whitehead's Doctrine of Causal Efficacy," *Journal of Philosophy,* 46 (1949), 85–100.

Lawrence, N., "Locke and Whitehead on Individual Entities," *Review of Metaphysics,* 4 (1950), 215–38.

——, "Single Location, Simple Location, and Misplaced Concreteness," *Review of Metaphysics,* 7 (1953–54), 225–47.

——, "The Vision of Beauty and the Temporality of Deity in Whitehead's Philosophy," *Journal of Philosophy,* 58 (1961), 543–53. Revised version in Kline, *op. cit.,* pp. 168–78.

——, "Whitehead's Method of Extensive Abstraction," *Philosophy of Science,* 17 (1950), 142–63.

Leclerc, Ivor, "Whitehead and the Problem of Extension," *Journal of Philosophy,* 58 (1961), 559–65. Reprinted in Kline, *op. cit.,* pp. 117–23.

——, "Whitehead's Transformation of the Concept of Substance," *Philosophical Quarterly,* 3 (1953), 225–43.

Lenzen, V., "Scientific Ideas and Experience," *University of California Publications in Philosophy,* 8 (1926), 175–89.

Litman, A., "Prehension as a Relation," *Journal of Philosophy,* 44 (1948), 234–40.

Loomer, B. M., "Ely on Whitehead's God," *Journal of Religion,* 24 (1944), 162–79.

Lowe, Victor, "Influence of Bergson, James and Alexander on Whitehead," *Journal of the History of Ideas,* 10 (1949), 267–96.

——, "James and Whitehead's Doctrine of Prehension," *Journal of Philosophy,* 38 (1941), 113–26.

——, "Mr. Miller's Interpretation of Whitehead," *Philosophy of Science,* 5 (1938), 217–29.

——, "The Philosophy of Whitehead," *Antioch Review,* 8 (1948), 223–39.

McEwen, W. P., "Whitehead's View of Personal Growth," *Personalist,* 24 (1943), 46–56.

MacKenzie, W. L., "What Does Dr. Whitehead Mean by 'Event'?" *Proceedings of the Aristotelian Society,* N.S. 23 (1922–23), 229–44.

Malik, C., "An Appreciation of Professor Whitehead," *Journal of Philosophy,* 45 (1948), 572–83.

May, W., "Determinism and Free Will in Whitehead," *Philosophy and Phenomenological Research,* 15 (1954–55), 523–34.

——, "Whitehead's Theory of Abstraction," *Proceedings of the Aristotelian Society,* 52 (1951–52), 95–118.

——, "Whitehead's Account of Speculative Philosophy in *Process and Reality,*" *Proceedings of the Aristotelian Society,* N.S. 46 (1945–46), 17–46.

Miller, D. L., "Purpose, Design and Physical Relativity," *Philosophy of Science,* 3 (1936), 267–85.

——, "Whitehead's Extensive Continuum," *Philosophy of Science,* 13 (1946), 144–49.

Moore, M. H., "Mr. Whitehead's Philosophy," *Philosophical Review*, 40 (1931), 265–75.

Morgan, C. L., "The Bifurcation of Nature," *Monist*, 40 (1930), 161–81.

———, "Subjective Aim in Professor Whitehead's Philosophy," *Philosophy*, 6 (1931), 281–94.

Morgan, G., "Whitehead's Theory of Value," *International Journal of Ethics*, 47 (1937), 308–16.

Morris, C. W., "Mind in *Process and Reality*," *Journal of Philosophy*, 28 (1931), 113–27.

Moxley, D. J., "The Conception of God in the Philosophy of Whitehead," *Proceedings of the Aristotelian Society*, N.S. 34 (1933–34), 157–86.

Murphy, A. E., "The Anti-Copernican Revolution," *Journal of Philosophy*, 26 (1929), 281–99.

———, "The Development of Whitehead's Philosophy," *New World Monthly*, 1 (1930), 81–100.

———, "Ideas and Nature," *University of California Publications in Philosophy*, 8 (1926), 193–213.

———, "Objective Relativism in Dewey and Whitehead," *Philosophical Review*, 36 (1927), 121–44.

———, "Review of *Symbolism*," *Journal of Philosophy*, 26 (1929), 489–98.

———, "What Is an Event?" *Philosophical Review*, 37 (1928), 574–86.

Palter, Robert, "The Place of Mathematics in Whitehead's Philosophy," *Journal of Philosophy*, 58 (1961), 565–76. Revised version in Kline, *op. cit.*, pp. 41–52.

Robinson, D. S., "Dr. Whitehead's Theory of Events," *Philosophical Review*, 30 (1921), 41–56.

Robson, J. W., "Whitehead's Answer to Hume," *Journal of Philosophy*, 38 (1941), 85–95. Reprinted, slightly abridged, in Kline, *op. cit.*, pp. 53–62.

Root, Vernon, "Eternal Objects, Attributes, and Relations in Whitehead's Philosophy," *Philosophy and Phenomenological Research*, 14 (1953–54), 196–204.

Rotenstreich, Nathan, "On Whitehead's Theory of Propositions," *Review of Metaphysics*, 5 (1951–52), 389–404.

Sellars, R. W., "Concerning 'Transcendence' and 'Bifurcation,'" *Mind*, 31 (1922), 31–39.

Sheen, F. J., "Professor Whitehead and the Making of Religion," *The New Scholasticism*, 1 (1927), 147–62.

Smith, N. K., "Whitehead's Philosophy of Nature," *University of California Publications in Philosophy*, 4 (1923), 197–224.

Stapledon, O., "The Location of Physical Objects," *Philosophy*, 4 (1929), 64–75.

Stebbing, L. S., "Concerning Substance," *Proceedings of the Aristotelian Society*, N.S. 30 (1929–30), 285–308.

———, "Mind and Nature in Professor Whitehead's Philosophy," *Mind*, 33 (1924), 289–303.

———, "Professor Whitehead's 'Perceptual Object,'" *Journal of Philosophy*, 23 (1926), 197–213.

———, "Review of *Process and Reality*," *Mind*, 39 (1930), 466–75.

Stebbing, L. S., "Universals and Professor Whitehead's Theory of Objects," *Proceedings of the Aristotelian Society,* 25 (1924–25), 305–30.

———, Braithwaite, R. B., and Wrinch, D., "Symposium: Is the 'Fallacy of Simple Location' a Fallacy?" *Aristotelian Society: Supplement,* 7 (1927), 207–43.

Taylor, A. E., "Dr. Whitehead's Philosophy of Religion," *Dublin Review,* 181 (1927), 17–41.

Taylor, H., "Hume's Answer to Whitehead," *Journal of Philosophy,* 38 (1941), 409–16.

Turner, J. E., "Dr. A. N. Whitehead's Scientific Realism," *Journal of Philosophy,* 19 (1922), 146–57.

Urban, W. M., "Elements of Unintelligibility in Whitehead's Metaphysics," *Journal of Philosophy,* 35 (1938), 617–37.

Ushenko, A. P., "A Note on Whitehead and Relativity," *Journal of Philosophy,* 47 (1950), 100–02.

———, "Whitehead's Theory of Negative Prehensions," *Journal of Philosophy,* 34 (1937), 263–67.

Vlastos, G., "Organic Categories in Whitehead," *Journal of Philosophy,* 34 (1937), 253–62. Reprinted in Kline, *op. cit.,* pp. 158–67.

———, "The Problem of Incompatibility in the Philosophy of Organism," *Monist,* 40 (1930), 535–51.

———, "Whitehead, Critic of Abstraction," *Monist,* 39 (1929), 170–203.

Wahl, J. A., "La Philosophie Speculative de Whitehead," *Revue Philosophique,* pp. 111–12 (1931), 341–78, 108–43. Expanded version in *Vers le Concret* (Paris: Vrin, 1932), pp. 127–221.

Watson, J., "A. N. Whitehead's Philosophy as in 'The Concept of Nature,'" *Proceedings: 8th International Congress of Philosophy,* Prague, 1936, pp. 903–12.

Weber, P. L., "Significance of Whitehead's Philosophy for Psychology," *Personalist,* 21 (1940), 178–87.

Wieman, H. N., "Professor Whitehead's Concept of God," *Hibbert Journal,* 25 (1927), 623–30.

———, "Value and the Individual," *Journal of Philosophy,* 25 (1928), 233–39.

Wind, E., "Mathematik and Sinnesempfindung. Materialen zu einer Whitehead Kritik," *Logos,* 21 (1932), 239–80.

Winn, R. B., "Whitehead's Concept of Process," *Journal of Philosophy,* 30 (1933), 710–14.

INDEX